Historic Canada

St. George and Its Neighbours

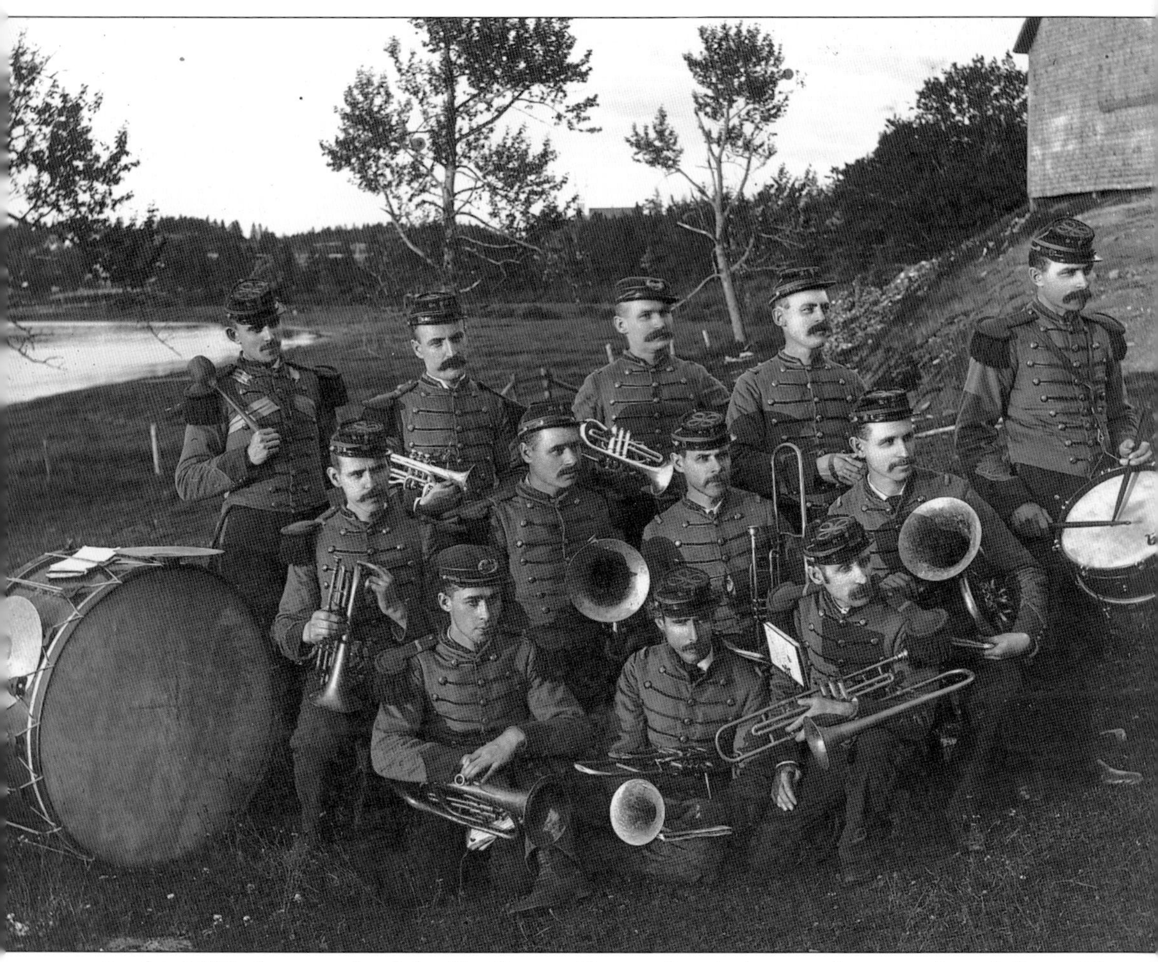

In this 1890 photograph of the St. George Cornet Band, the members are, from left to right, as follows: (front row) George Craig, Robert Murray, and Sam Murray; (middle row) Thomas Meating, Henry Meating, Joseph Meating, and French Meating; (back row) Robert Dodds, Charles Lynott, John Mooney, Fred Bogue, and Jimmy Dodds. (Courtesy PA, 18-246.)

Historic
Canada

St. George and Its Neighbours

David Goss with Elizabeth Toy

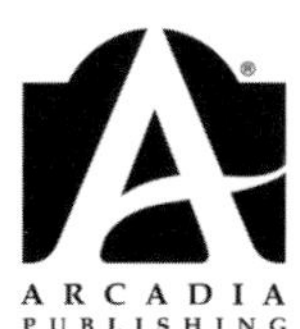

ISBN 978-0-7385-1149-8

Published by Arcadia Publishing
Charleston SC, Chicago IL, Portsmouth NH, San Francisco CA

Printed in the United States of America

Library of Congress Catalog Card Number: 2002113040

For all general information contact Arcadia Publishing at:
Telephone 843-853-2070
Fax 843-853-0044
E-mail sales@arcadiapublishing.com
For customer service and orders:
Toll-Free 1-888-313-2665

Visit us on the Internet at www.arcadiapublishing.com

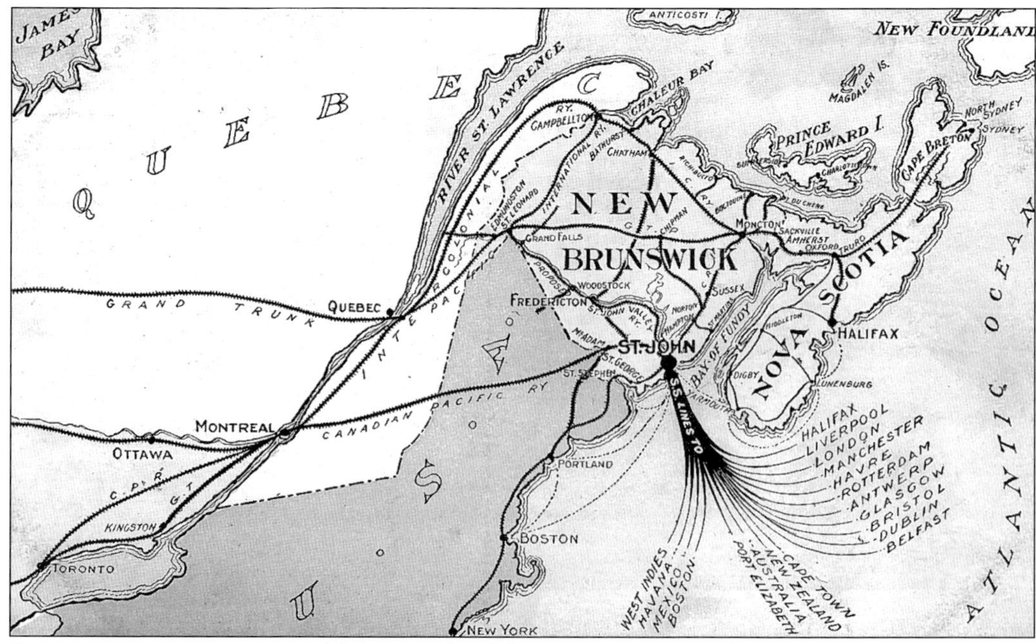

Sea routes connecting to world ports and rail lines connecting with the rest of Canada are the focus of this postcard view of New Brunswick, the Bay of Fundy, and the St. George area.

Contents

Acknowledgments

Where does one begin? Well, with Elizabeth herself. She had misgivings about taking on this project. "If I was only 10 years younger," she said again and again, "I'd do it in a minute." Finally, she agreed, so long as I would work with her, and it has been a delight to do so. Every time we sat down to work on a chapter, she would bring out a photograph or photographs we should have considered at our previous meeting. I then would go back and fit it in. This happened right down to the very last minute when she finally agreed to use the picture of her 90th birthday that she had not wanted to use before. That image was worked into the book on page 128. That was one of the easier changes. After we made that change, she invited me into the room from where she had been bringing the boxes, envelopes, and albums for the six weeks we worked together and showed me a framed overhead view of the entire pulp mill operation measuring one metre square. I could not believe it. It had every building and dam in the complex—at least a dozen locations—all hand-tinted in red. I stood there with my mouth agape. For the first time, I really understood how the damming of the Magaguadavic worked and the extent of the mill operation. My mind raced: does she want this in the book? No, she explained; she just wanted to show me something that was presented to her father and framed by her mother. I was so glad to hear that because it was just too late for such a big change. It then dawned on me; she was just being mischievous, tantalizing me with one more photograph that she knew I would want to use but for one reason or another could not. "When are you going to stop digging out these treasures?" I asked her. She laughed. "You haven't seen the half of it. . . I think there's enough for another book just in this room," she said. I looked around. She struck me as a lady who had not thrown out a thing in her nine decades. And I think she is likely right; there could be another book. So if you enjoy this one, keep you eyes open. For, if she is willing, I sure would be.

Elizabeth would like to thank the following persons who helped confirm information, provided photographs, or did both: her brother Eugene Toy, Alice Boyd, Lewis Dillman, Anita Grearson, Mary Jackson, M. and L. Leland, Wendy Murray, and Bea Stewart. To this list, I would like to add Steve and Bernice Campbell, as well as those identified in the credit lines throughout the book. The *St. Croix Courier* was also an invaluable, though inanimate, source of information, especially the 1866–1990 "Journey Through Time" collection that Elizabeth gave me to use. Finally, a word of thanks to my wife, Donna, for sharing me with Elizabeth these past few weeks and to my daughter Christy, who typed, sorted, then retyped, and resorted again and again.

—David Goss

Introduction

The town of St. George is found on the Bay of Fundy coast, at the mouth of Magaguadavic River, about equidistant between the province's busiest entry point from the United States, St. Stephen, and the biggest city to the east of St. George, Saint John. These two factors stimulated economic activity in the town as those traveling between the two points in times past found St. George to be a convenient rest stop and its magnificent falls on the Magaguadavic an interesting scenic attraction.

But based on these factors alone, St. George would have remained but a whistle-stop after the railway pushed through in 1882 connecting the two points. However, by that time New York entrepreneurs vacationing at Lake Utopia had discovered workable quantities of granite in the hills, and the town soon became a major exporter of polished granite. St. George granite was used in the United States to finish the Roman Catholic Cathedral in Boston and the Museum of Natural History in New York, as well as in Canada for the Sir John A. Macdonald Memorial in Montreal, the Parliament Buildings in Ottawa, and a number of post offices. Early in the 20th century, another group of New Yorkers established a pulp mill at the Magaguadavic Falls, and the town had a second industry to add to its economic base.

The granite industry started to peter out in the 1920s, and the last major building constructed of native granite was the post office built during the depression years. For all intents and purposes, the granite industry was dead by the 1940s.

The pulp mill too was a shaky operation. Following a major fire in 1946, it may well have closed, but it continued to operate under a new owner and expand through the 1950s. When the mill closed in 1967, St. George's future looked dismal. The railway had ceased to operate, a new highway was about to bypass the town, and thus, even tourists who passed through on their way to St. Andrews or Saint John or on trips to the Bay of Fundy Isles would not longer do so.

Some predicted the end of the community. However, a new pulp mill was established at Lake Utopia, and the \$150-million-per-year salmon aquaculture industry now flourishing in the Bay of Fundy breathed new economic life into the town.

Elizabeth Toy has lived through these changes, and in her role as a reporter and correspondent for the *Quoddy Tides*, the *St. Croix Courier*, the *Fredericton Gleaner*, and the *Telegraph Journal*, she has written about many of them. She has come to know the people as few others have through her reporting of the social and commercial life of the town. Elizabeth has taken and collected photographs that now can be used to illuminate the community's history—how it has evolved and developed over the years. Because of her wide range of interests, her travels around the area, her family's involvement in the pulp mill, her membership in the Baptist church, and her joyful times spent at her family cottage on Lake Utopia, all aspects of town life can be found in Elizabeth's collection.

Elizabeth's collection of photographs exceeds 2000, and from this enormous archive, we have selected but 10 percent to best represent life in the community of St. George and its surrounding neighbours.

For the most part, Elizabeth knew the "who's" and "when's" of her photographs, so only the best and most appropriate images were used to tell this story and move it along. Some photographs she has collected date back to the 1890s. Some have come from Pheobe Toy, Elizabeth's mother, who took and developed many of the earliest images of the town and its people. While some of these photographs are not as sharp as we might like, they provide an important record and, in some cases, the only available visual documentation of town life in that era.

To augment Elizabeth's photographs, we have drawn upon the collections of the Provincial Archives (PA) and my own collection I have built over the years with the help of friends and acquaintances who live up and down the coast. In each case, the individual or individuals who donated the photograph are identified. Their photographs depict the neighbouring communities to good advantage and fill in the few gaps in Elizabeth's collection. The text with each will explain the relationship to St. George or reason the photograph was chosen.

While Elizabeth Toy has a very good recollection of many of the events that have been of importance or just of delight to the residents of St. George and nearby coastal communities, we also interviewed persons in all of the neighbouring areas pictured in order to add interesting detail to the photographs, be it factual or from the realm of folklore.

Overall, the reader should finish the book with a good idea of the delights of living in St. George, as well as the challenges the town has faced. Readers are invited to experience the history of St. George, from fire to flood and through the ups and downs of industry, and catch glimpses of the coastal areas where town residents have visited, played, and worked over the past 100-plus years.

One

St. George and Its Neighbours

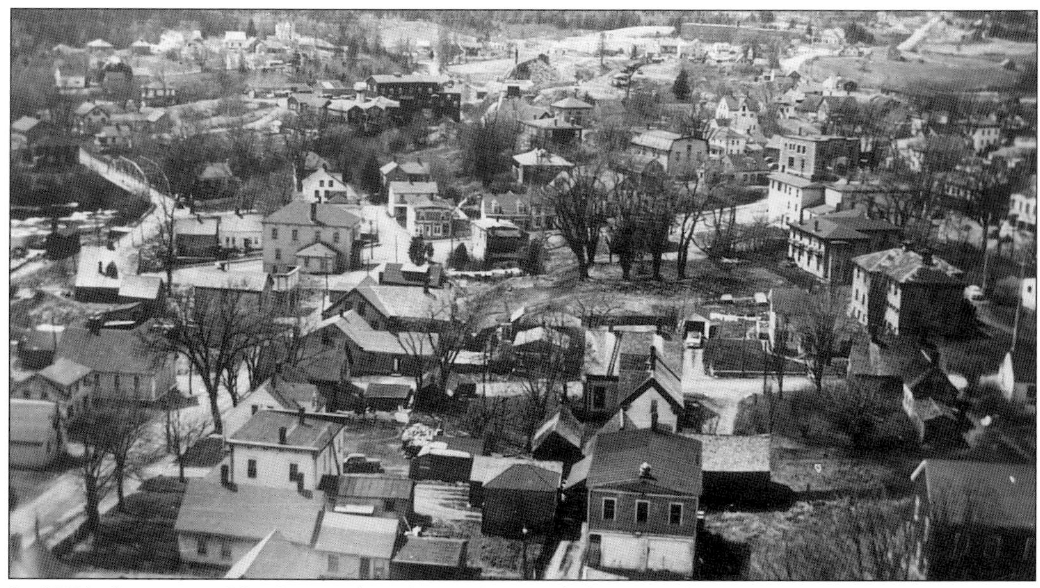

In 1954, the town of St. George hired a professional photographer to prepare some promotional images of the town from the top of the recently constructed water tower. It is believed that photographer Don Kimbell is responsible for this postcard view and those that follow. In this image, he shot a view across town toward the west. Though subdivided into many lots now, the entire town to the east of the river was granted to Peter Clinch in 1783. In the lower left side of this photograph, Carleton Street crosses South Street and meets Breadalbane via the lower bridge. Below the bridge, foam swirls in the saltwater tidal basin. The sheds of the pulp mill can be seen on the hill mid-picture to the right of the lower bridge. The upper bridge is not visible nor is the famed Magaguadavic Falls (sometimes called Rainbow Falls). But Highway One, the main road that links St. George with its neighbours, can be seen snaking toward the mountain range in the upper right of the photograph. Kimbell picked a good clear day to do his work, and these photographs offer a great view from which to begin this book.

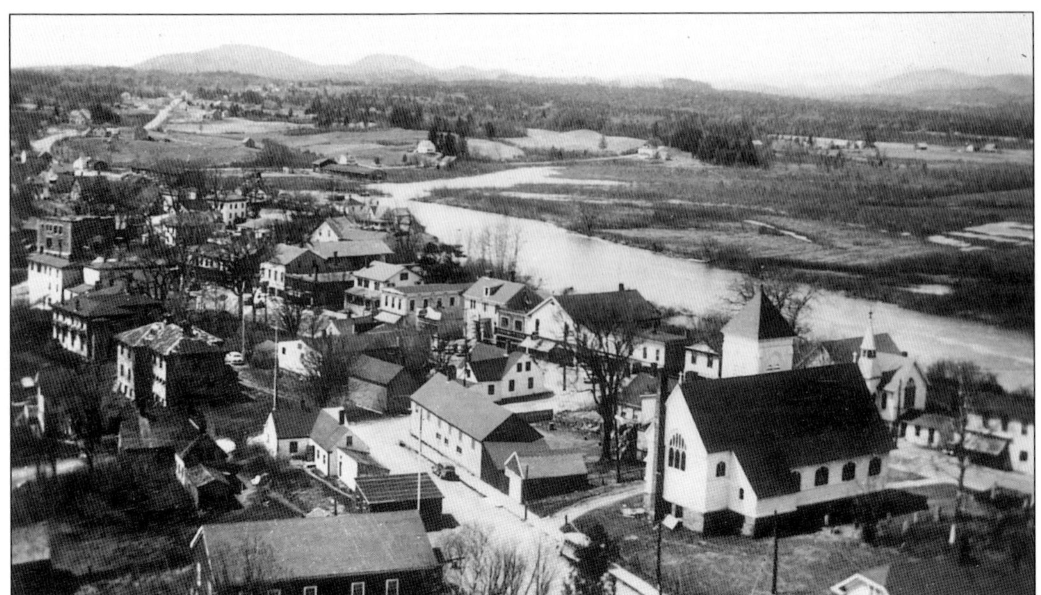

The second picture in the series shows Main Street (former Route One). The businesses and churches will be seen up close in later chapters. Of particular interest is the Anglican church, which burned on December 31, 2001. It is in the front right, and to its side is the first cemetery where town-founder Peter Clinch is buried. The Baptist church is just across Main Street on the south bank of the Magaguadavic River.

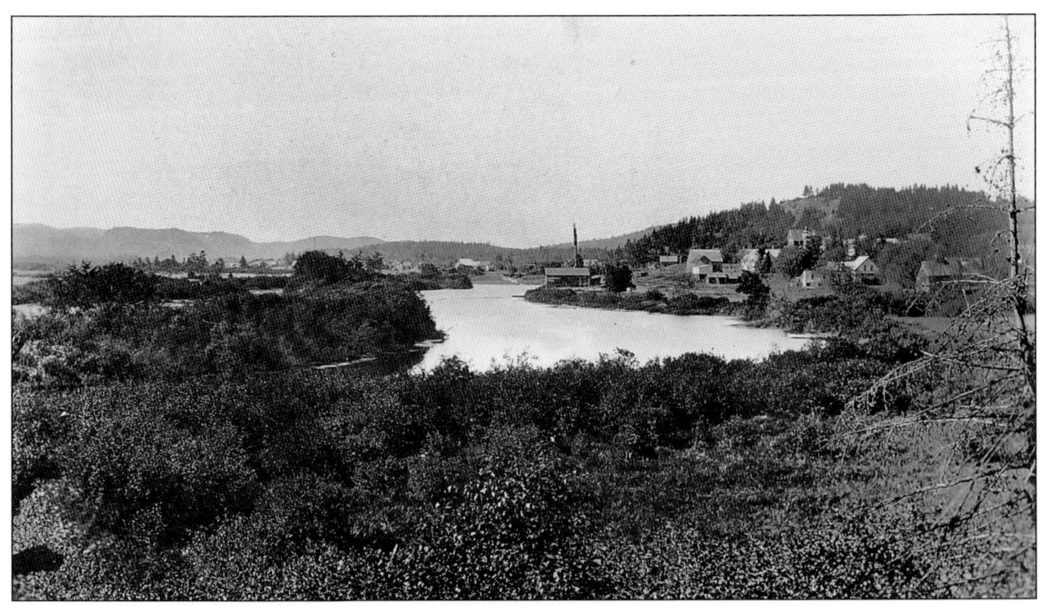

This postcard photograph was taken from Main Street, just behind the Baptist church shown in the previous photograph, looking upriver to a bend in the Magaguadavic River. Magaguadavic is Micmac for "river of big eels," though some say it means "big hill place." The natives knew the river well and used it as a waterway (with portages) from the St. John River running through the centre of the province to the clam flats along the Bay of Fundy.

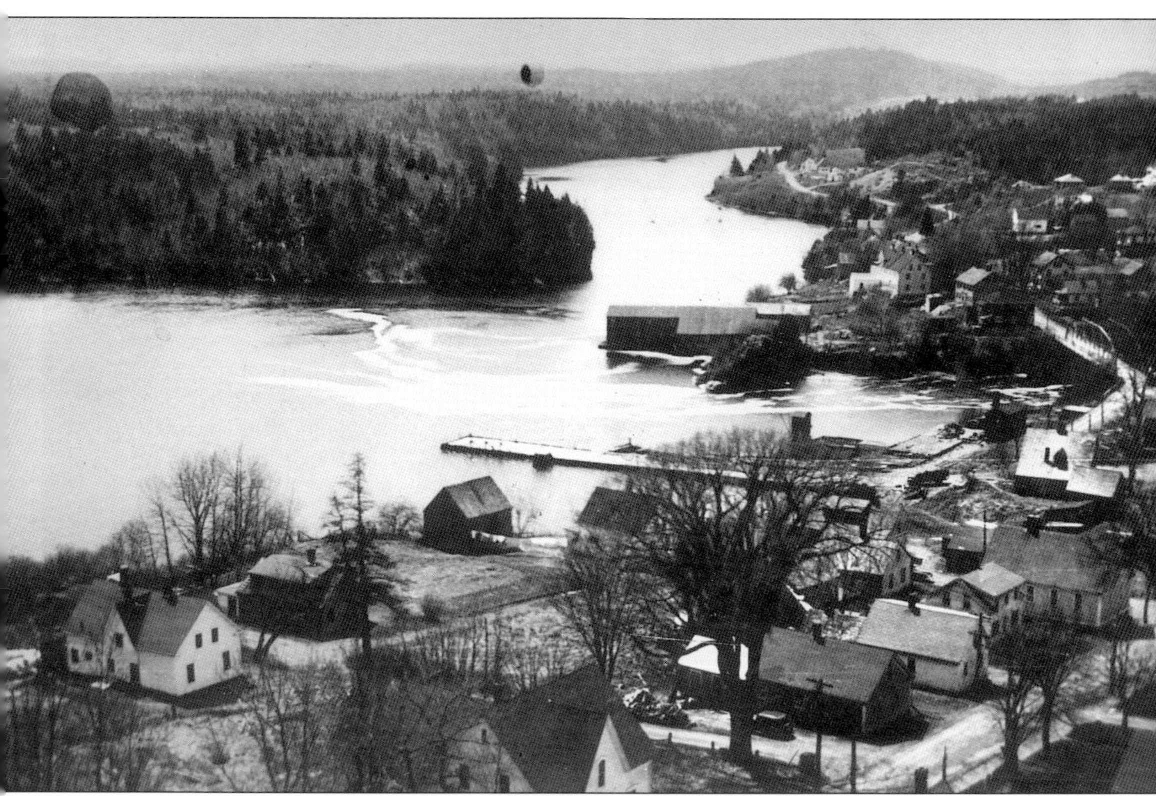

This fourth picture in the series shows the saltwater basin below Magaguadavic Falls and the lower bridge. The basin is tidal in nature and is filled by the famed Bay of Fundy eight-metre tides, which are at their high point in this view. The town wharf, and downstream the so-called "Red Store Wharf" used for storing and shipping granite products, protrudes into the basin from the shoreline below South Street.

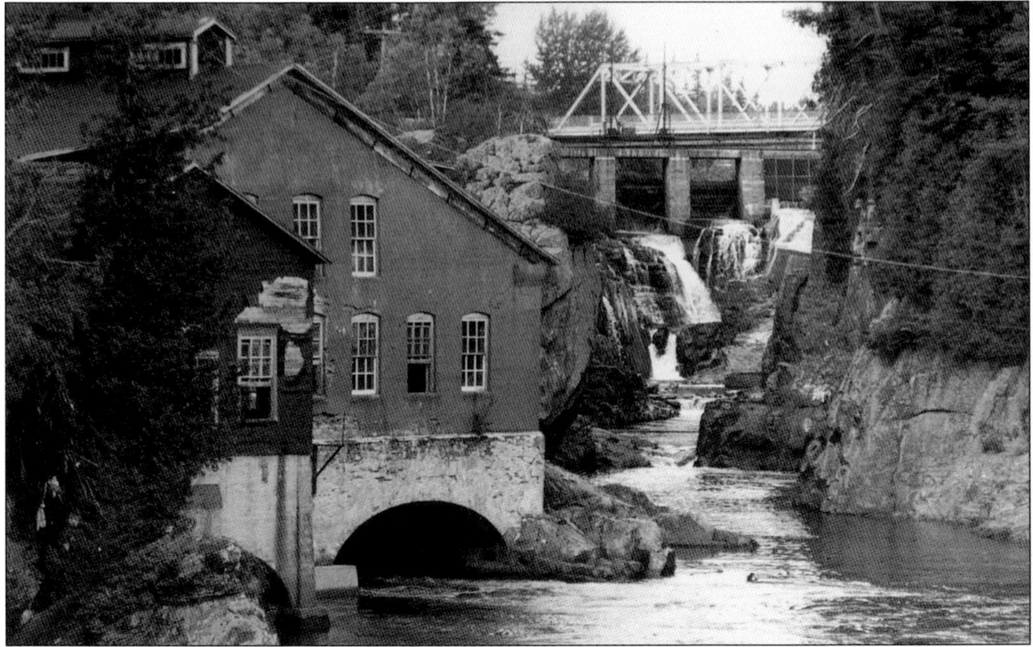

The most widely used promotional view of St. George is of the pulp mill and power plant below Magaguadavic Falls, as shown here. The river's massive concrete dam, approximately 20 metres high, is seen at the top of the gorge, and though it seems in the photograph above that the trusses of the highway bridge sit atop the dam, they are about 30 metres upstream. Some water filters through the dam, flows over, especially in spring, and down the fishway, but most travels via the penstock to the pulp mill and power plant seen above on the left. The interior of this plant is shown below.

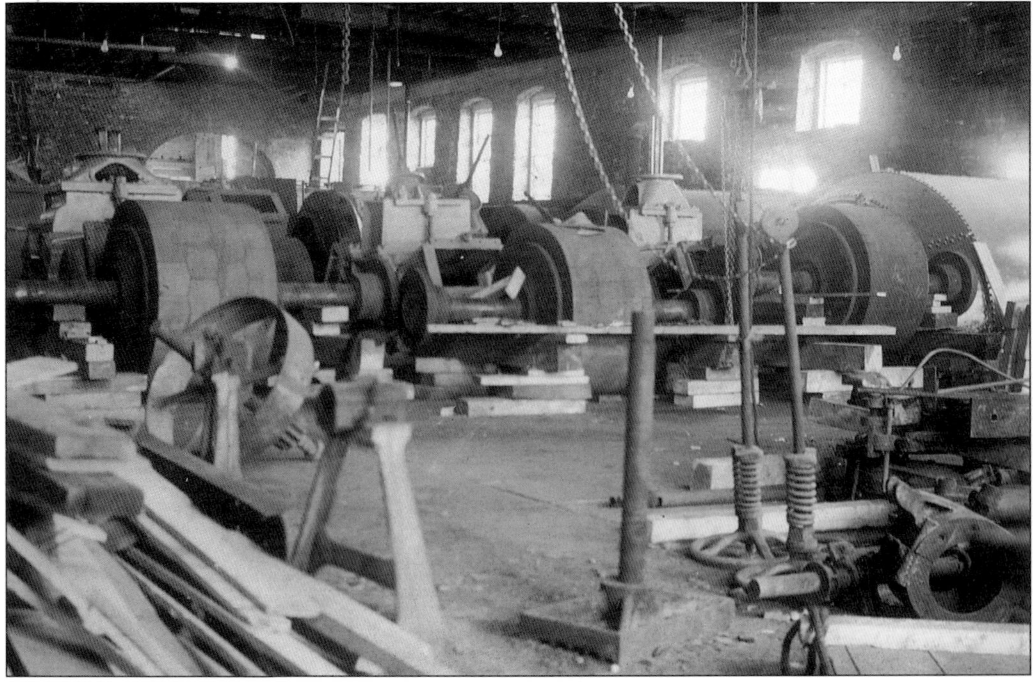

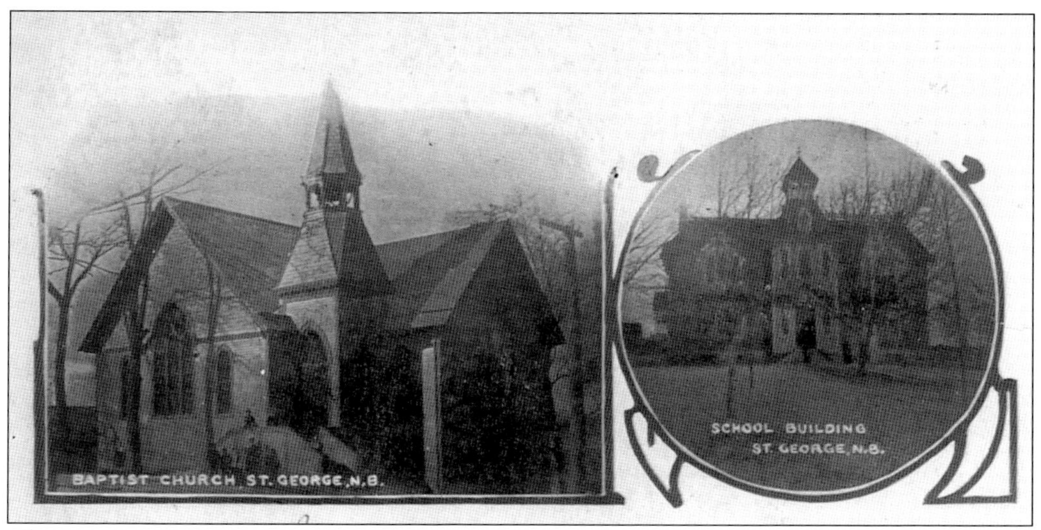

This is a postcard view of the second Baptist church, built in 1904–1906, and the St. George Superior school, constructed in 1888. The card itself was sent to Leila Logan of Eastport, Maine, from St. George on December 31, 1907, and received the next day in the United States. Such service is unknown today, but back then railways and steamboats linked the two areas. Since the postcard was faint, a later photograph of the school, torn down in 1989, is shown below.

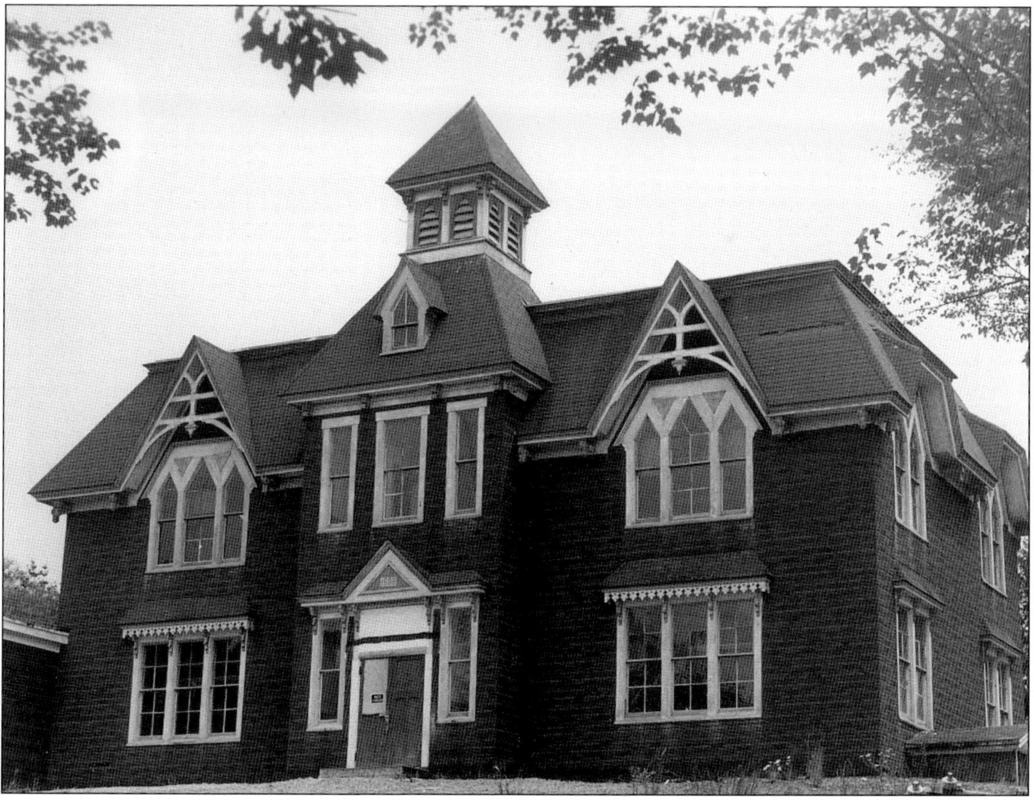

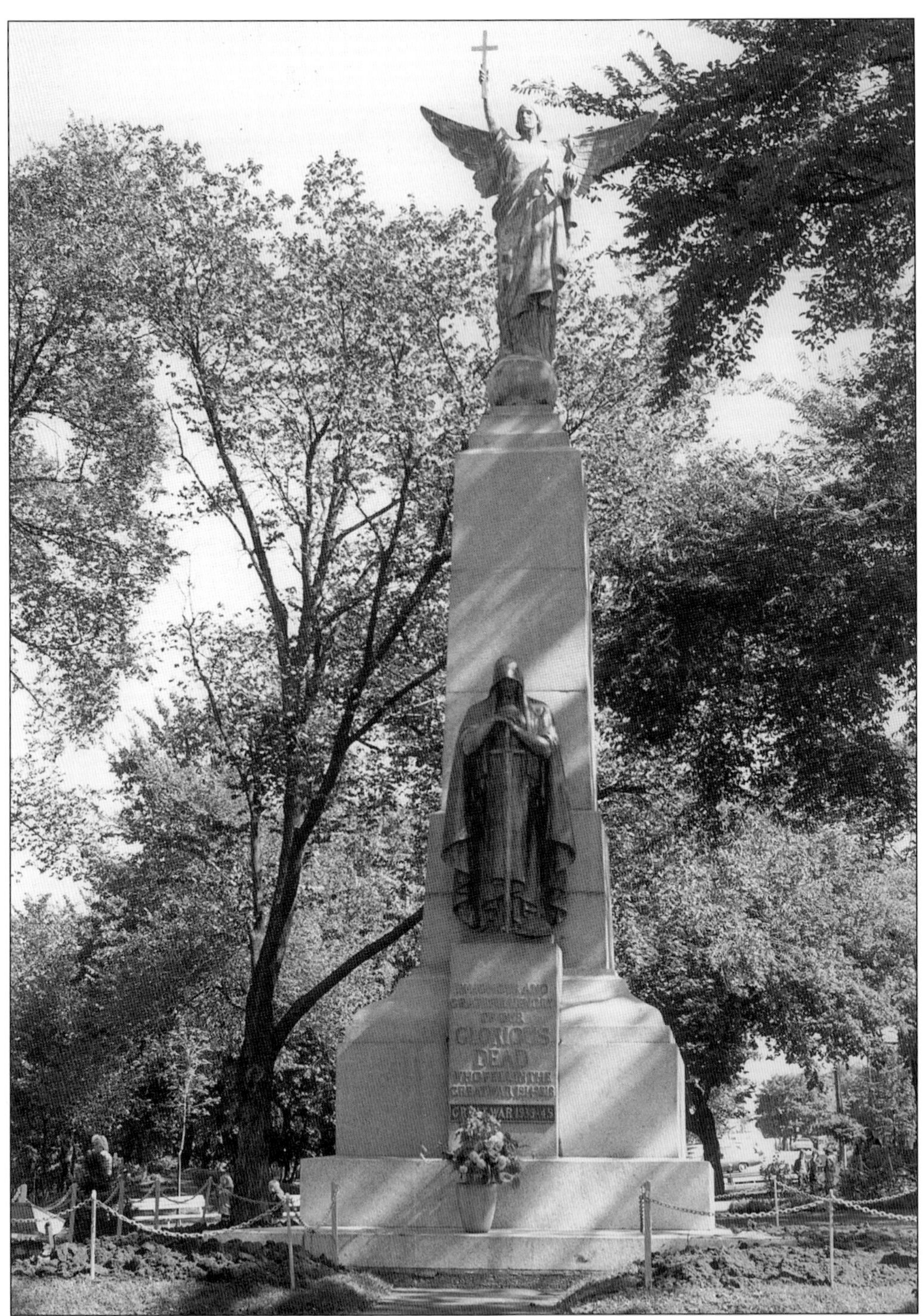

The cenotaph in Saint John's King's Square was unveiled June 10, 1925. It features Spoon Island granite prepared in St. George by the Meating and Epps Company. Alfred Howell, the Ontario designer, wanted to use granite from his home province but was persuaded to use native granite and workmen by the local committee overseeing the event. Thus a link with St. George and its granite industry still stands in neighbouring Saint John. (Courtesy Goss.)

St. George residents visiting Saint John for doctor and dental care also enjoyed shopping at big uptown stores like Woolworth's. To do so, they would have walked by the St. George cenotaph in this park at the head of King Street and seen the Admiral Beatty hotel at the southern edge of the park from whose rooftop this photograph of the area was taken. (Below) At the foot of King Street, visitors would have looked out into the harbour from Market Slip and seen a scene similar to this 1954 postcard view. (Courtesy Goss.)

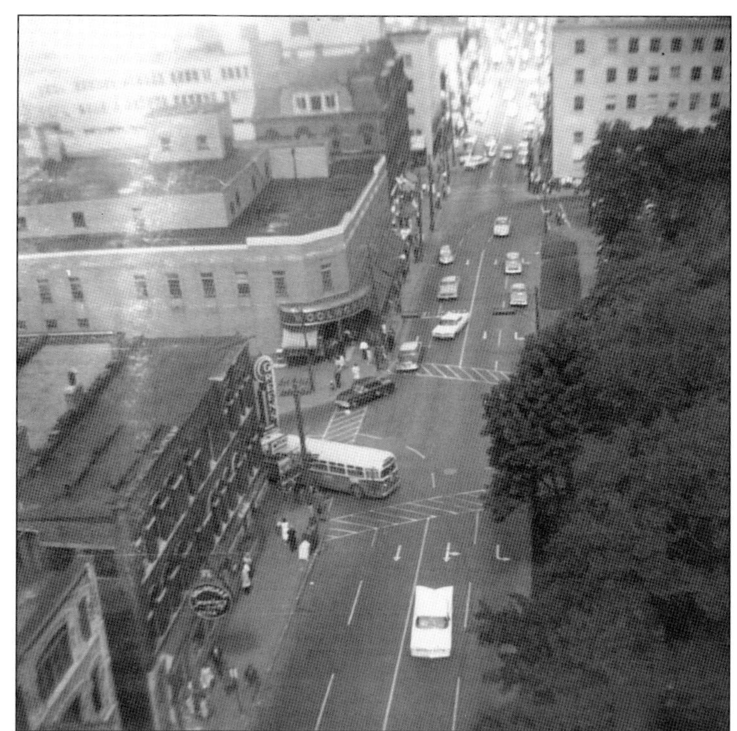

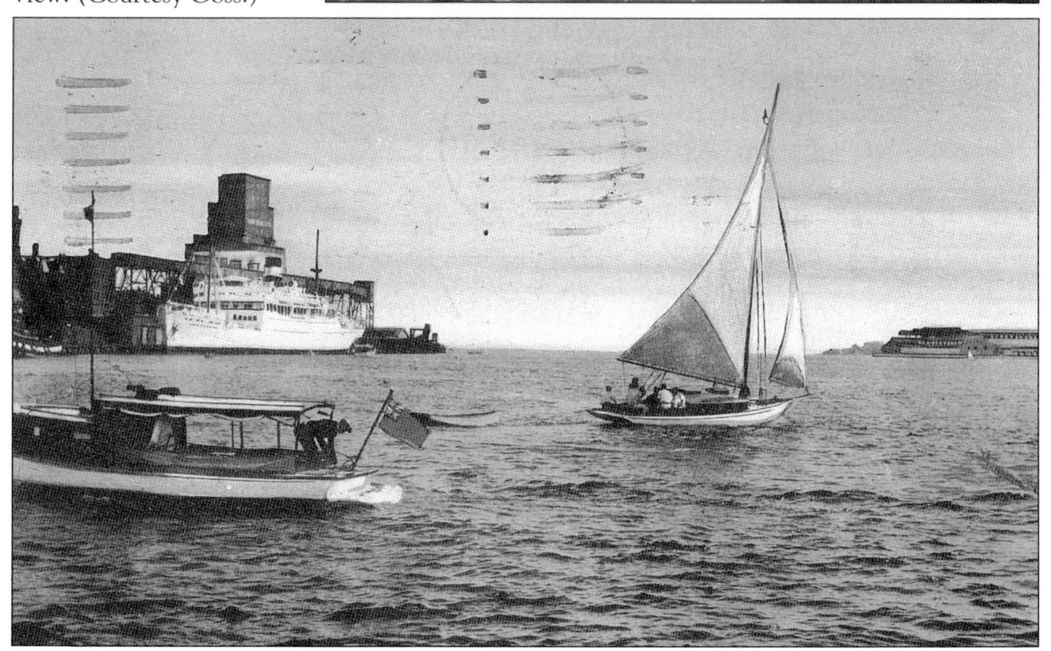

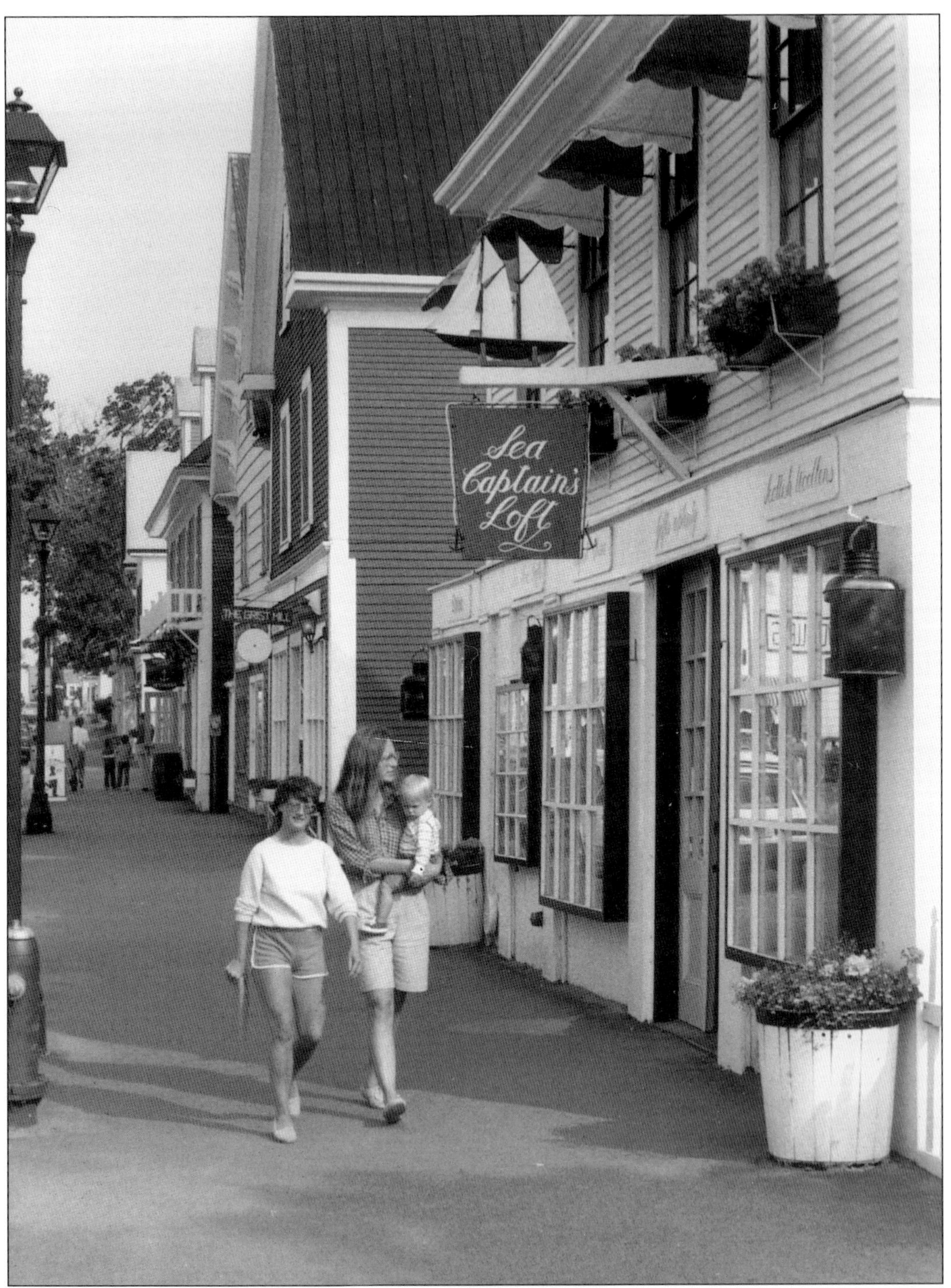

To St. George, Saint John was the industrial neighbour while, at the opposite end of the Bay of Fundy, the town of St. Andrew's, with its quaint shops and the palatial Algonquin Hotel, was the resort neighbour. The town was Canada's first to develop its attractions as a seaside resort based on the railway and steamer links to the eastern United States and as a convenient retreat from the heat of the big cities.

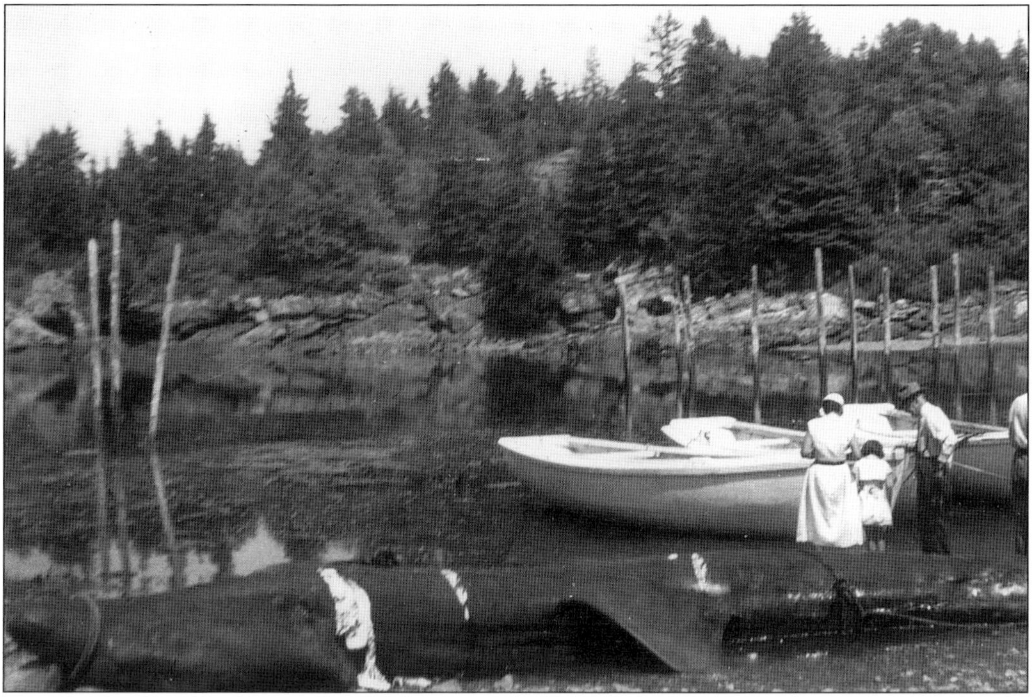

When traveling between Saint John and St. Andrew's, there are dozens of places that invite exploration for their scenic beauty, historic attraction, or commercial importance. In the photograph above, we see a beached shark that is being examined by visitors at L'Etete. It was not the largest shark on record—which was caught in waters off Grand Manan Isle in 1930 and measured 11 metres long—but it was worth a visit. And so are the many pretty spots featured within this volume, such as the fisherman's wharf at Lord's Cove, Deer Island, shown below, where the area's lobster industry is centred.

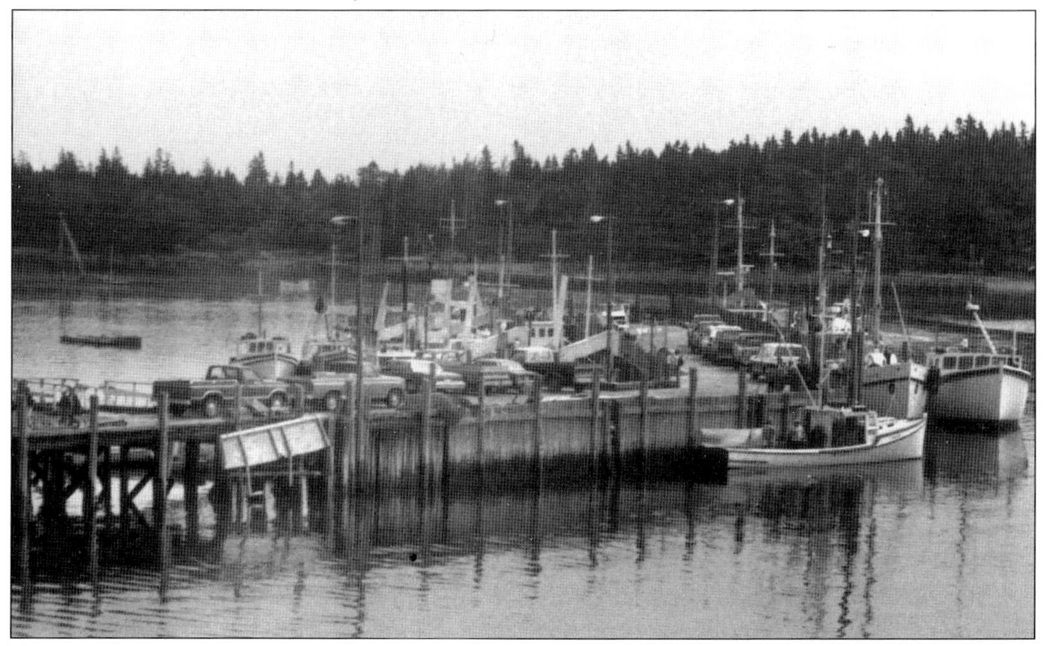

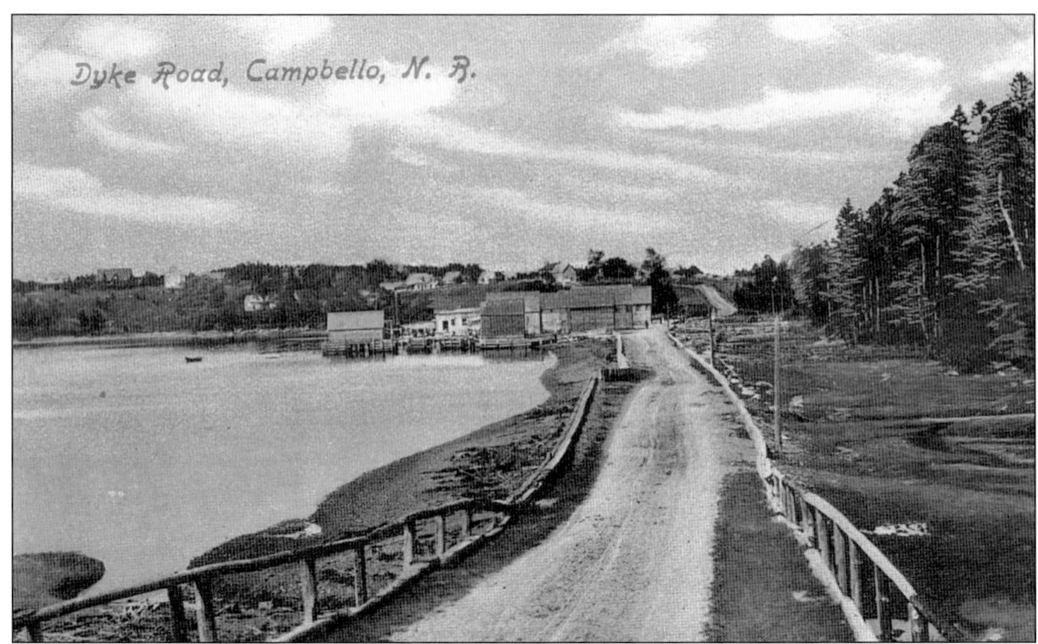

It is said that there is an island in Passamaquoddy Bay for each day of the year. One of those islands, Campobello Island, is shown here, above. This postcard is of Dyke Road and was sent by S.B.R. to G.G. Murdock of Douglas Avenue in Saint John with the following note: "Campobello is just as lovely here as ever, the weather has been very fine. . . and lovely moon lite nights." The cool climates of Campobello and Grand Manan were attractive to American visitors in the days before air conditioners. Simple activities like hiking, beachcombing, and rowing, as shown in the scene below off Gannett Light, were attractive to the city dwellers, who were as adverse to crowds and noise as they are today. (Courtesy PA, 8-716.)

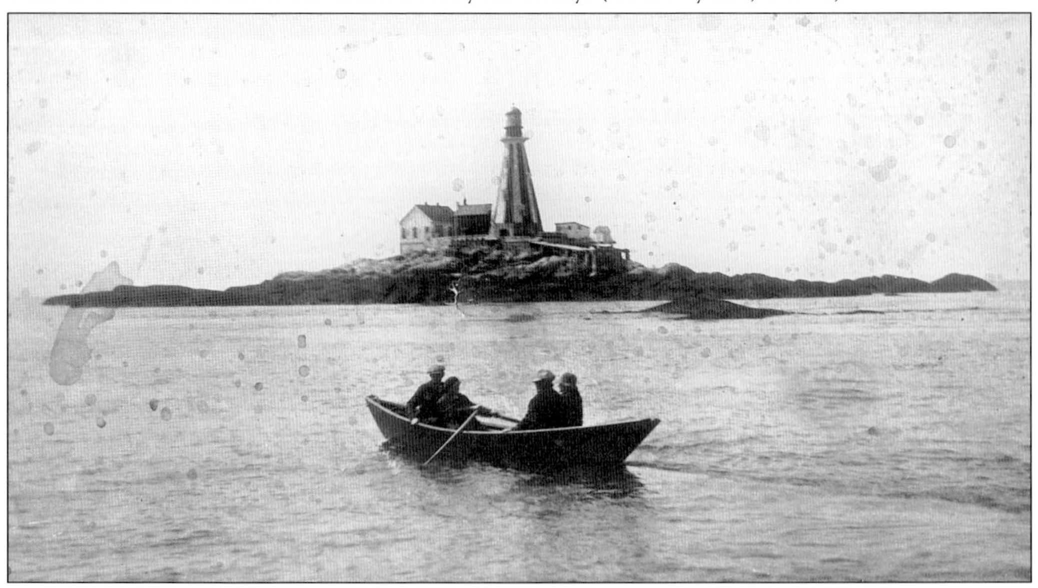

Pictured here is Eugene Toy and his sailboat near his family's cottage at Grey's Mountain, Lake Utopia, in July 1931. A full chapter of this book is devoted to this beautiful eight-by-two-kilometre lake to the north of St. George where many area residents had summer cottages and enjoyed fishing, hunting, hiking, and picnicking. Some adventurers claim to have seen the monster of the lake and speculate about its origins and the origins of a mysterious granite medallion found on the lake's shores. Canoeing and rafting, as shown below, are still popular activities on the lake. In fact, some of the more remote regions and island cottages can only be accessed via boat.

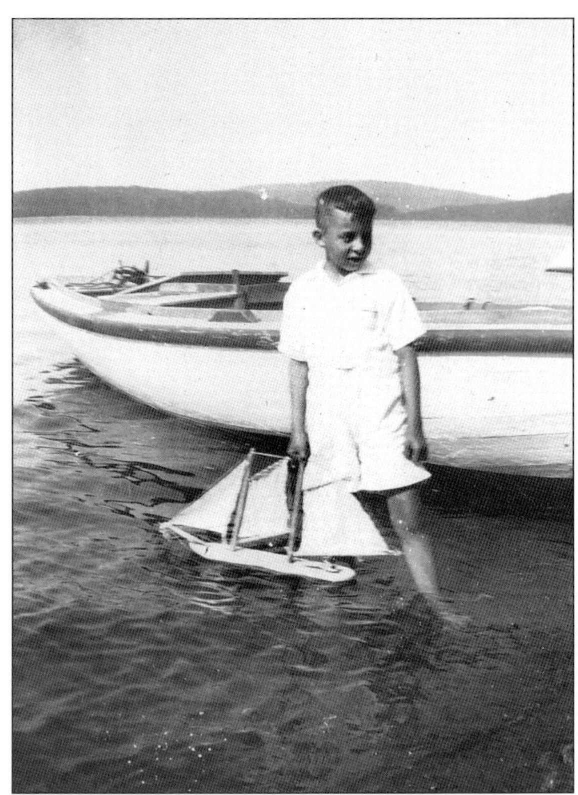

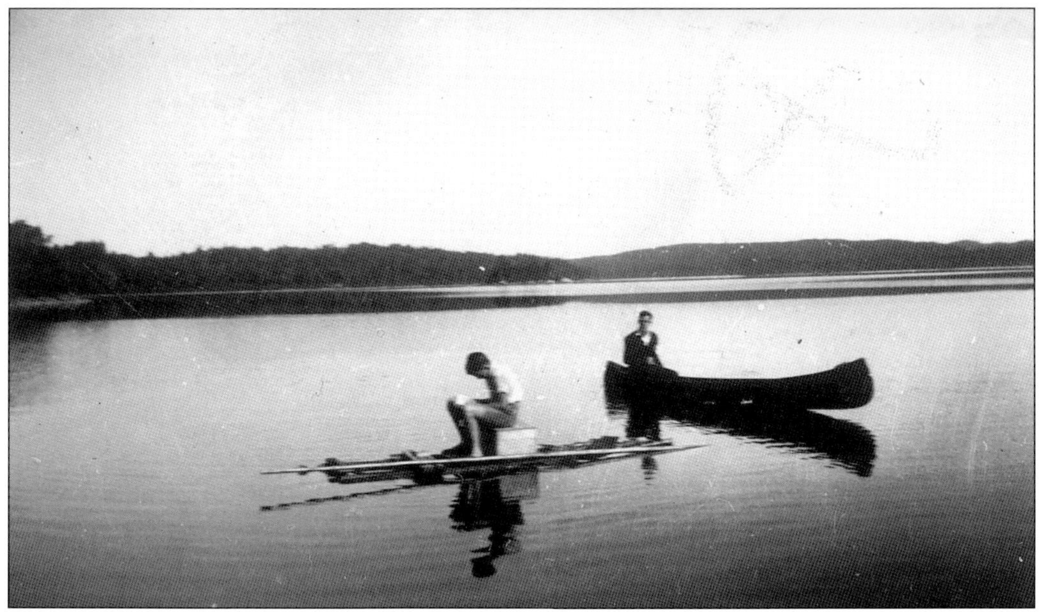

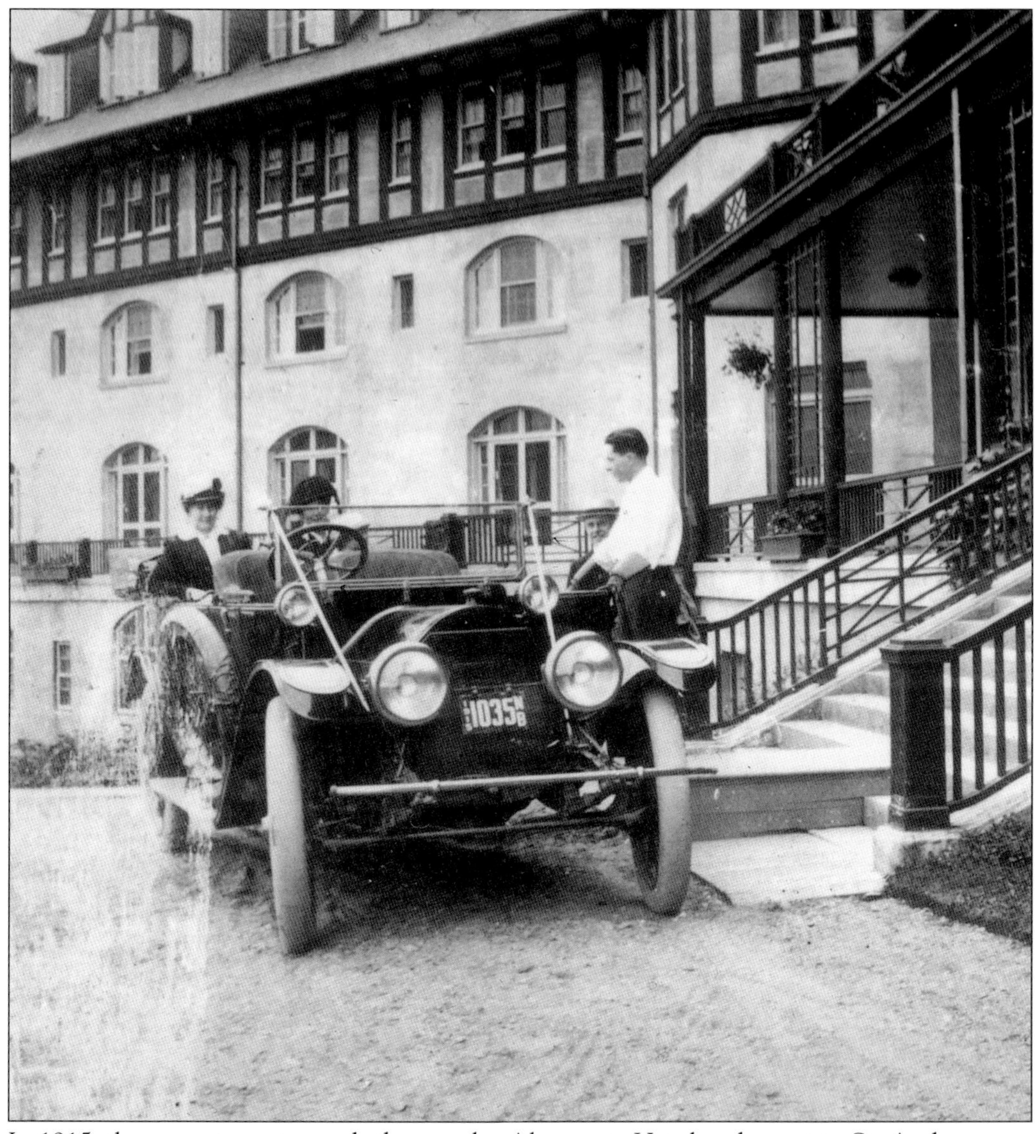

In 1915, the newest way to reach the popular Algonquin Hotel and resort in St. Andrews was via the car. Opened in June of 1889, the hotel first received guests by train or by steamer, and then by horse-drawn coaches. But by 1915, some guests were beginning to arrive in the most modern form of transportation, the car. As will be seen in the pages to follow, St. George residents enjoyed a variety of attractions in the local region and used a variety of transportation methods to get to them. (Courtesy Anne Baker.)

Two

The Magaguadavic River and Falls

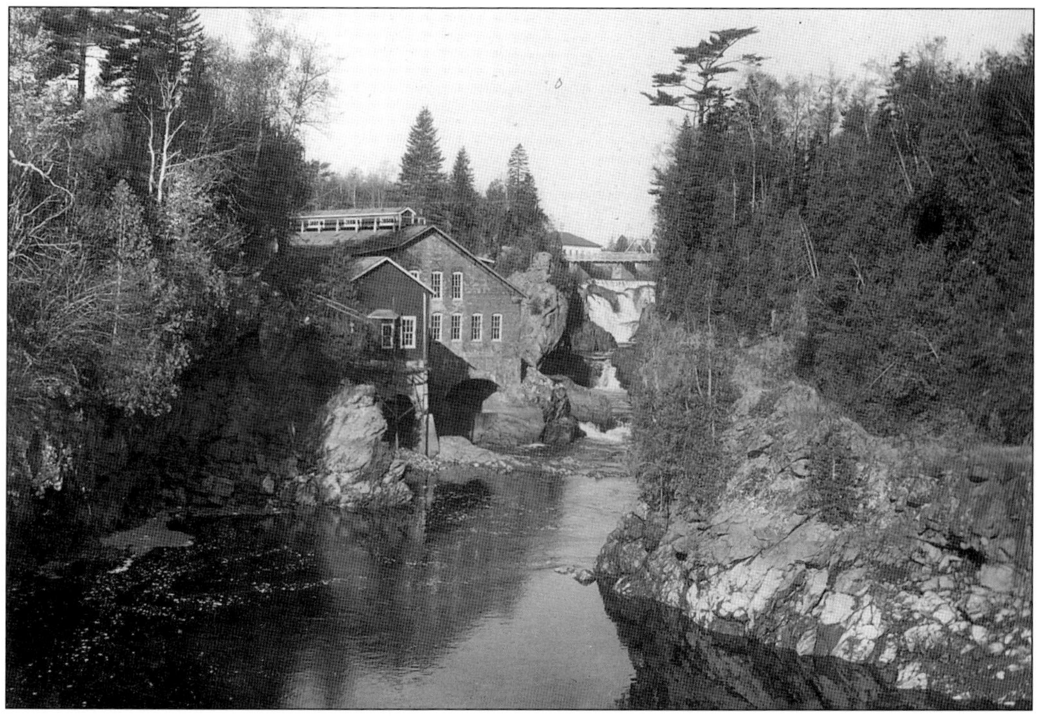

When the Loyalists settled in New Brunswick (then known as Nova Scotia) following the American Revolution in 1783, there were about 2,600 settlers already established in what would become New Brunswick. They were widely scattered and primarily involved in fur trading, fishing, and lumbering. Most lived not far from the coast or convenient inland waterways and considered the interior to be wild lands.

Peter Clinch was granted a 700-acre tract of land east of the falls on the Magaguadavic River. Arriving in November of 1783, too late to build, he wintered in neighbouring Saint John and then began development of a mill on the river in the spring of 1784. He called the settlement "Little Falls."

Eight kilometres south of Clinch's location, some 150 men had settled on the peninsula of L'Etang and named it St. George. There were thoughts that it would become "the principal port of British North American." However, when the village burned in 1790, the settlers abandoned the site, joined Clinch at Little Falls, and changed the name to St. George in honor of their king. The Magaguadavic Falls location presented both a challenge and an opportunity, and both will be seen in the photographs in this chapter. Above is a view of the falls and the 1902 brick powerhouse, which is still in use, though no wood is sawn or pulp ground at the location today.

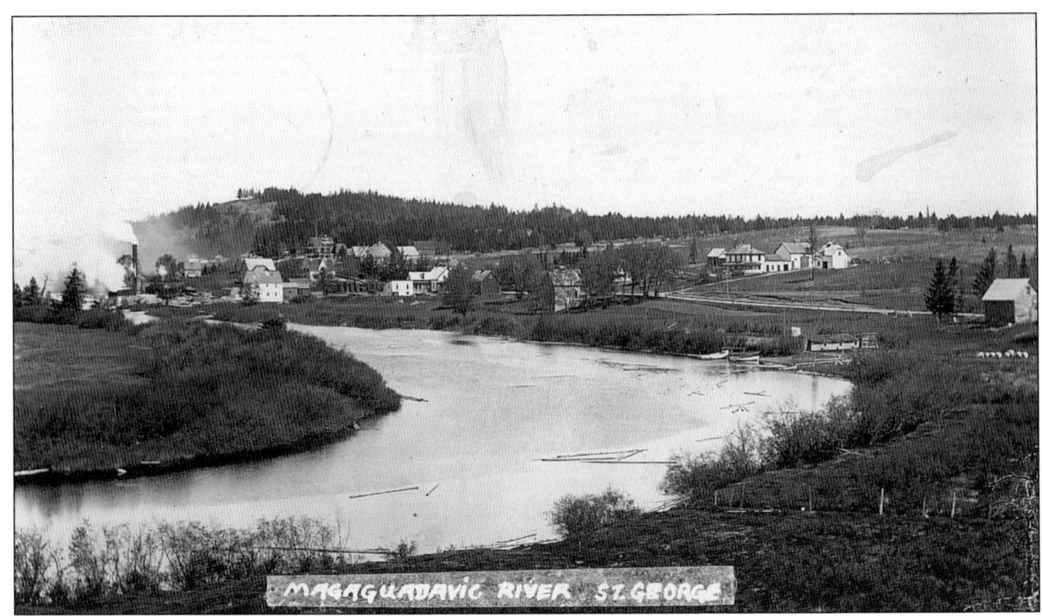

The Magaguadavic River begins as a stream, which can be jumped in spots, where it flows out of the 16-kilometre-long Magaguadavic Lake deep in the woods of York County and 60 kilometres north of the waterfall at the town of St. George. Clinch, it is said, became smitten with the area's great beauty when he was taken upriver in a canoe by the Passamaquoddy Indians. In a scene like this, it is easy to see why.

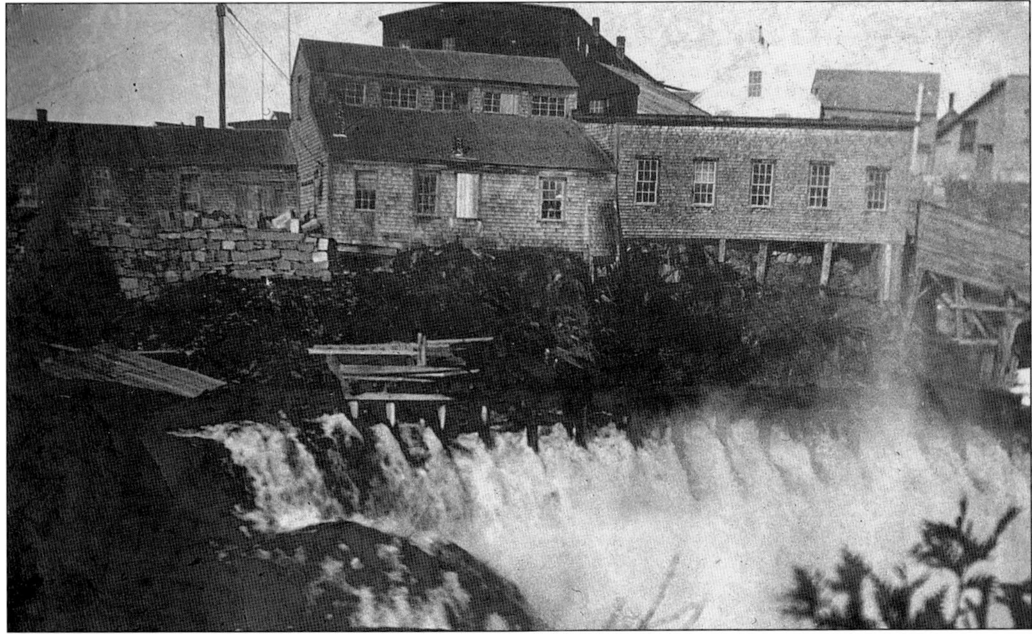

No one alive today has seen the river un-dammed at First Falls. The early dams, as shown here, were all wooden structures, and the damage in the spring freshets was great. The power of the 21-metre falls has been used for milling lumber, cutting and polishing granite, and driving machinery in the pulp mill. In early times, it was not realized that the dams were impeding the passage of alewives, shad, and salmon to upriver spawning grounds.

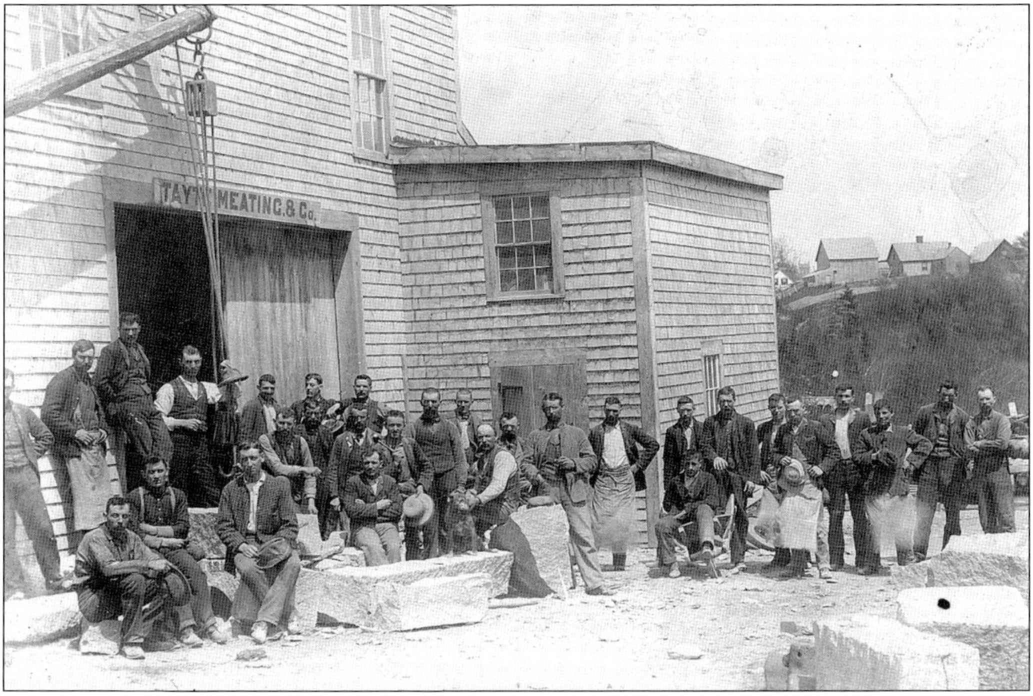

One of the industries that depended on the power of the falls was the cutting and polishing of granite. The industry began in the 1870s when New York fisherman Charles Ward noted immense ledges of red granite on the shores of Lake Utopia. He was instrumental in forming the Bay of Fundy Granite Company, and later there were many other companies, including the St. George Granite Company, Milne, Coutts & Company, New Brunswick Red Granite Company, Epps, Dodds & Company, and Tayte, Meating & Company, whose sheds and workers are shown in these turn of the century views. Some 50 sites were worked during the period of 1872–1940, and it was by the utilization of this natural resource that St. George became known as the industrial centre of Charlotte County.

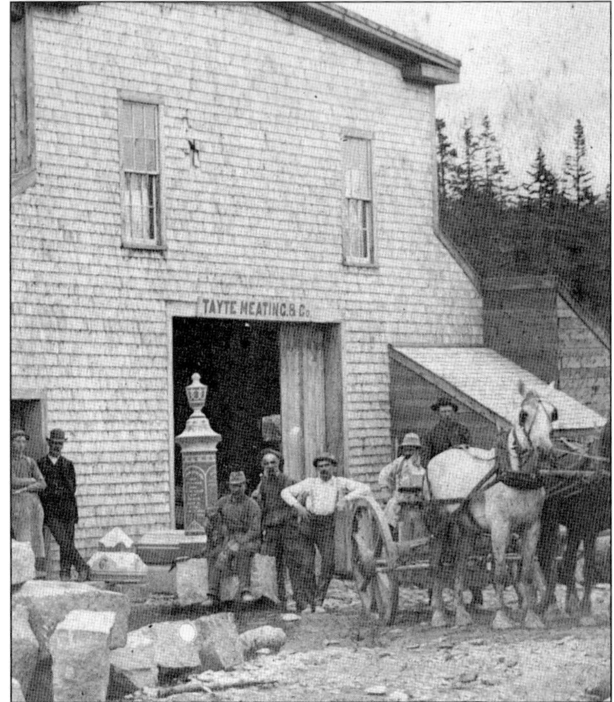

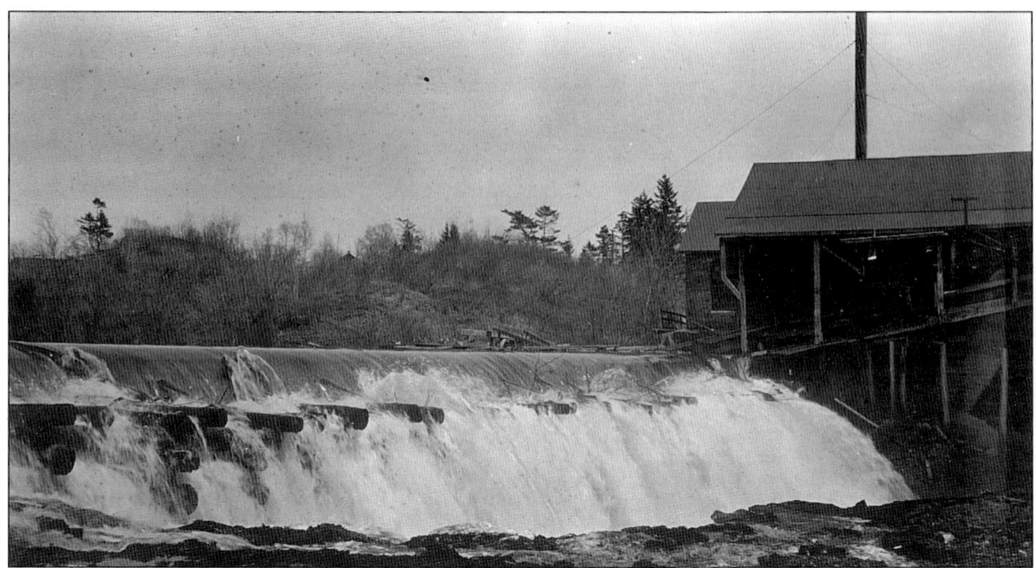

It was spring runoff time when this picture was taken in 1933 at the wood mill on the Magaguadavic. By that time, the Roberge Dam, the first big dam on the river, had already been completed. The dam was above the wood mill, below what was then the upper bridge (now middle bridge) where the logs were received, debarked, and fed into the sluice to go into the grinding and pulping stage at the pulp mill site farther downstream.

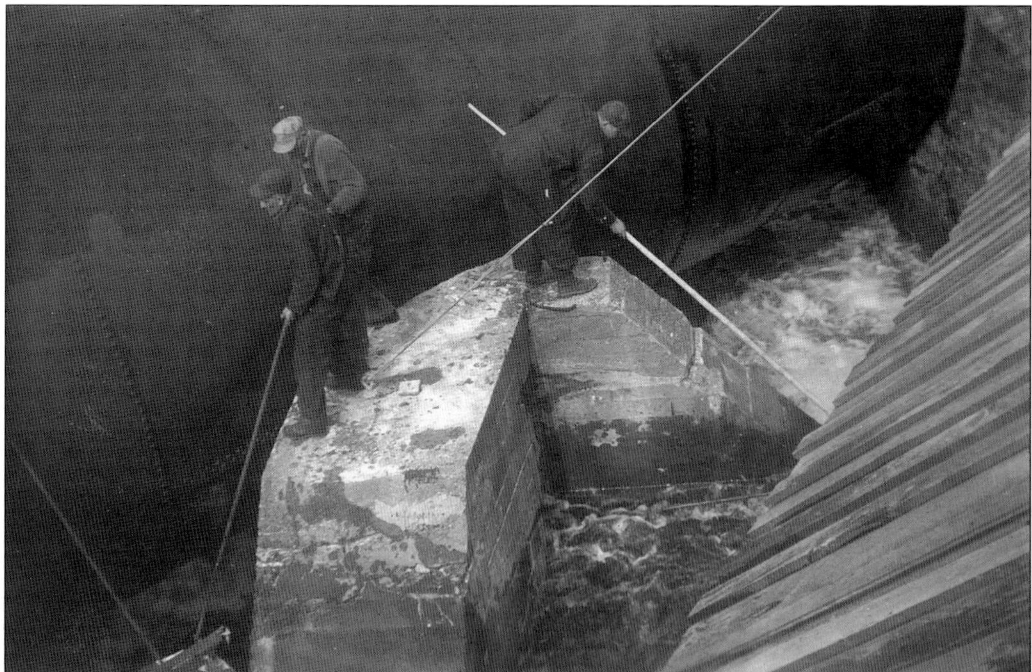

These men are near the pulp mill trying to catch salmon with hooked spears. They are standing on granite and concrete piers, which supported the steel penstocks that fed water to the mill. The Dominion government built a major fishway in 1885 when it became obvious the fish needed an assist over the dams. Still, it was not considered much of a crime to catch salmon when times were tough and the fish still seemed plentiful.

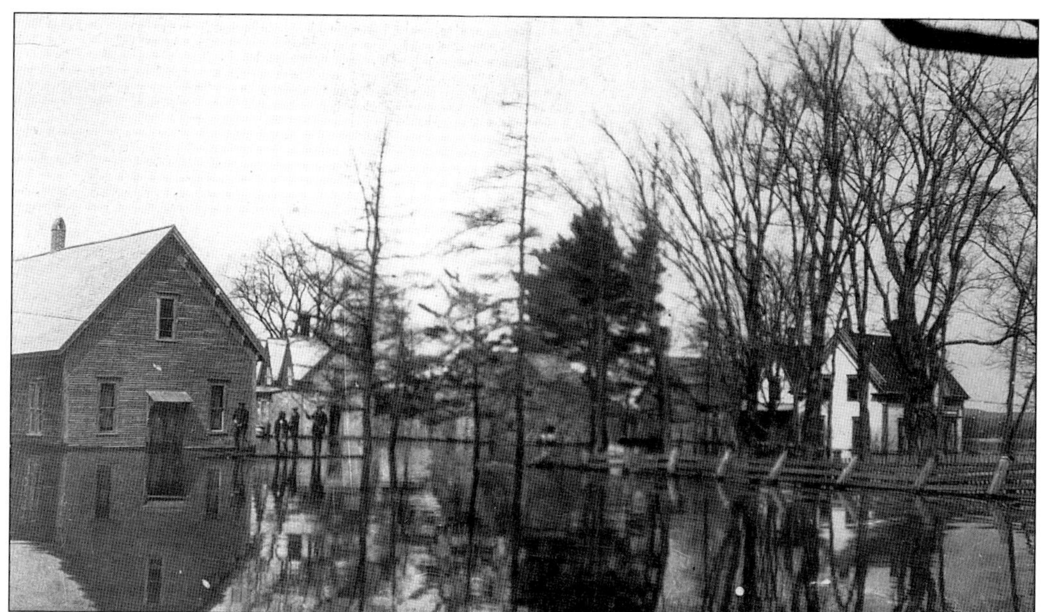

The damming of the Magaguadavic created perfect conditions for water backup during the spring runoff, and sometimes homes were flooded and inaccessible except by raft, as seen here in this photograph taken on May 1, 1923. The men are floating outside Alvah C. Toy's home on Riverview Avenue. In the background are the Dregorgian Hall and Tom Meating's home and barn.

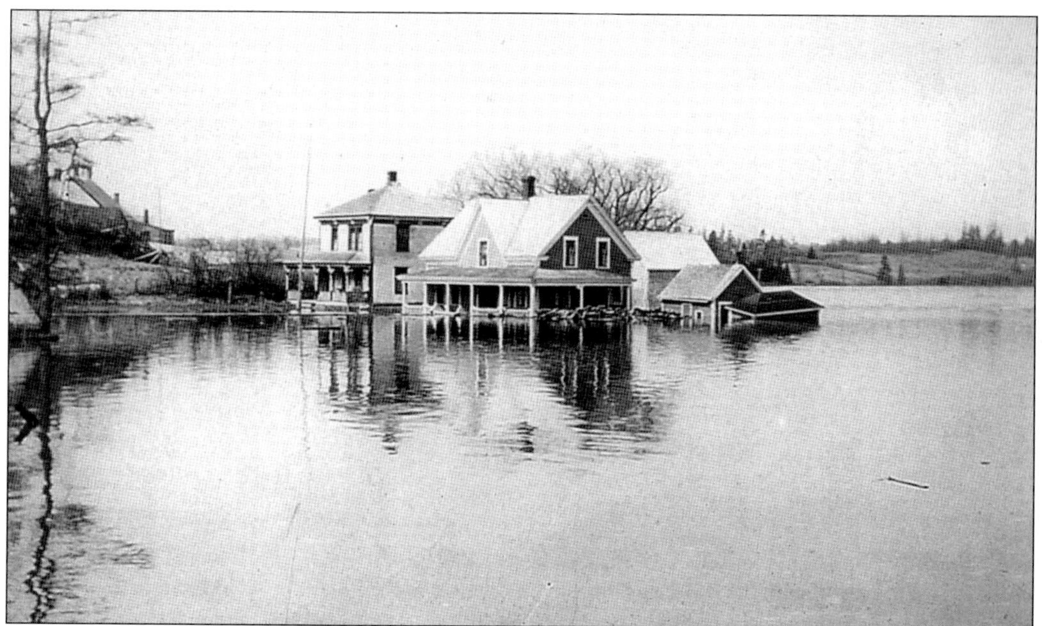

Also in 1923, the homes of Alex Herron (later Alan and Nadine Holmes) and Mattie Dodds (later Barbara and Richard Boone) are shown surrounded by the Magaguadavic in this second view of freshet conditions.

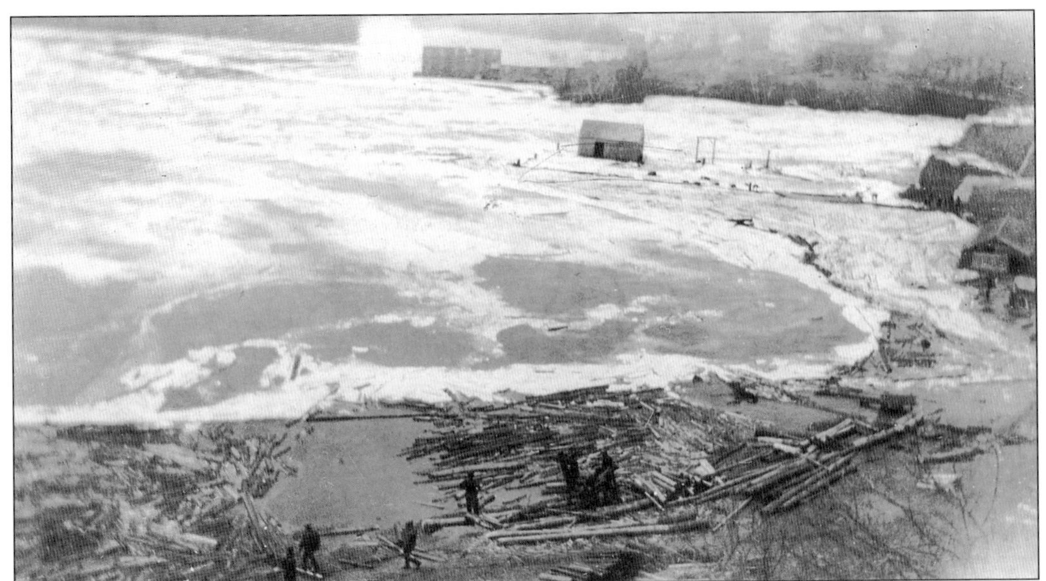

On the last day of April 1923, at high water, the saltwater basin below the Magaguadavic was receiving so much water that the town wharf, shown in other sections of the book with ships loading pulp, was almost underwater. The men in the foreground are trying to save logs that had broken free of the upriver booms and floated over the dam in the raging river.

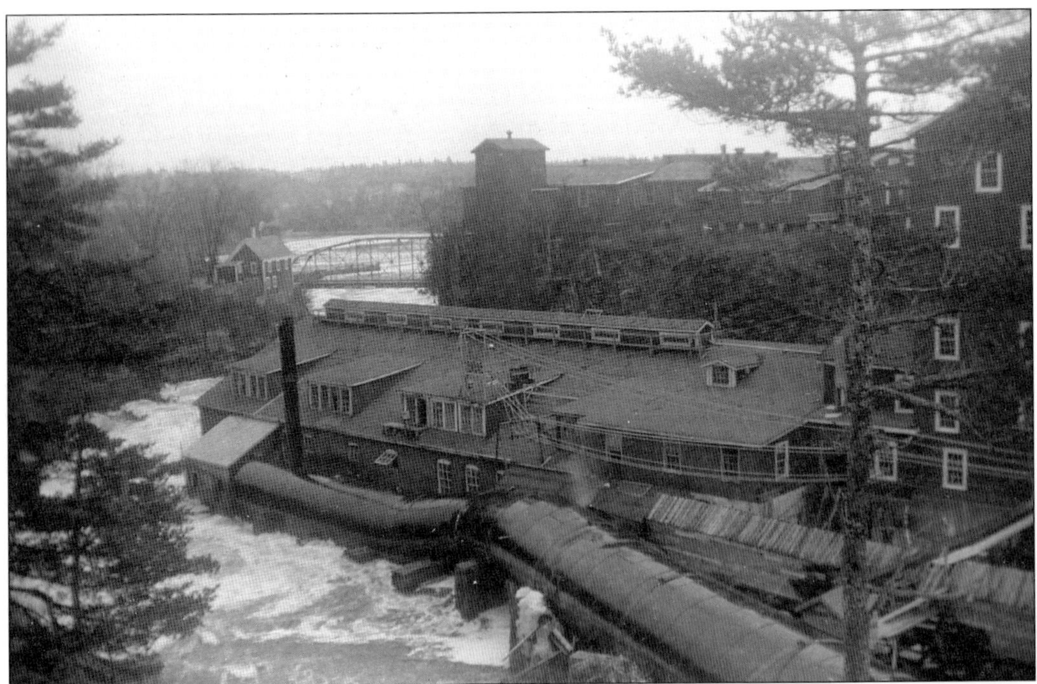

Before it was dammed, the Magaguadavic surged over five ledges in a 450-metre-long channel with 33-metre-high walls that led to the saltwater basin at its mouth. It created a pretty picture and dense spray. After damming, the water used to run the generators was sluiced through the 5.5-metre penstock shown running into the mill in this photograph, but in spring conditions, the falls looked more like they did in olden times.

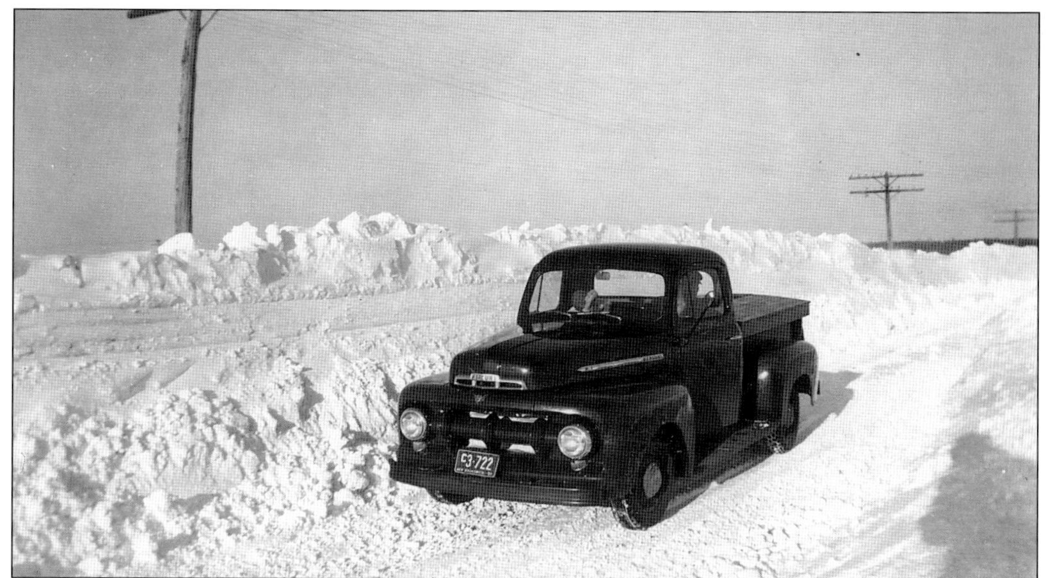

Winters brought varying amounts of snow, and in early times, snow was welcome as it smoothed rutted roads and made traveling by sleigh comfortable and convenient. With the era of automobiles, snow was not as welcome, and it could result in closures of roads, as was the case in this storm at Pennfield Ridge on February 29, 1952. Heavy snow usually led to the high-water conditions in springtime, as seen in several of these photographs.

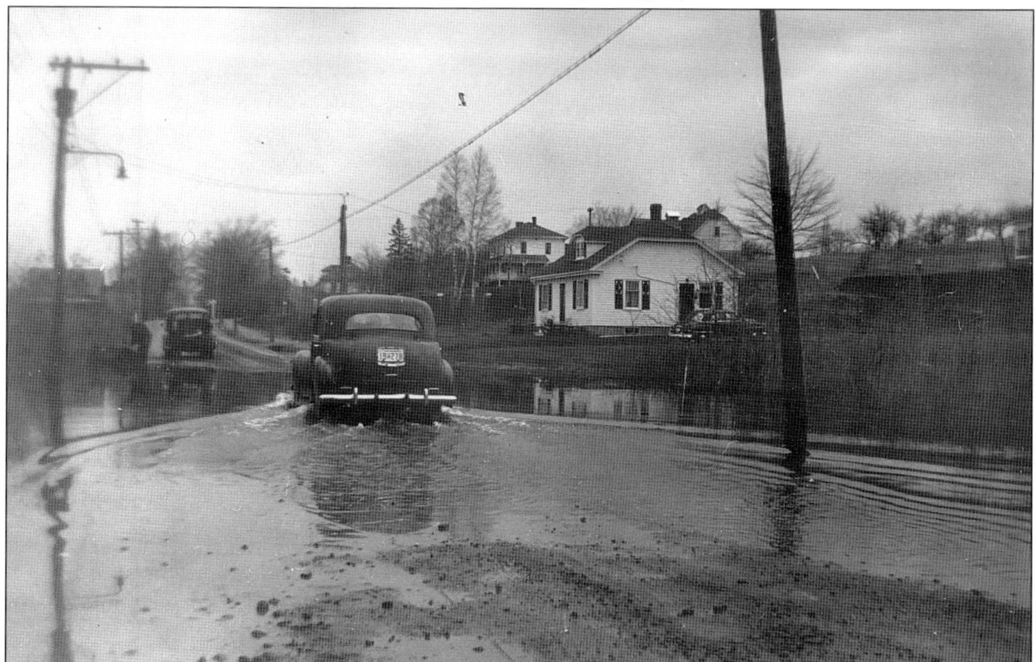

In the late afternoon of April 19, 1954, the swelling Magaguadavic's water reached Riverview Avenue and lapped at the lawn of Don Goodeill's home. Cars are seen working their way carefully through the water as men on the far side of the swollen river lift a boat with an outboard motor from their truck and place it in the river, perhaps to aid some stranded family up or down the river.

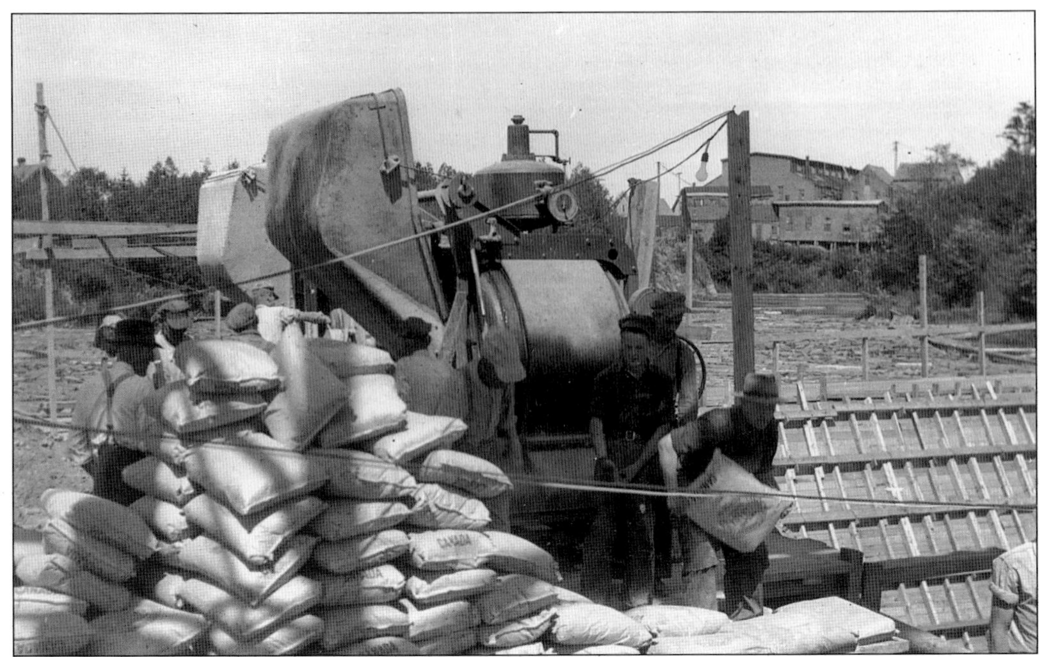

This crew of men is busy at work, in August 1945, building a new dam in what was known as the "Gully" at the wood mill. The dam was the first cement dam on the Magaguadavic River. Across the river are the old granite sheds. Only two companies were still active in the early 1940s, namely O'Brien-Baldwin and Milne-Coutts. In 1953, the latter was the last operating and was bought out by the St. George Pulp and Paper Company.

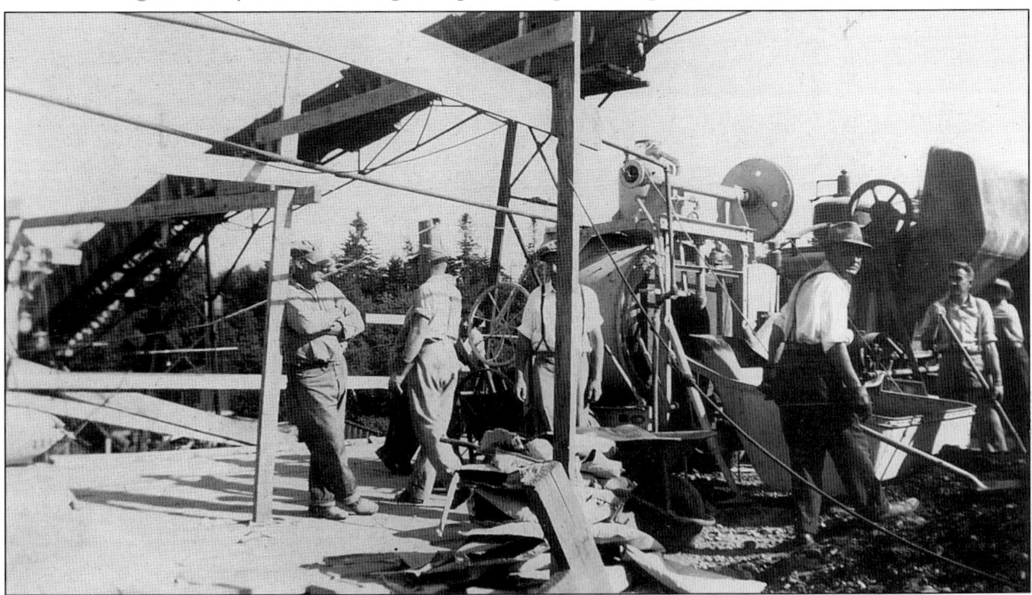

This second view of the concrete dam under construction also shows the pulpwood conveyor that carried the four-foot sticks across the pond and into the debarking building. The gent with his sleeves rolled up and turned looking toward the photographer is Steven Campbell (also shown on page 90). His first-hand knowledge of the pulp mill, lumbering, cold winters, freshets, and town business has been shared freely and been very helpful over the years.

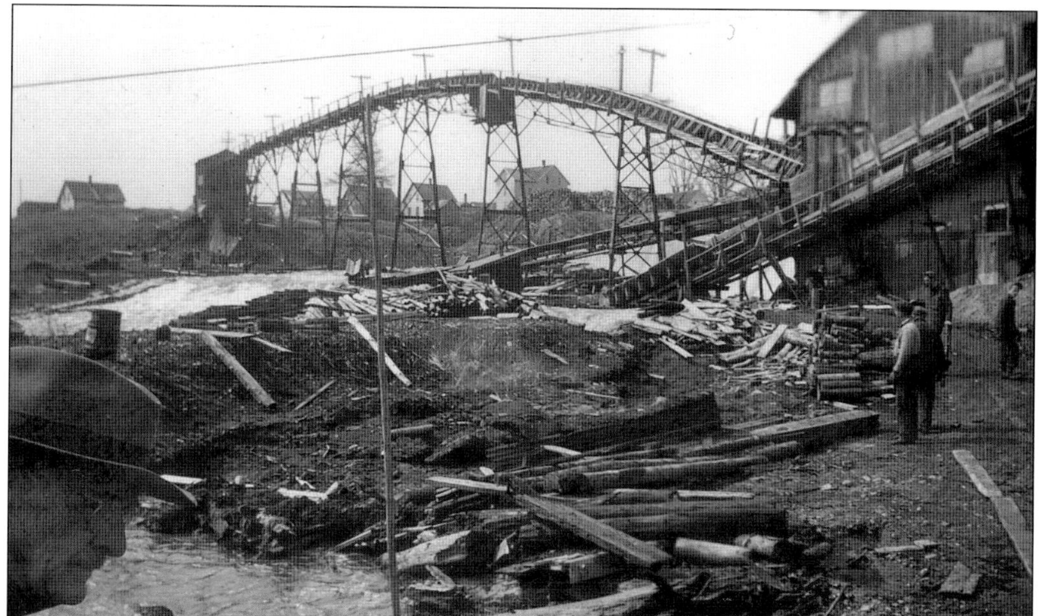

In this general view of the pulp mill operations and the pulp stick conveyors, Alvah C. Toy can be seen in the lower left corner. He was a New York–trained accountant and bookkeeper for the company and came to New Brunswick to assume those positions when the mill first opened up in 1902. He had retired and died before the mill closed in July 1967 putting 100 mill workers and 300 woods workers out of work.

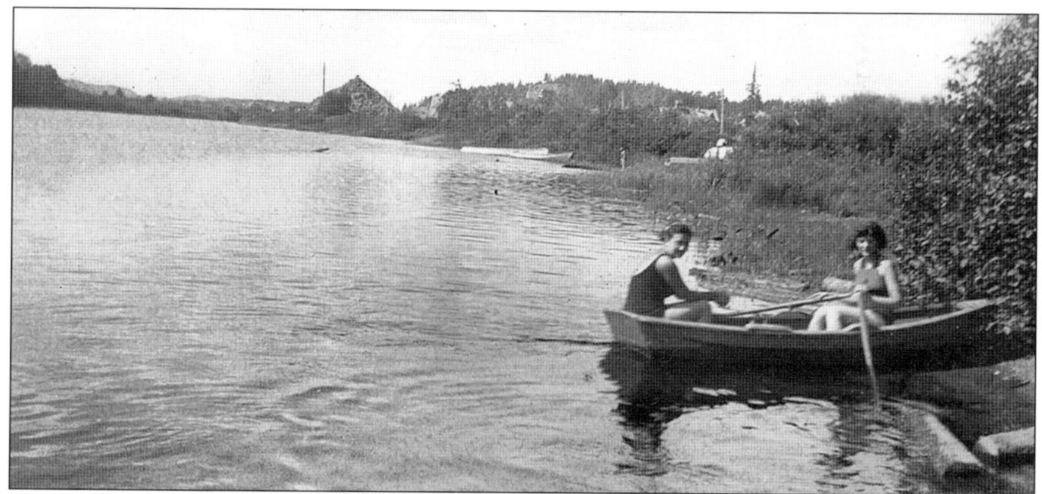

Up the Magaguadavic from the pulp mill, two teens, Frances Toy and Audrey MacDonald, are seen rowing on the river in July of 1935. In the background is Patterson's sawmill with a huge pile of logs ready to be sent down to the mill through a five-metre steel penstock and then chewed in the grinders and pressed dry to make the 100-pound bales of pulp, which were shipped off to mills in the United States for further processing.

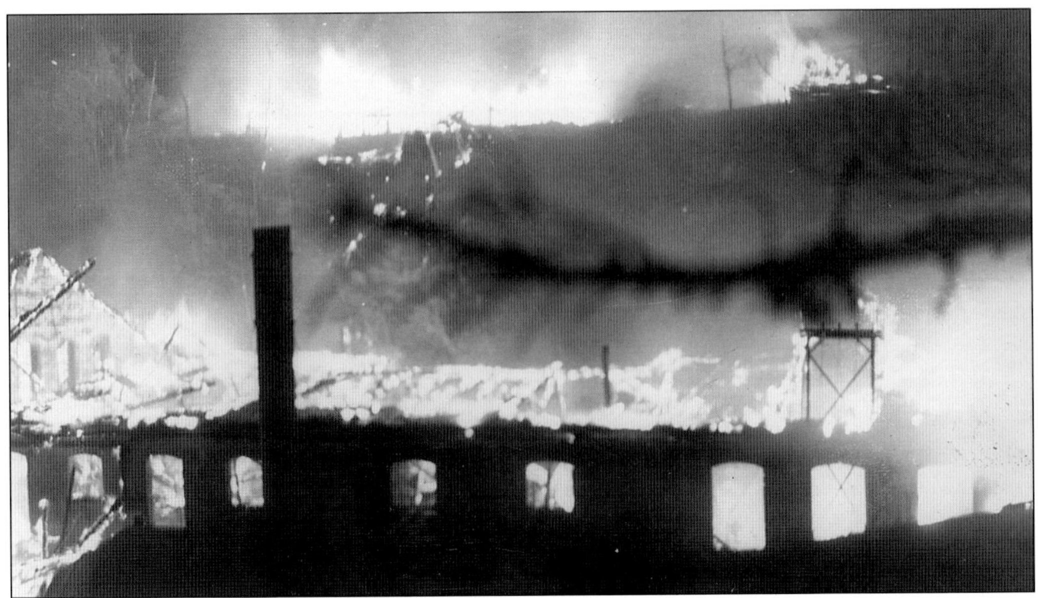

On the night of October 20, 1946, a fire struck the mill. Most of the walls remained standing, and some of the machinery, like waterwheels, pulp grinders, parts of the wet machines, and hydraulic presses, was salvageable. Reconstruction of the mill was undertaken by owner A. J. Lacroix of Saint John, who had taken over the mill after International Paper had sold it to Edouard Lacroix of St. George's, Quebec, and Senator B.W. Page of Maine.

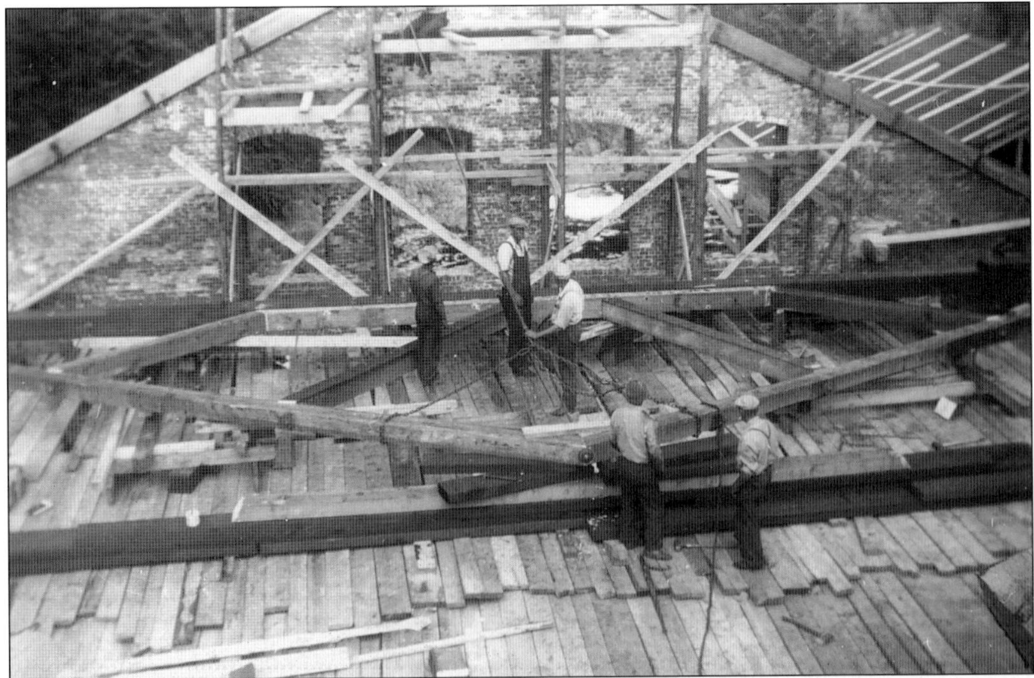

Through the summer of 1947, reconstruction was undertaken as shown above, and by Christmas, the *St. Croix Courier* was able to note St. George would have a "Happy Christmas," as ". . . after a silence of more than a year, the old whistle of the St. George Pulp and Paper Company. . . will probably resume its daily duties before the end of the year."

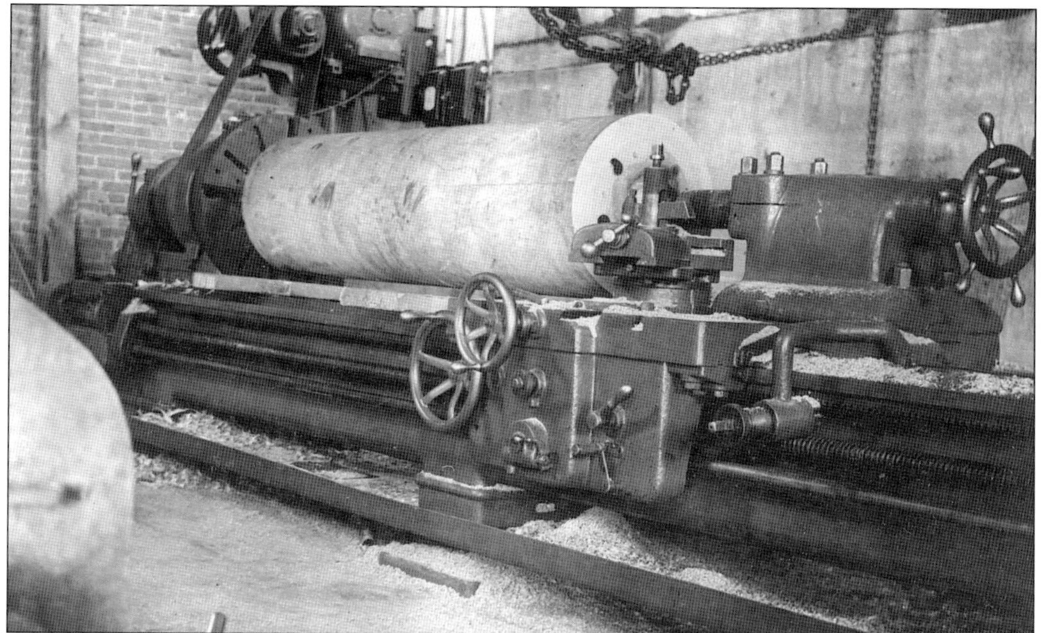

The top photograph shows the machine shop of the pulp mill with hardwood rollers 2.5 metres long, which were made of maple or yellow birch. Here the wet-machine workers used a sharpened hardwood stick about a half-metre long to cut and peel the ground wood pulp sheets off the roles. The sheets were then folded and put on an endless belt that took them to the hydraulic presses. The bottom photograph shows a new generator, which was added to the mill after the 1946 fire and changed the direct current operation to that of a 550-volt alternating current.

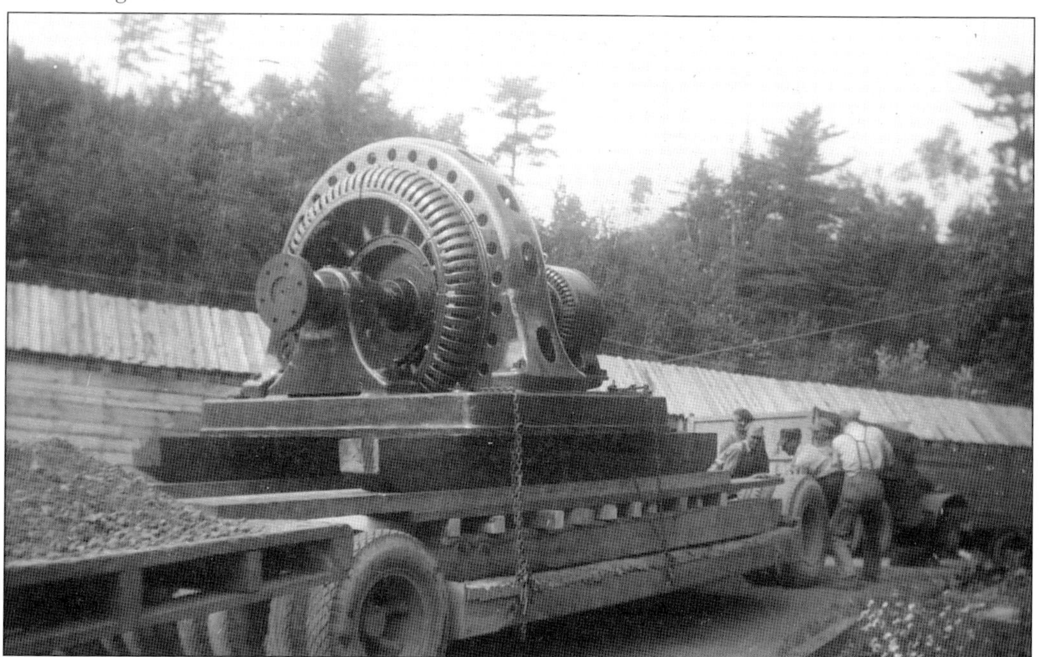

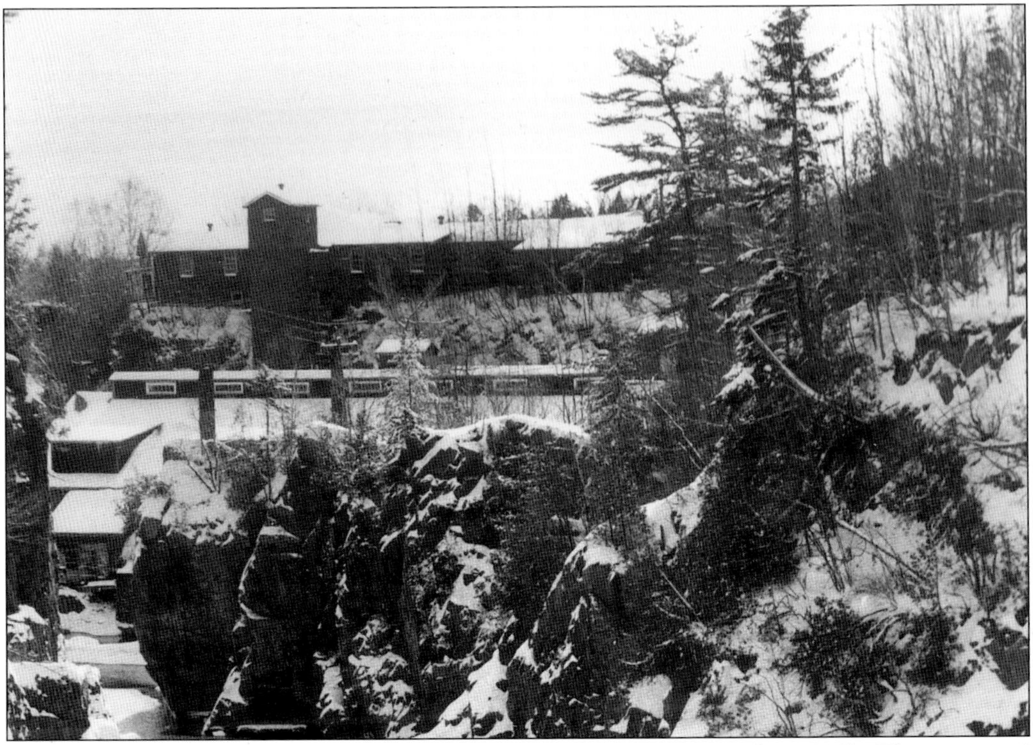

Some people find winter the most beautiful time of year at Magaguadavic Falls. The perpetual mist turns to crystals of ice that cling to the trees and crevices in the cliffs. Eventually, the falls ice over, and all is quiet. Still, water churns through the penstocks to the old pulp mill building, today to generate power for the town—by J.D. Irving, the present owners of the building—rather than pulp. Thus, Clinch's falls still serve his decedents.

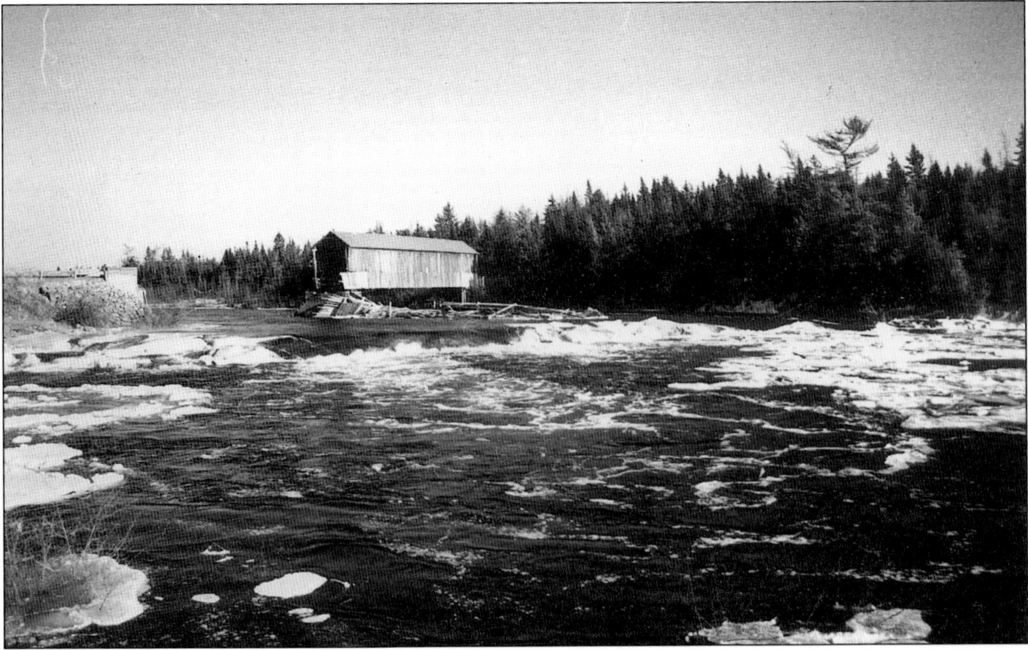

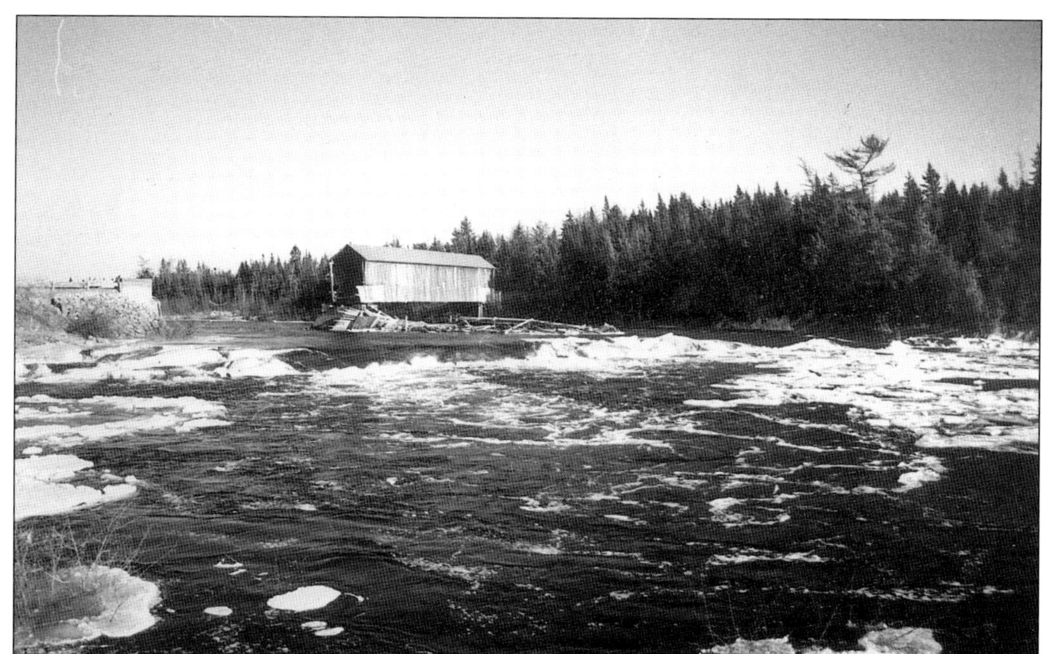

Covered wooden bridges likely crossed the river both below and above the Magaguadavic Falls in earlier times. In the top picture, we see the covered bridge at Second Falls on the Bonny River. Half of the bridge was blown off its foundation by gale-force winds on Monday, February 2, 1976, in what later became known as the "Groundhog Gale." The picture to the right was taken by Phoebe Toy of the lower bridge probably just after the pulp mill was opened. Note how its timbers were used for advertising various teas available at the time.

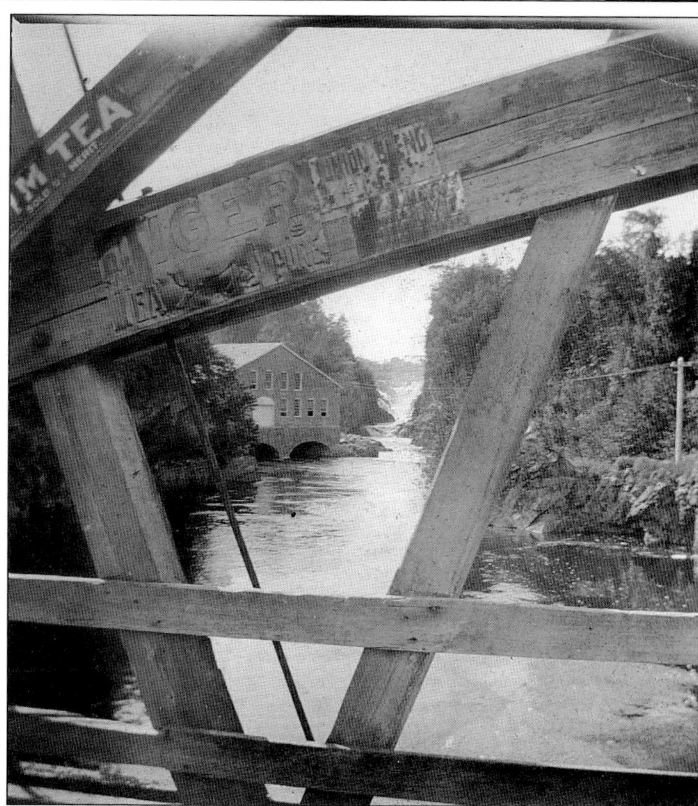

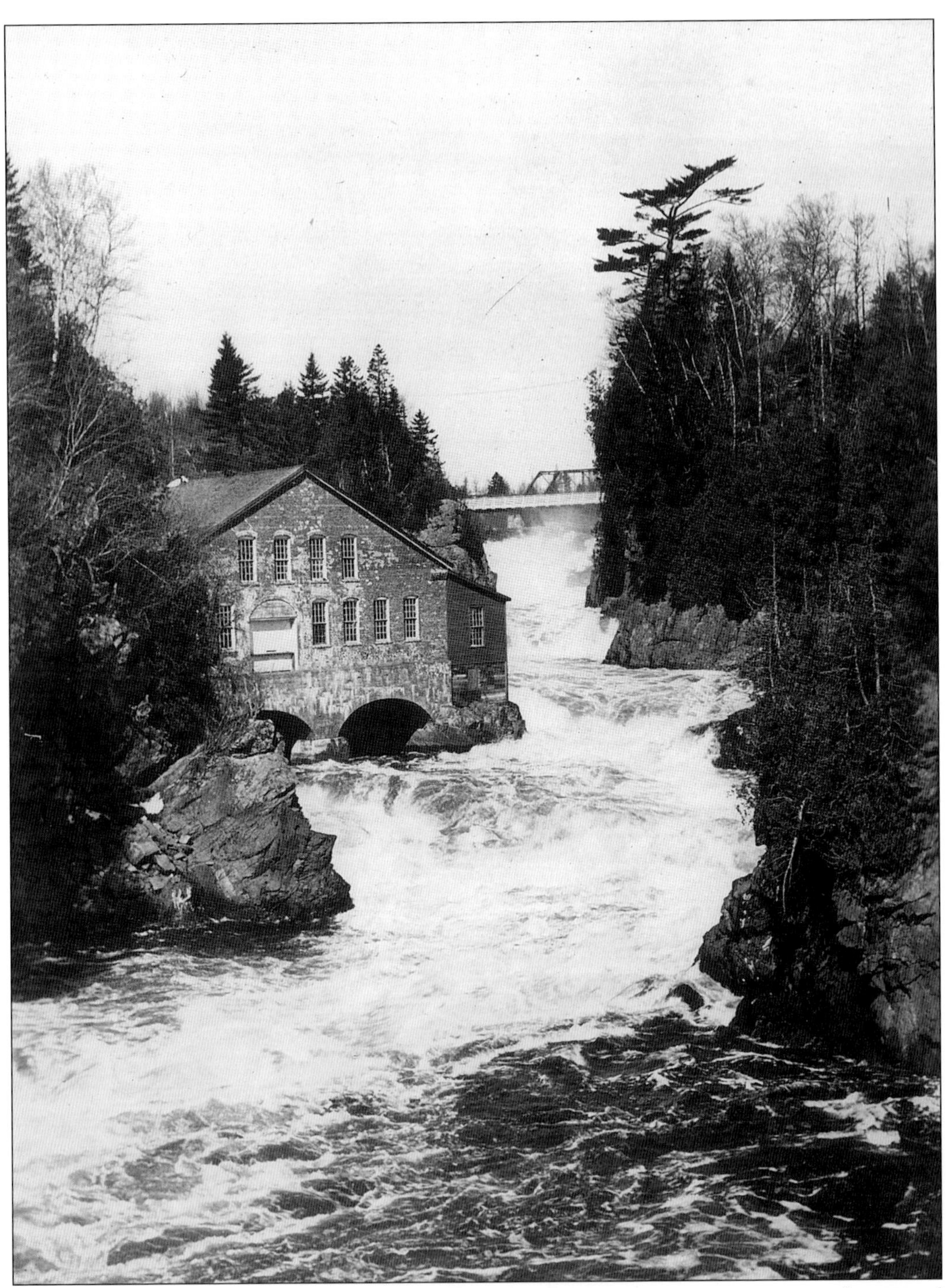

The most often used image for promoting St. George is an interesting contrast of a rugged natural gorge and man-made structures. The pulp mill and powerhouse stand on the left, and atop the cliff is a huge windswept pine tree. The oldest photographs show the tree as it stands now. Perhaps, it was there when Peter Clinch first saw the falls and recognized the combination of timber and water that was just right for his new home.

Three

BUILDING THE TOWN

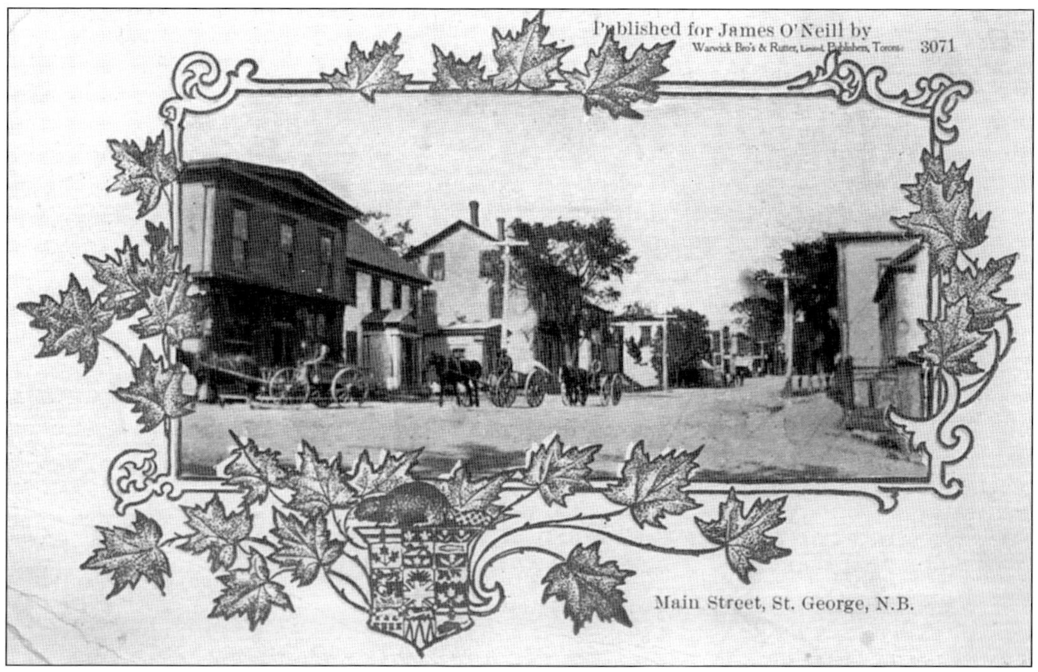

Soon after Peter Clinch settled on his grant at the Magaguadavic Falls in the heart of what is now the town of St. George, he established a sawmill to take advantage of the energy generated by falls. Others soon followed his lead, and by 1833, there were nine sawmills operating in the area. The town streets began to spread out from the falls toward the east and the west and along the shore. In 1839, some quarrying of granite began, and by the 1870s, it was a significant factor in the further expansion of the town's streets. In 1902, a pulp mill was built by New York businessmen and fueled another growth spurt in town. By 1904, the village was incorporated as a town. At that time, there were four towns incorporated in Charlotte County, then the most of any county in the province. The granite industry, which was strongest before the 1900s, had its ups and downs in the early part of the 20th century, and by the 1940s, (though some was still shipped in the 1950s) it was all but closed. The pulp mill employed about 100 men in the mill and some 300 in the woods, but it had periods of inactivity over the years until its final closure in 1967. However, population grew to nearly 1,000 by the beginning of the 20th century, and businesses built up to the extent that St. George became the choice for shopping and the place to access dentists, doctors, lawyers, and other business needs for surrounding areas. In addition, the railway had come to town, and by the 1880s, it became the easiest way to reach the town from places along the line between St. Stephen and Saint John. In the 1950s, the town fell on hard economic times. When a new controlled-access highway bypassed Main Street in the late 1960s, the town seemed to bottom out. However, in recent years, there has been a revival due to fish farming (mostly salmon) in the Bay of Fundy. This has resulted in new growth and new building in the town. Sadly, it has also resulted in the loss of many of the earlier buildings, which can be seen now only in photographs, such as this postcard view that shows gravel wagons on Main Street, *c.* 1910.

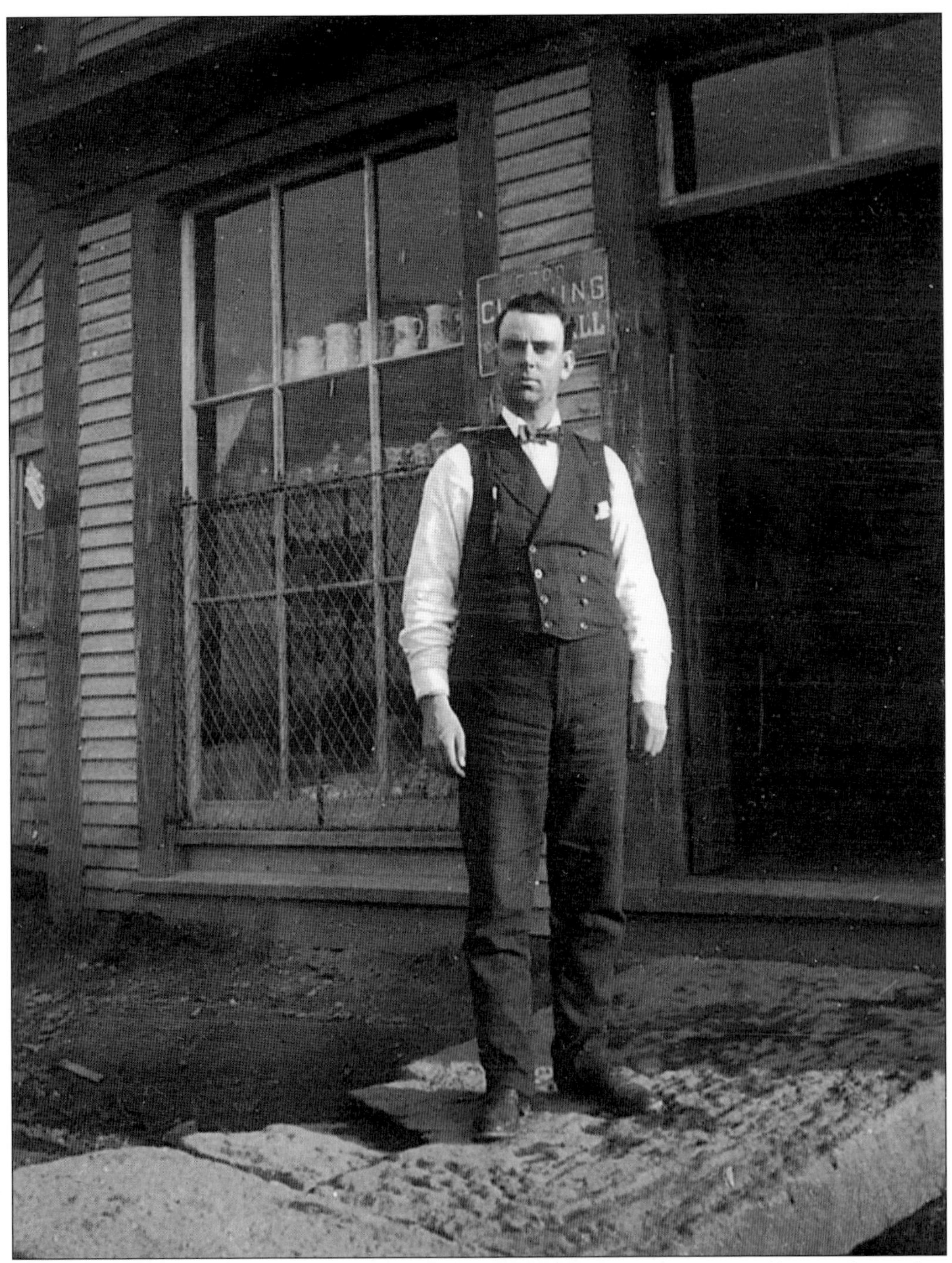

Edward Millighan stands in front of the Epps, Dodds & Company granite mill store, located at the east end of the upper bridge, in Phoebe Toy's 1900-era photograph. The St. George area was one of five areas in the province that was involved in the quarrying of granite, the others being at nearby Bocabec, up the St. John River at Hamstead, and at the north end of the province at Bathurst and Antinouri Lake.

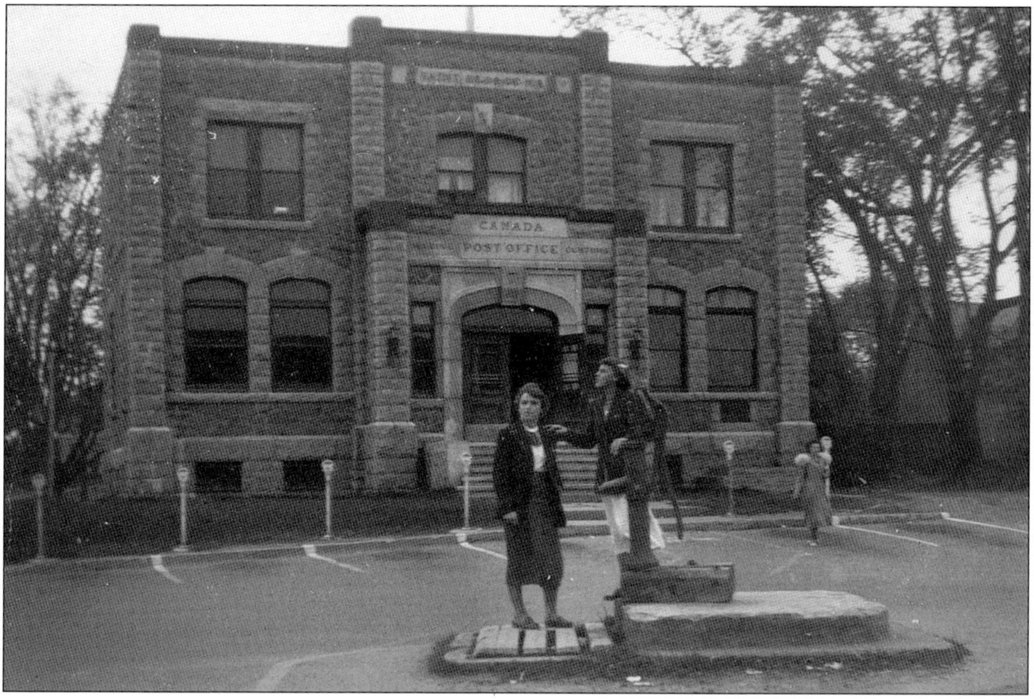

The post office was constructed in 1935–1936, and granite was used largely through the efforts of A.D. Ganong, a member of parliament, as a way of keeping local men at work in the Great Depression. The 1902 Presbyterian manse is the only other town building that is completely granite. This October 1952 photograph shows the daughters of Mr. and Mrs. Harry Hooper at the town pump and Barbara Hoyt leaving the post office.

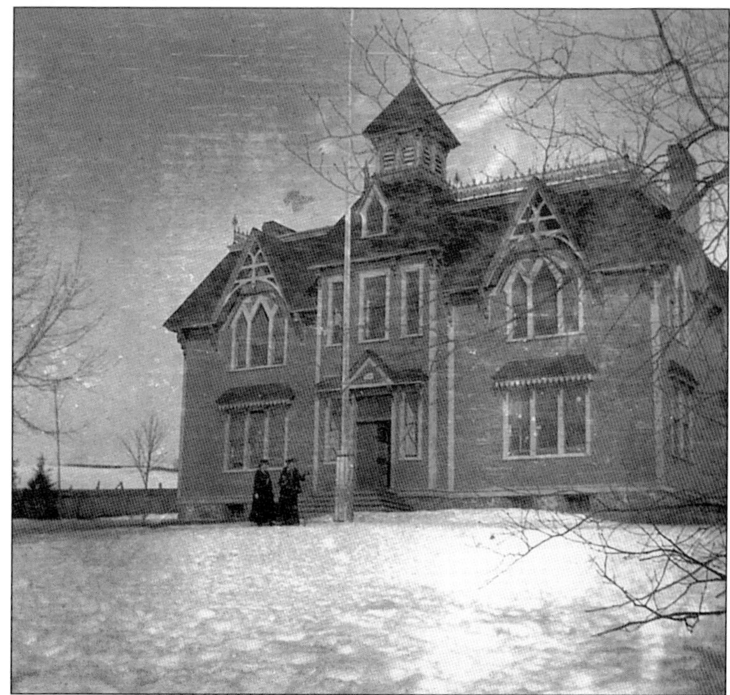

Had granite been chosen to build the St. George Superior School in 1888, it might still be standing. Upon the opening of the school, the *St. Croix Courier* noted "it's one of the handsomest school buildings in the province. . . 19 by 12 meters. . . will accommodate four departments of the town's school. . ." G.M. Johnson was principal and also taught, along with Thomas O'Malley and Mary and Elisa Magowan who are thought to be standing in front of the school in this Phoebe Toy photograph.

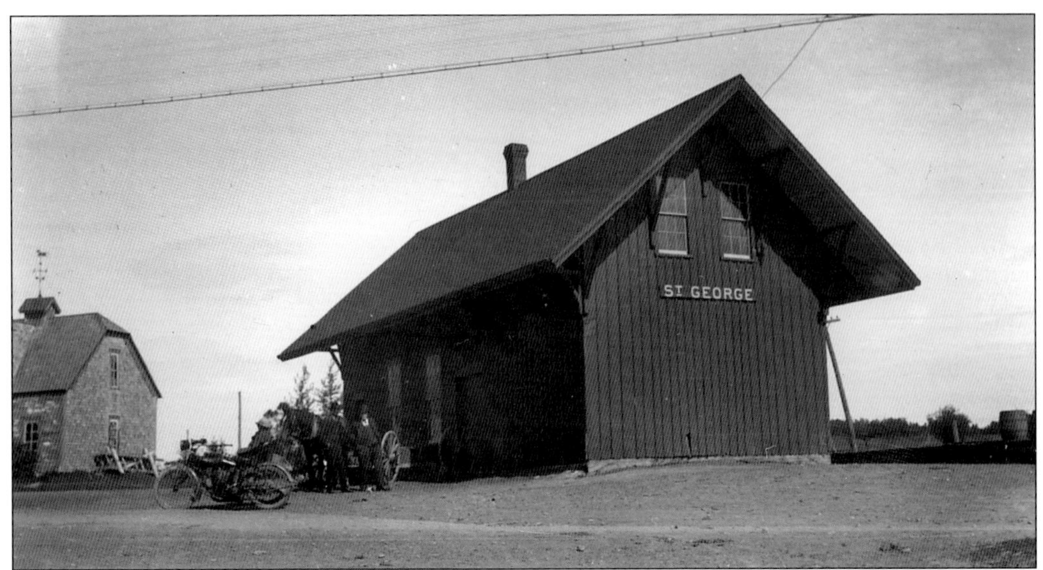

The railway came to St. George officially in January of 1882 and became an important way of moving cut and polished granite to Saint John and on to destinations in upper Canada or the eastern United States. A.V.F. Duffy took this photograph in 1920 while on a motorcycle trip from Saint John to St. George. His motorcycle is seen between the station and John O'Neill's gable-roofed barn.

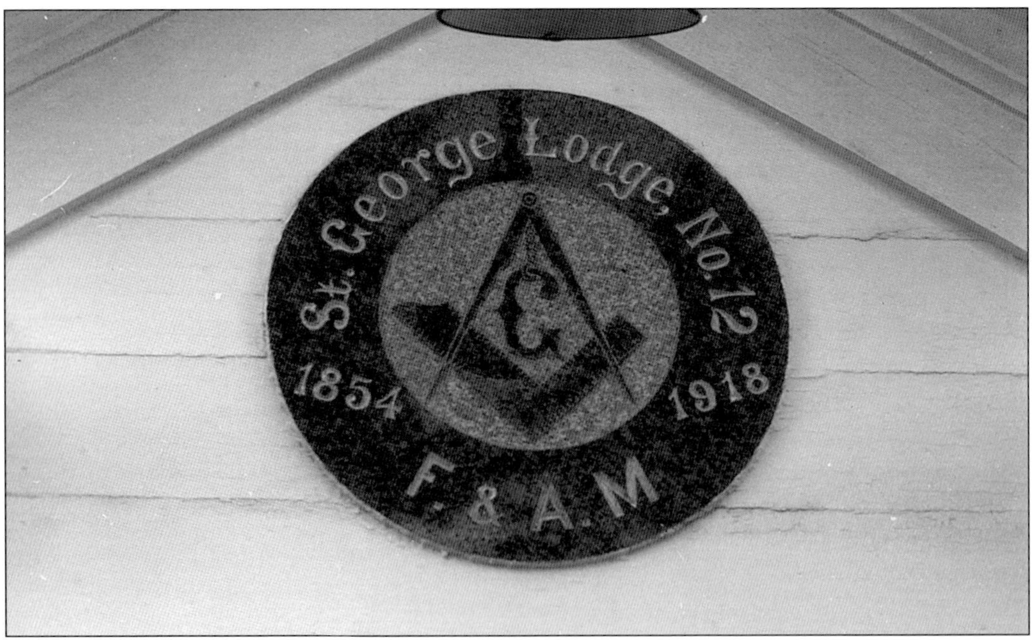

This keystone placed over the door of the St. George Lodge No. 12 of the Free and Accepted Masons commemorates their founding in 1854 and the fact that they opened this building, which still stands, in 1918. It is one of the best public examples to be found in St. George of the skill of the tradesmen in cutting, shaping, and polishing granite.

Probably the best place Duffy could have gone to appreciate the skill of the granite workers that led to the selection of their work for buildings in cities across North America would have been the St. George Rural Cemetery. The Maxwell stone is one example of hundreds in this location and shows how the men could work in rectangles, columns, shaped columns, and ball forms with the very hard material.

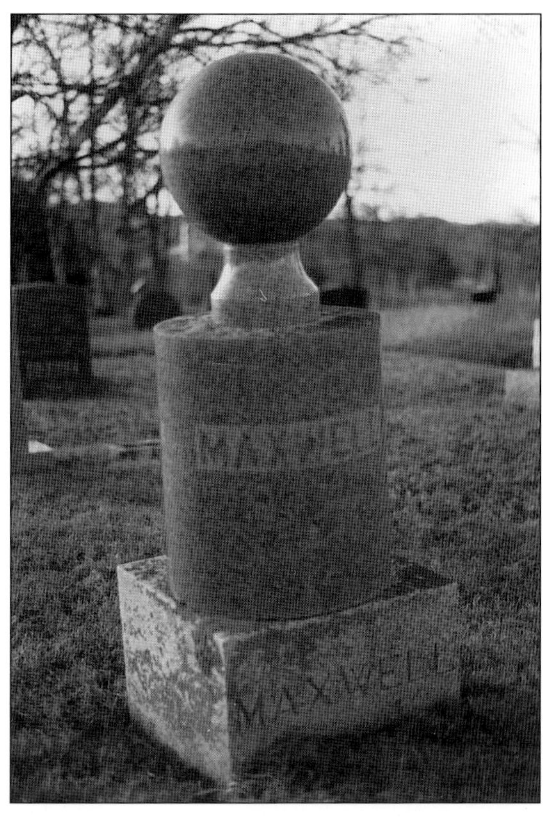

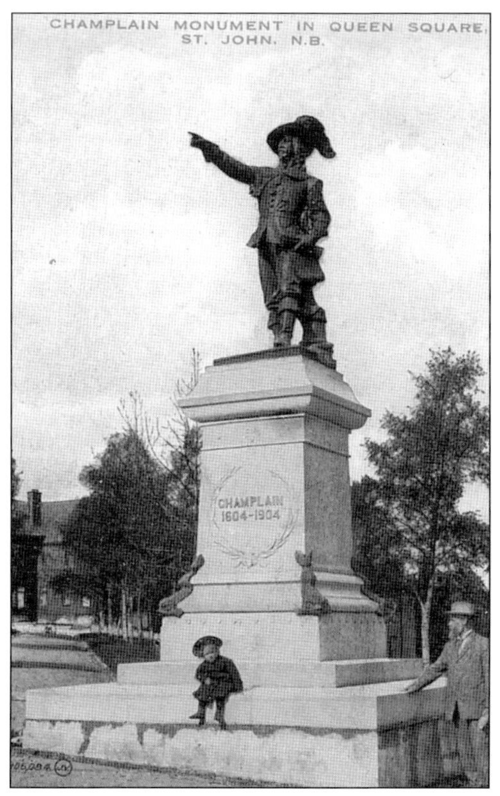

The first visitors to the Charlotte County area in which St. George is located was Champlain and DeMonts, who spent the winter of 1604–1605 on Dochet's Island in the St. Croix River. The base of the tricentennial commemorative monument to Champlain that stands in Queen Square in Saint John was made by granite workers of St. George at the Meating and Epps Company in 1910.

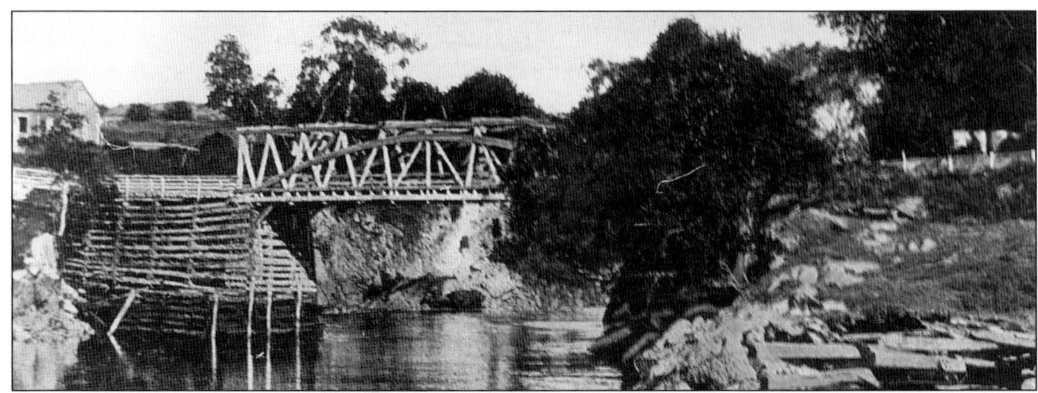

A covered bridge is believed to have been the first bridge built across the Magaguadavic to join the east and west sides of St. George at a point just below the falls near the lower basin. It was destroyed during the Saxby Gale of October 4, 1869, and was replaced by the single-span, unsupported log bridge shown in this photograph. A close-up of this bridge's truss work (with the tea advertisement) was shown on page 33.

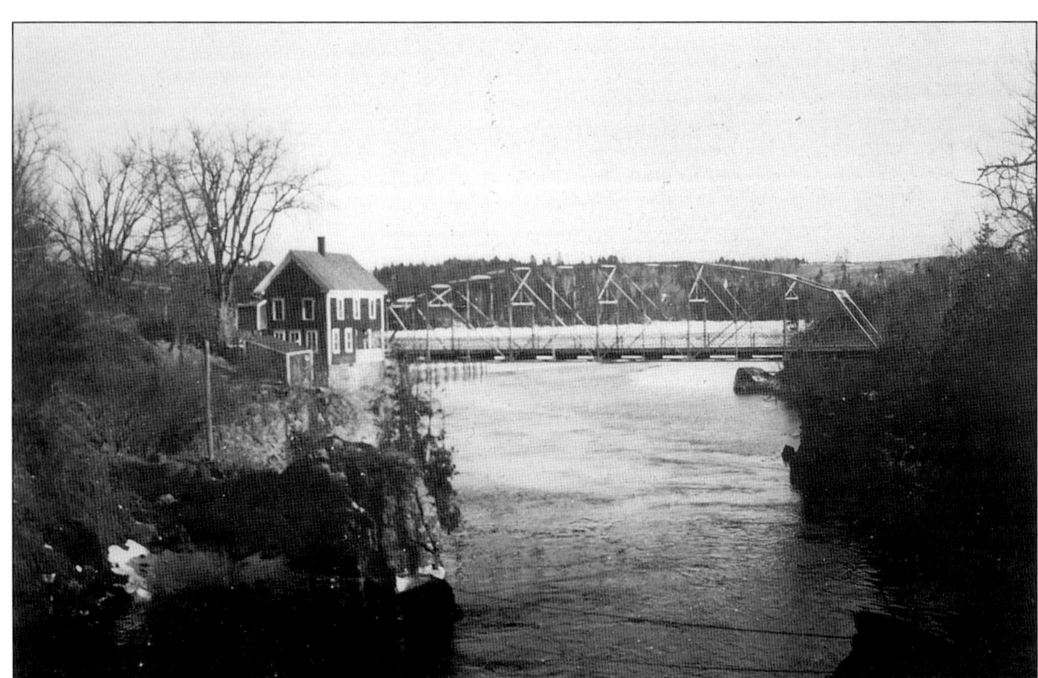

This 1938 photograph of the office where Alvah C. Toy worked at St. George Pulp and Paper Company shows the 1910 steel bridge, still standing today, that replaced the log structure below the falls. The upper steel bridge above the falls was a hand-me-down moved from another location and has since been replaced. It is now called the middle bridge, as a third bridge was completed north of the village for a bypass highway in 1967.

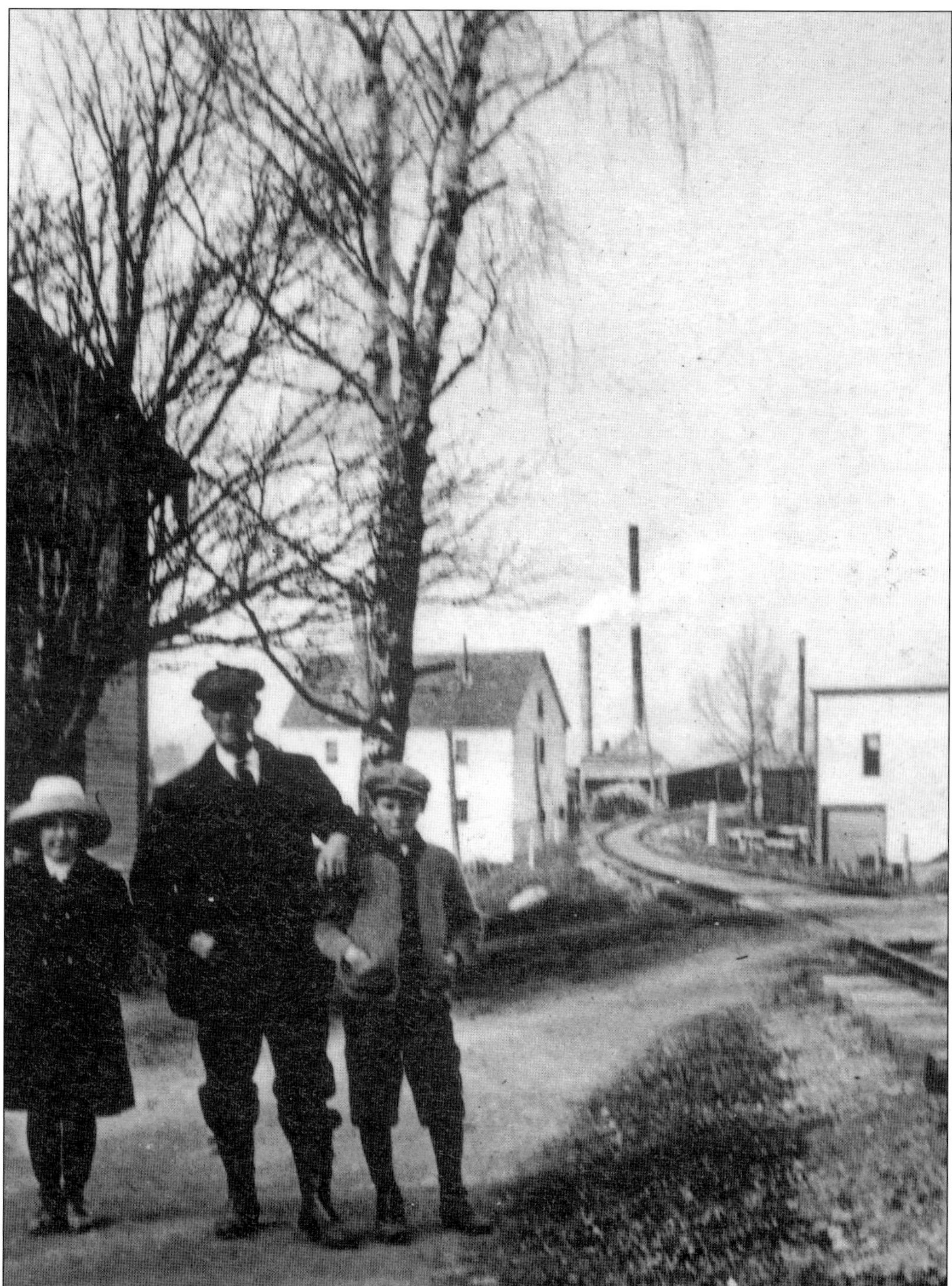

Henry Heinz, his daughter Helen Heinz, and Lester Grant are pictured here around the turn of the 20th century on Riverview Avenue. To their left is the Goss Inn and Funeral Parlor, and in the distance is the Patterson Mill (see page 29) and cookhouse on the Magaguadavic River. To their right is the Grant House, which, in 2002, was the home of Mayor Stanley Smith and his wife, Sybil.

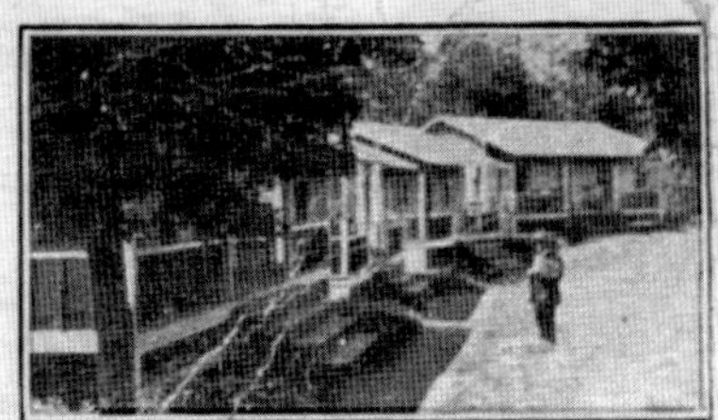

H. L. H. Hotel

THE HOME AWAY FROM HOME

THE MURRAY HOUSE

AND COMMUNITY CAMPS

WITH TOILETS AND RUNNING WATER

36 MILES FROM ST. STEPHEN **ST. GEORGE, N. B.** 50 MILES FROM SAINT JOHN

PICTURESQUELY situated on a hill commanding a superb view of the Magaguadavic River on the Main Road after passing the English Church on the right

BEAUTIFUL GROUNDS

Bathing, Boating, Hunting, Salt and Fresh Water Fishing, Large Airy Rooms

CAMPS TO LET AT UTOPIA LAKE

INFORMATION BUREAU

L. W. MURRAY, PROPRIETOR

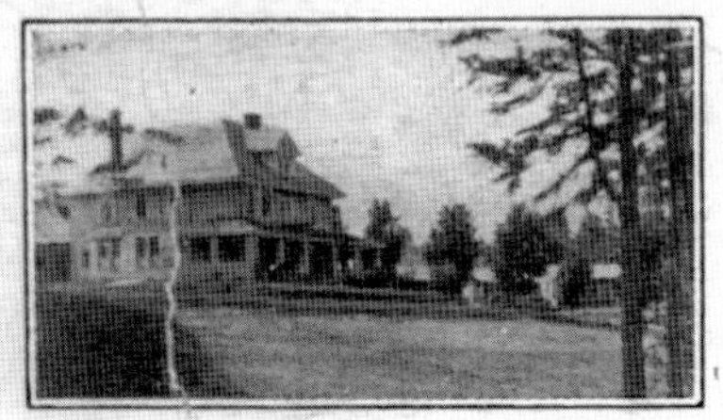

Look closely at the advertisement for the Murray House and note that it is 50 miles (80 kilometres) from Saint John. A 45-minute drive now, it could take 4 hours 75 years ago when this card was printed. The train took close to 3 hours to make the trip. So at the time, St. George was a considerable journey, and there were a number of establishments like the Murray House, in and around the town, where a visitor could spend the night. As the card shows, the Murray House could also accommodate guests in overnight cabins (similar to those tucked under the trees in the lower photograph) at nearby Lake Utopia.

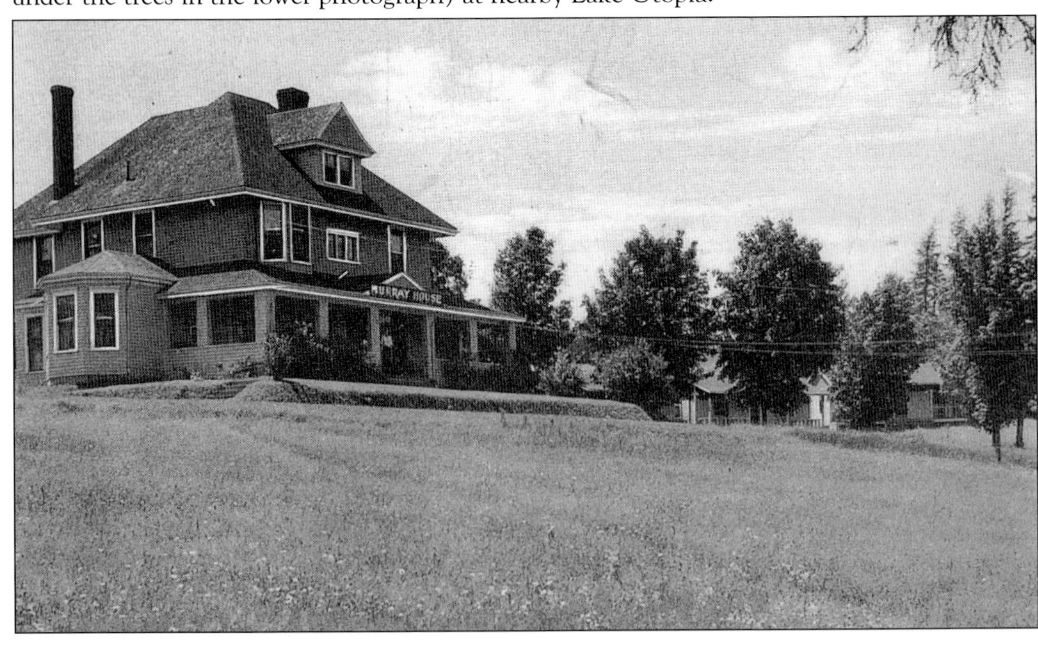

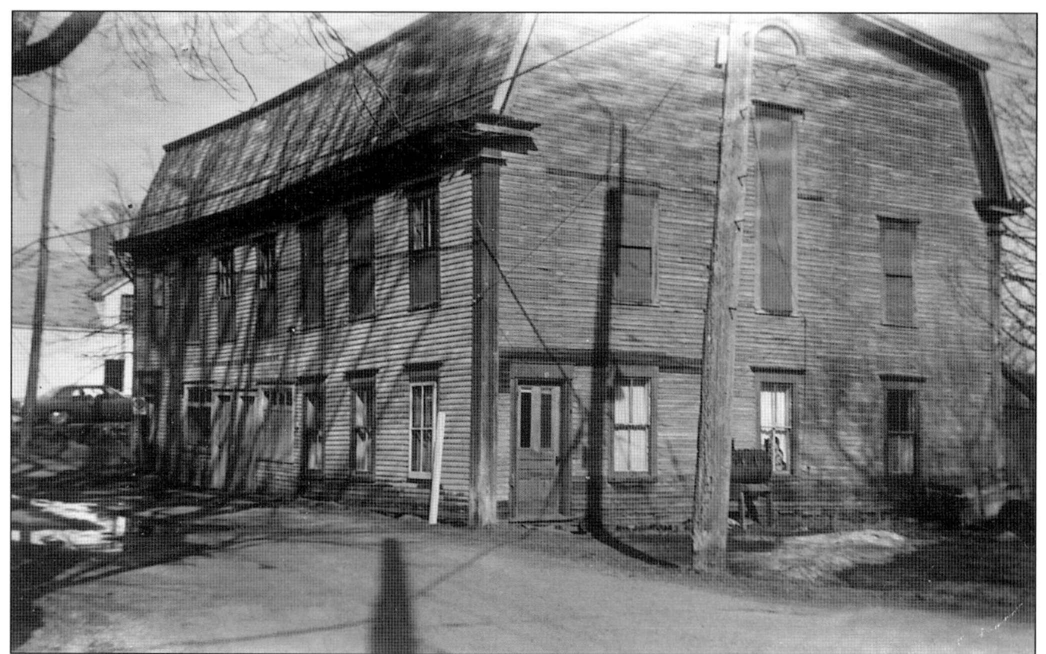

The Roseland Hall (Coutts Hall) was torn down in November 1983 when it was well over 100 years old. Some people have memories of dances, Christmas concerts, political rallies, and church and town suppers that were held in the hall. Others remember getting their hair permed or cut, and still others remember the drummers' rooms where traveling salesmen came to show their wares. Some may even recall friends who lived in the caretaker's lower-floor apartment.

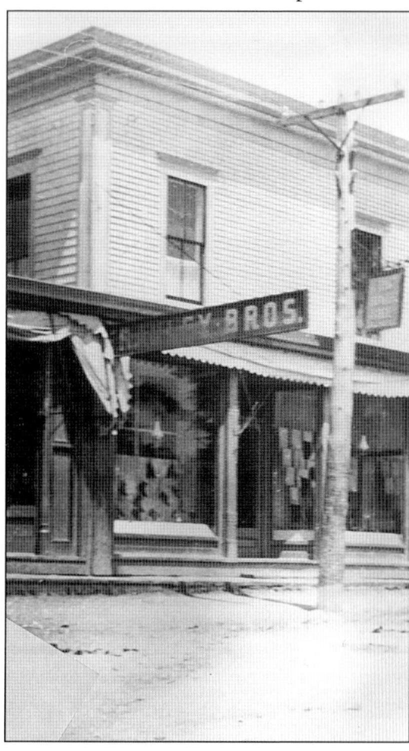

Frauley Brothers would have been one spot upon which the drummers would have called. They were the leading mercantile operation in town in the first third of the 20th century. On Main Street, they had a men's clothing store run by George Frauley, a ladies' shoe store run by Bessie Frauley, and a grocery store run by Artie Frauley, as well as a family-run theatre (the Opera House) over top of George and Ella Frauley's residence.

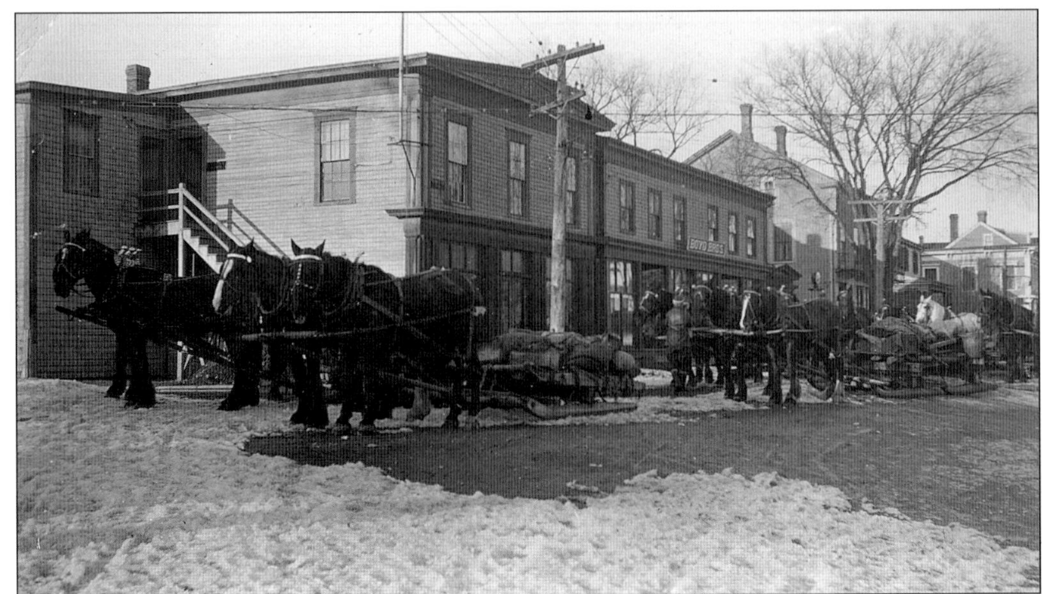

The Boyd Brothers Store is seen behind the horses and sleighs engaged in spring roadwork on Main Street, *c.* 1930. Simon Boyd first opened a hotel in the lower town; the hotel burned down in 1916. Soon after, William Boyd opened a general store on Main Street, which eventually specialized in hardware and operates today under new owners just outside of town. The huge elm beside the Boyd Store was likely the result of schoolchildren's Arbour Day efforts.

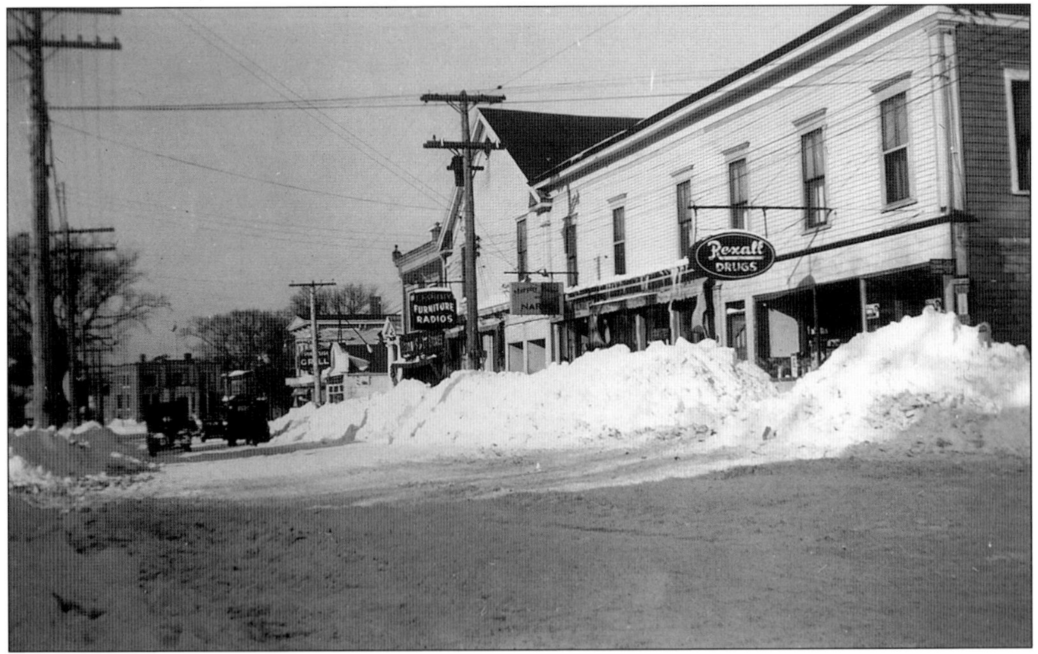

This winter scene of Main Street on February 29, 1952, was taken the same day a big storm closed the Pennfield Ridge Road, as seen in the photograph on page 27. This photograph was taken looking west with the granite post office building at the extreme back of the photograph. By then, Frauley's had closed, and their residence had been taken over by the Rexall Drug Store run by Harry H.R. Hersey.

To the right is a close-up of the scene in the previous photograph, now looking east and showing the parking meters almost buried on February 29, 1952. Of interest in the background are buildings that have all disappeared in the past 50 years. The house with the peaked dormer was formerly owned by James Bogue and later Neil MacMillian. It was torn down for a parking lot, as was the Hartley McGee Hotel to its left. Beyond them is the steeple of St. Mark's Church; the structure completely burned in 2001. The photograph below shows the St. George water tower, a town landmark since being built in 1950. In a national contest 10 years ago, the Canadian Broadcasting Corporation decided St. George had Canada's best drinking water.

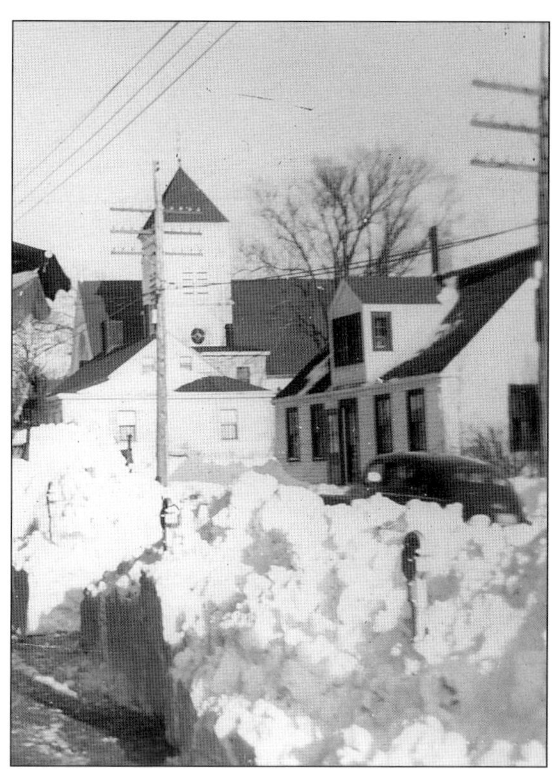

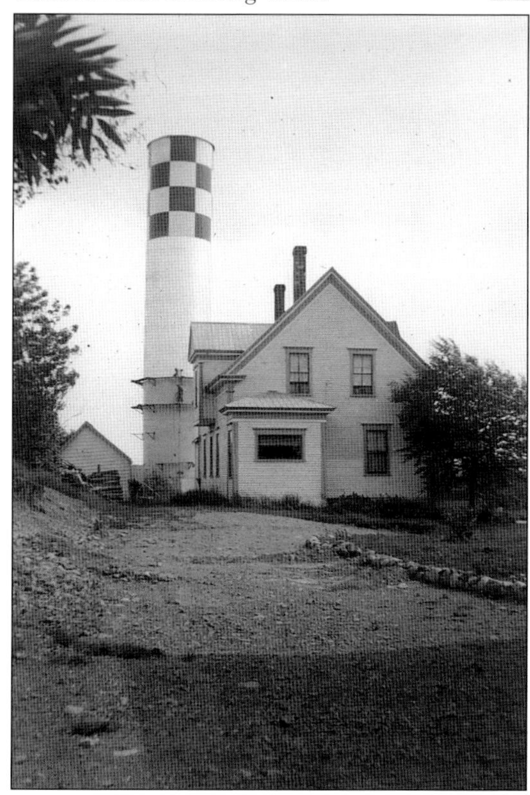

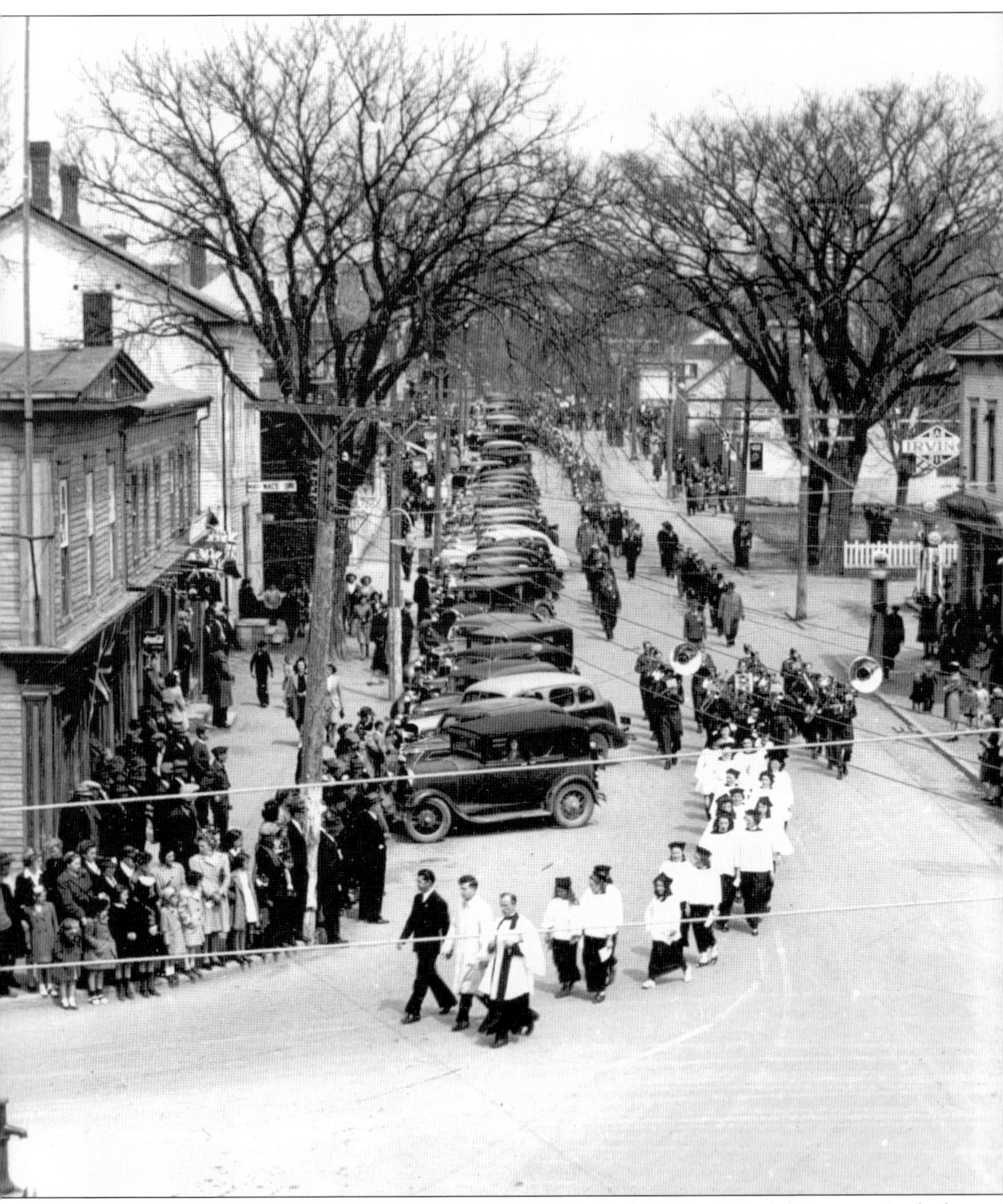

What would Main Street be without some folks enjoying the amenities of the street? And what greater occasion could there be than May 8, 1945, when the citizens of the community turned out en masse to celebrate Victory in Europe Day? Here they are marching down Main Street and turning by the town pump in front of the post office. They are led by the town's ministers, church choirs, and the military band from nearby Camp Utopia.

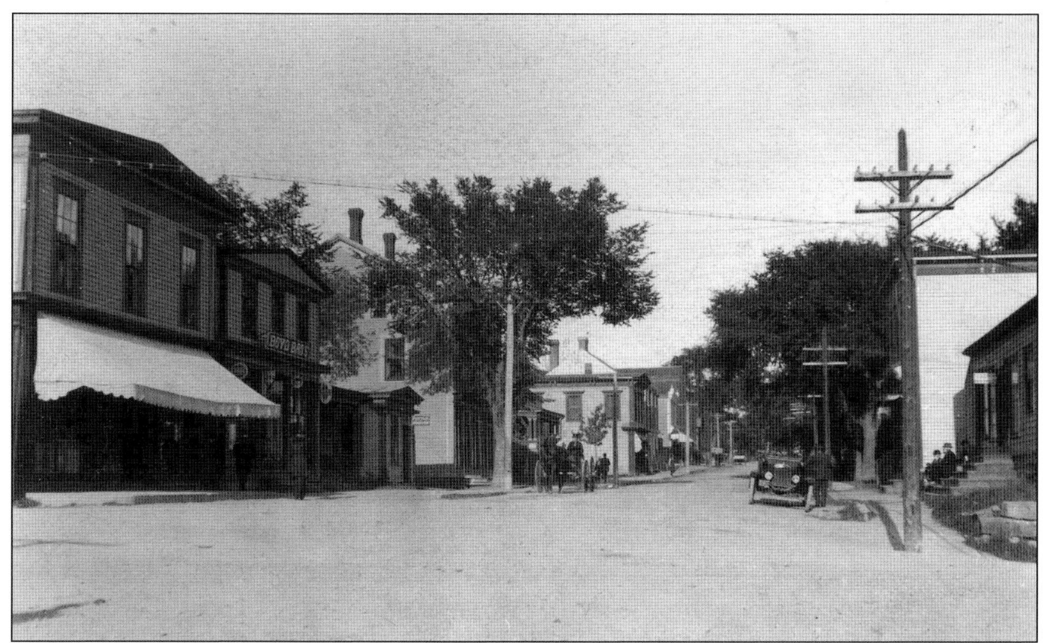

Here is Main Street and O'Brien's Corner in earlier times. The photograph was taken prior to the end of 1922, as there is a wagon traveling on the left side of the road. New Brunswickers switched to the right side on December 1, 1922. By August 17, 1921, 914 U.S. tourists had crossed the border, a 16 percent increase over 1920, and many complained not only about rutty road conditions but also folks driving on what they considered the wrong side of the road!

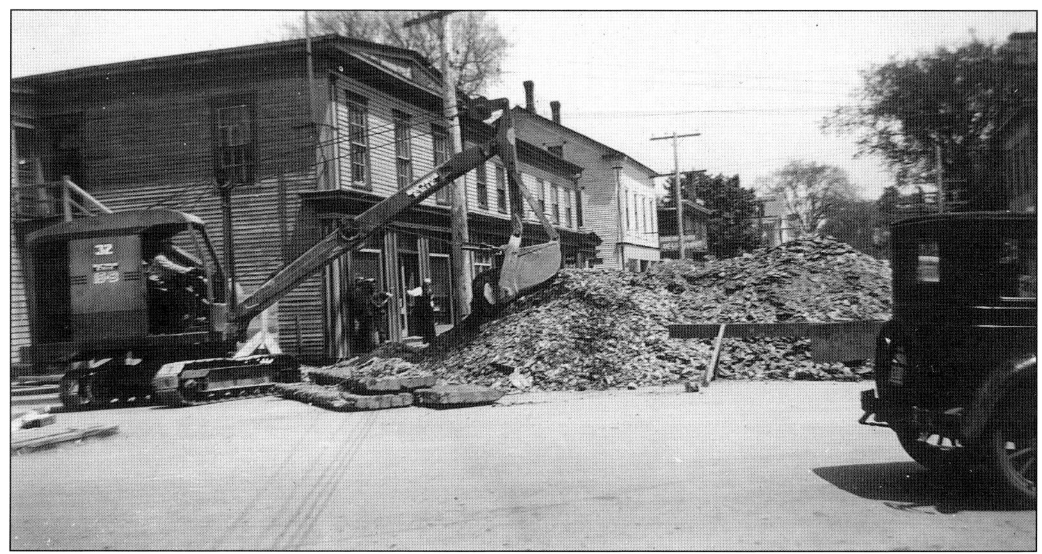

Shown is O'Brien's Corner in 1949 when water and sewer systems were being installed under the streets of St. George in a $350,000 project. That is Tim O'Brien, who gave the corner its name, in the doorway of his store. Note the old-time cars around. Did they last longer in times past than they do today, or did styles not change so frequently? Perhaps, a bit of both is true.

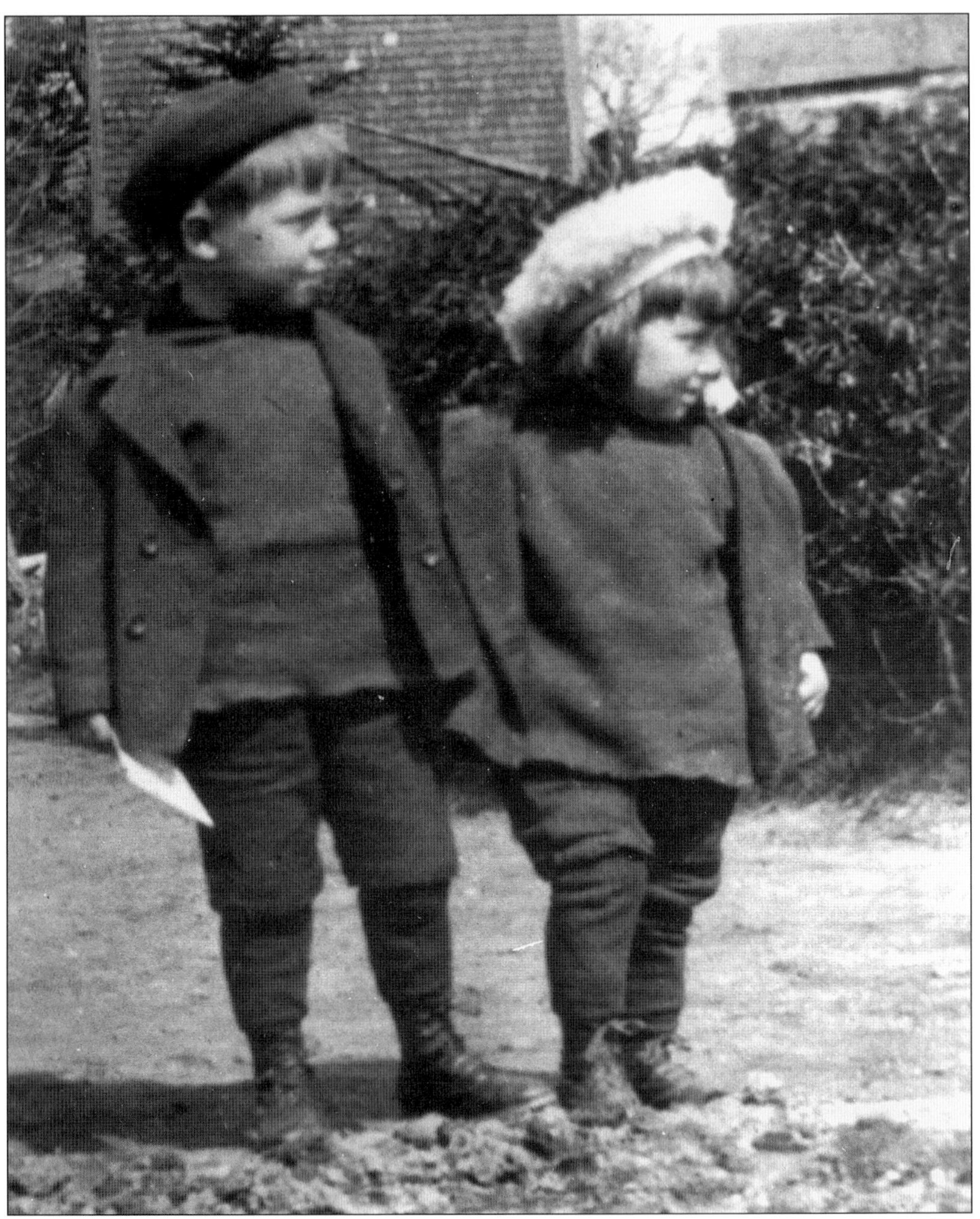

Pictured here are the children of Mr. and Mrs. Octave Plude. Octave Plude, who came from New York, was the manager and builder of the St. George Pulp and Paper mill in 1902. One may wonder what stories these children would tell if they were able to speak today about days gone by when they would walk hand in hand down the steps of their father's office and around the granite works, pulp mill grounds, and streets of old St. George.

Four

Fraternal, School, Church, and Social Life in St. George

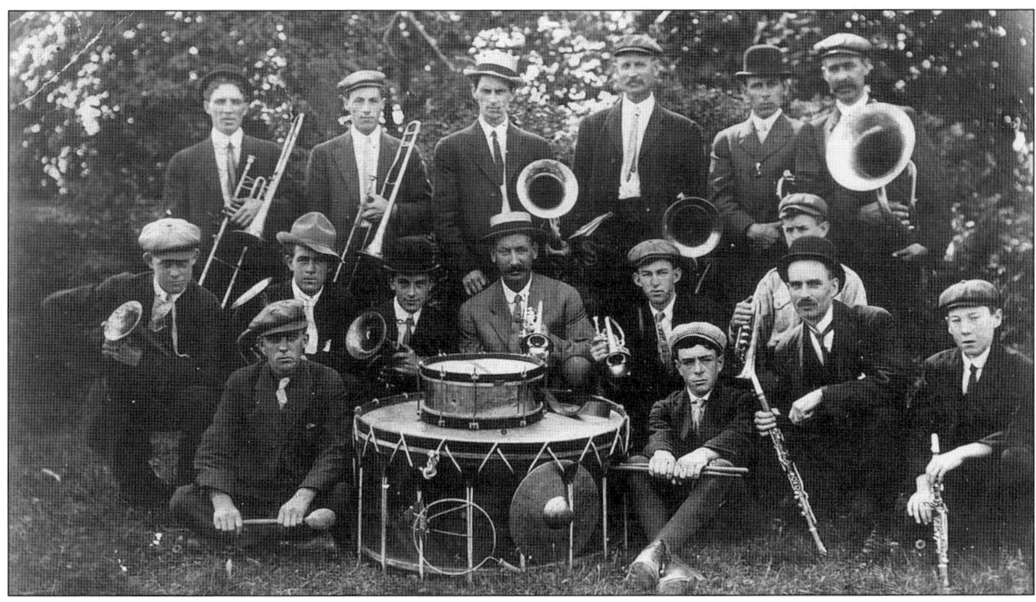

The St. George Band was known far and wide for its excellence in music. It epitomized the joy of the community that was also found in its fraternal organizations, churches, schools, clubs, and societies, which make life in any community more fulfilling. The band played public concerts and was hired for political rallies, picnics, and ball games, went on the steamboat excursions to Eastport and Grand Manan, and was invited to towns and villages up and down the coast to enliven community celebrations. They thereby gave the other communities a sense of the joy of life that existed in St. George. Thus, it seemed fitting to honor these bandsmen of 1912–1913. From left to right are the following: (front row) Earl Stewart, Horace Stewart, Joe Spear, Charlie Craig, Frank Hibbard, Harry McAdam, George Henry, Ralph Doyle, George McCallum, and Eugene Hennessey; (back row) Joe McHugh, James Watt, George Brown, French Meating, Gabrid Craig, and George Craig. (Courtesy Anita Grearson.)

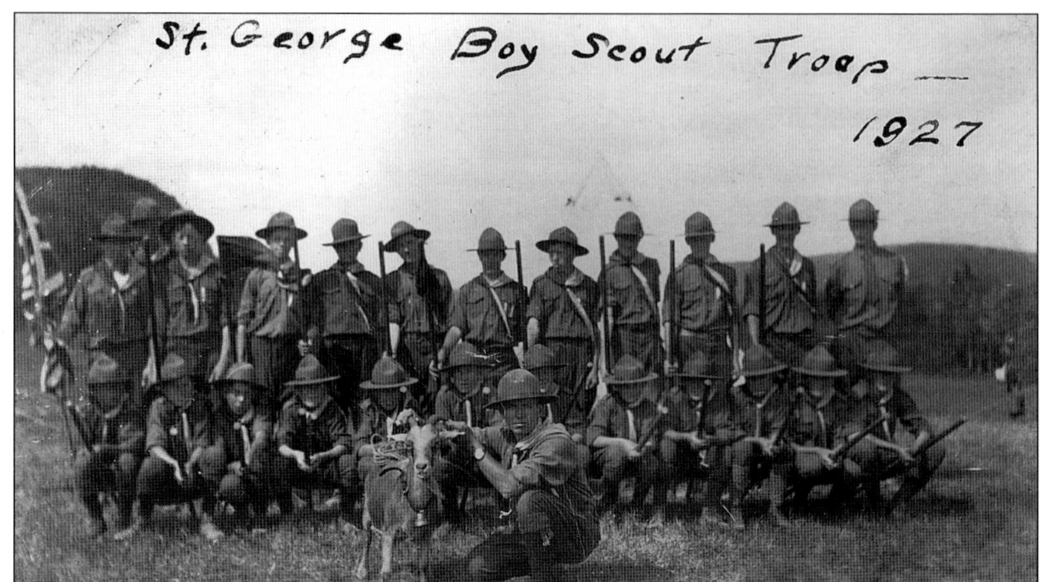

The Boy Scouts are now approaching their 100th year of operation, having started in 1907. They began in New Brunswick at Saint John's (Stone) Church in 1910 when a Boy's Brigade switched to the Scout program. When the St. George Troop got underway is unknown, but by 1927, they were well enough established that this postcard of the troop at White Field, Lake Utopia, was produced. Edwin Toy holds the goat mascot in front.

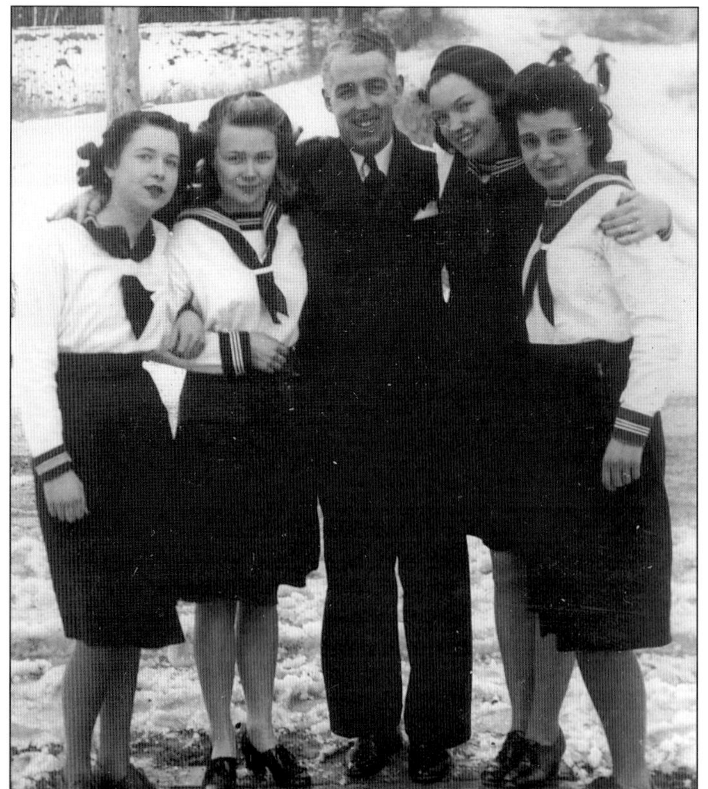

The Canadian Girls in Training and Girl Guides were also active in St. George as a counterbalance to the male-only scouting organization. From left to right are Jean Armstrong, Eileen Nason, Rev. Donald MacDormand, Marian Tabor, and Mary Patterson. They were ushers at the wedding of Frances Toy and Jim Waycott on January 20, 1942.

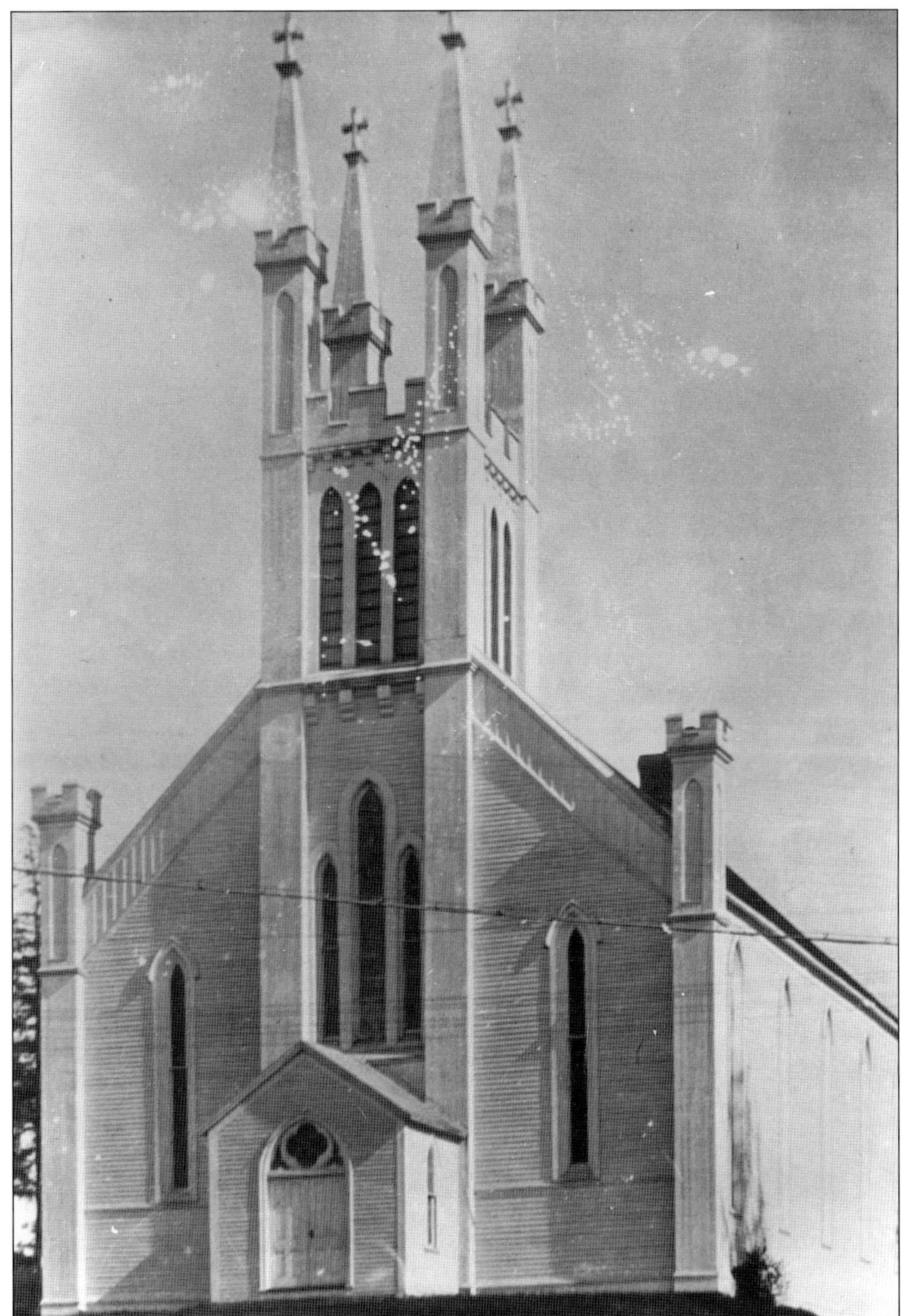

The Roman Catholic Church (known as St. George's), built in 1864, is a landmark at the intersection of Main Street and the road to L'Etete. Until the 1970s, it had pinnacles with crosses on the tower and outside corners, which were removed as they became rotted. In February of 2002, plans were made to restore the church's early appearance.

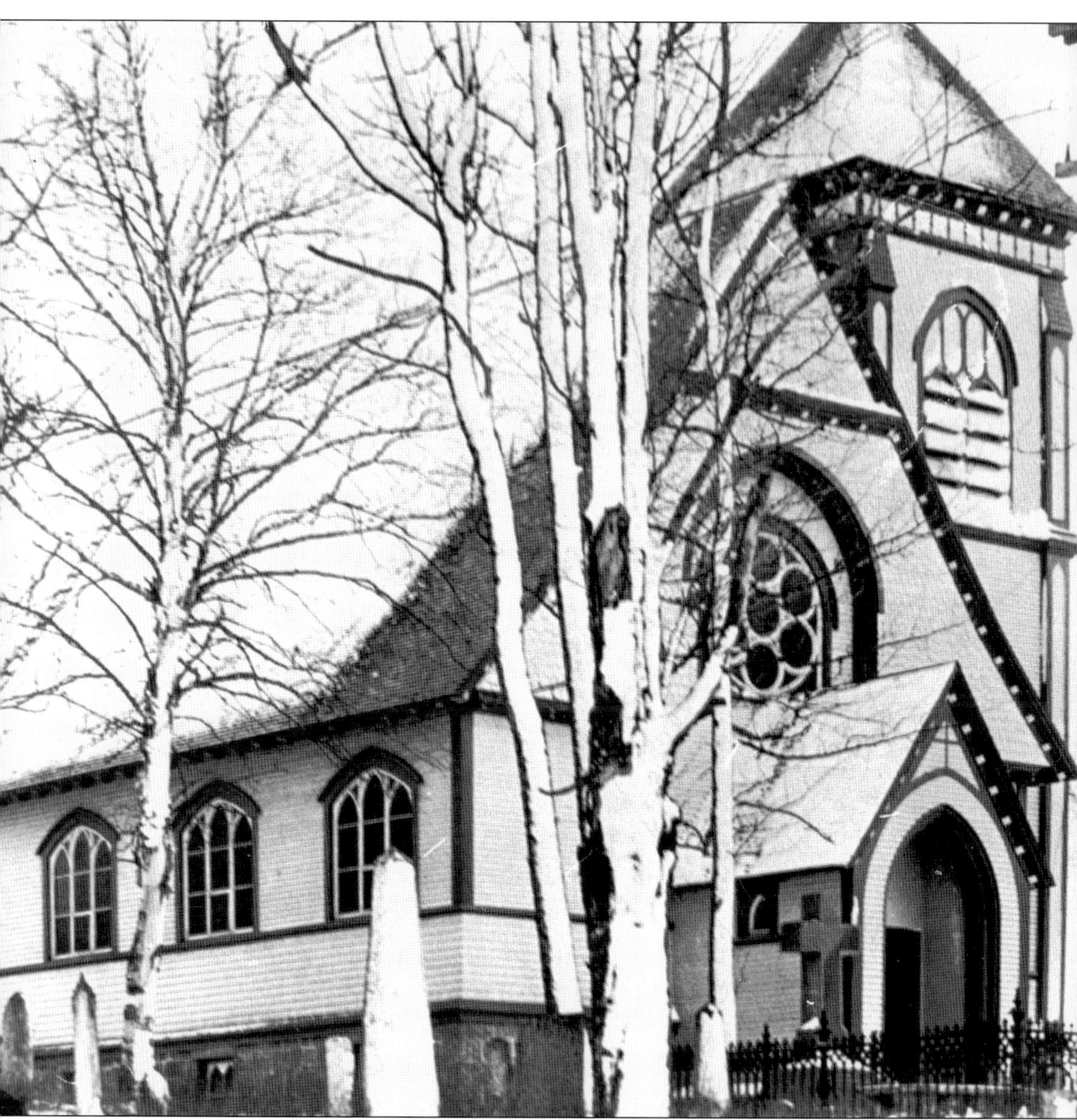

St. Marks (Anglican) Church was consecrated in1909 and served the congregation of 150, as well as the wider community, until its destruction in a conflagration on the evening of December 31, 2001. The church had just undergone a $180,000 extension to the west side in 1999 to make it more user-friendly for the handicapped and to provide needed space for its busy congregation. All was lost, including several irreplaceable stained glass windows, which are glimpsed in the photograph overleaf.

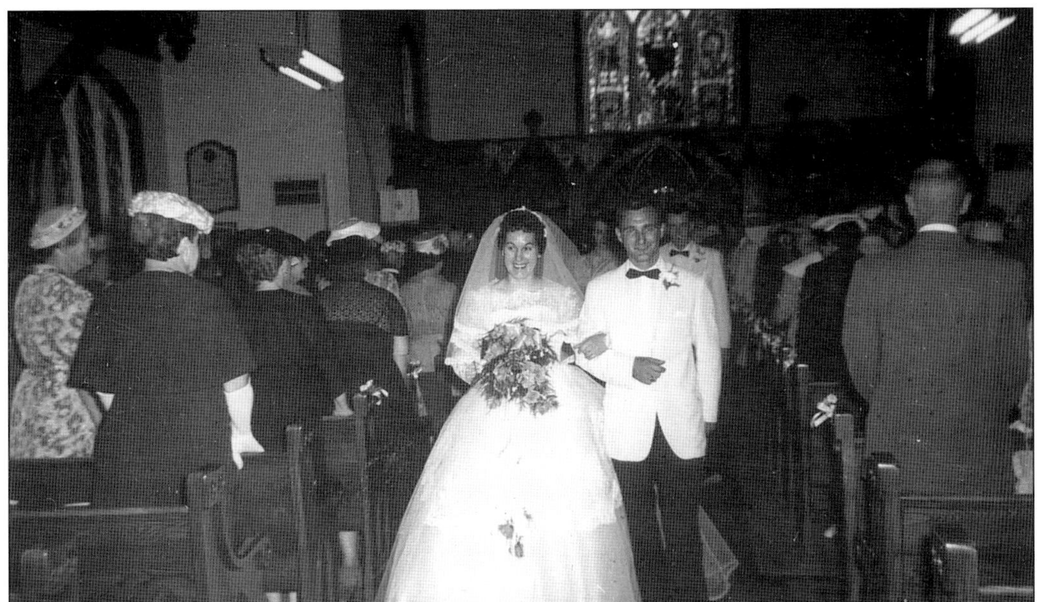

Though this photograph centres on bride and groom Joyce Taylor and Philip Parks at their September 17, 1960 wedding, it also provides an interior view that can no longer be enjoyed of St. Mark's Church, lost in the fire of December 31, 2001. In the background is the great east window, one of 15 priceless stained glass windows melted in the fire.

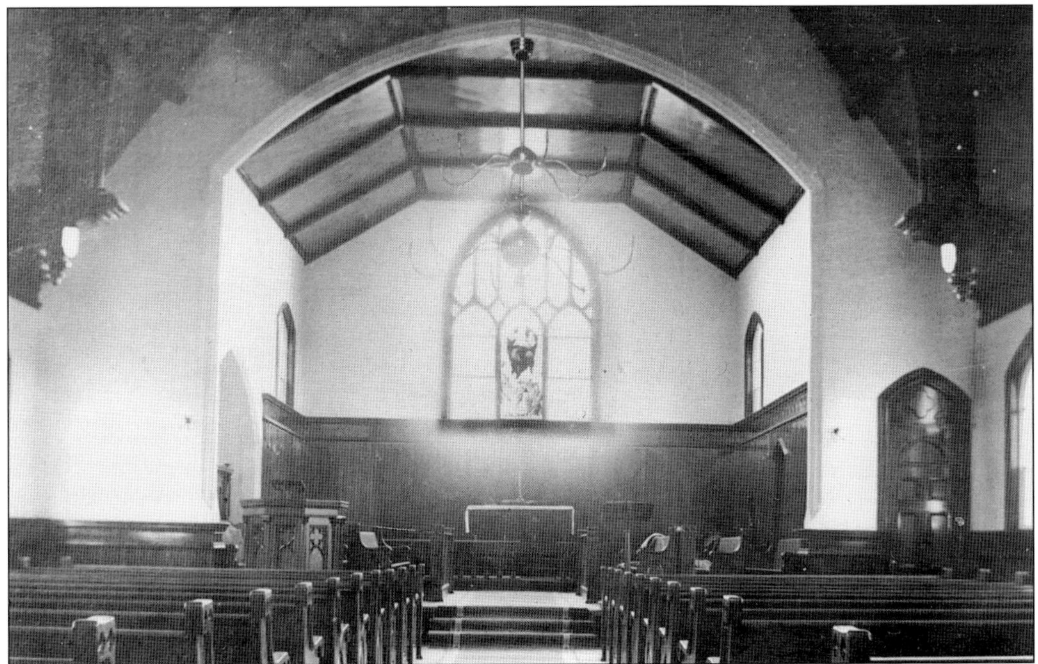

In the interior of St. Mark's Church, 1940, we see the decorative wood panels, roof beams, and inlaid ceiling of the interior and the front and side stained glass windows. Both were factors in its quick demise; the heavy coats of varnish on the wood combined with the drafts when the stained glass windows blew out caused the flames to accelerate. Fully insured, the church will be rebuilt. (Courtesy Anita Grearson.)

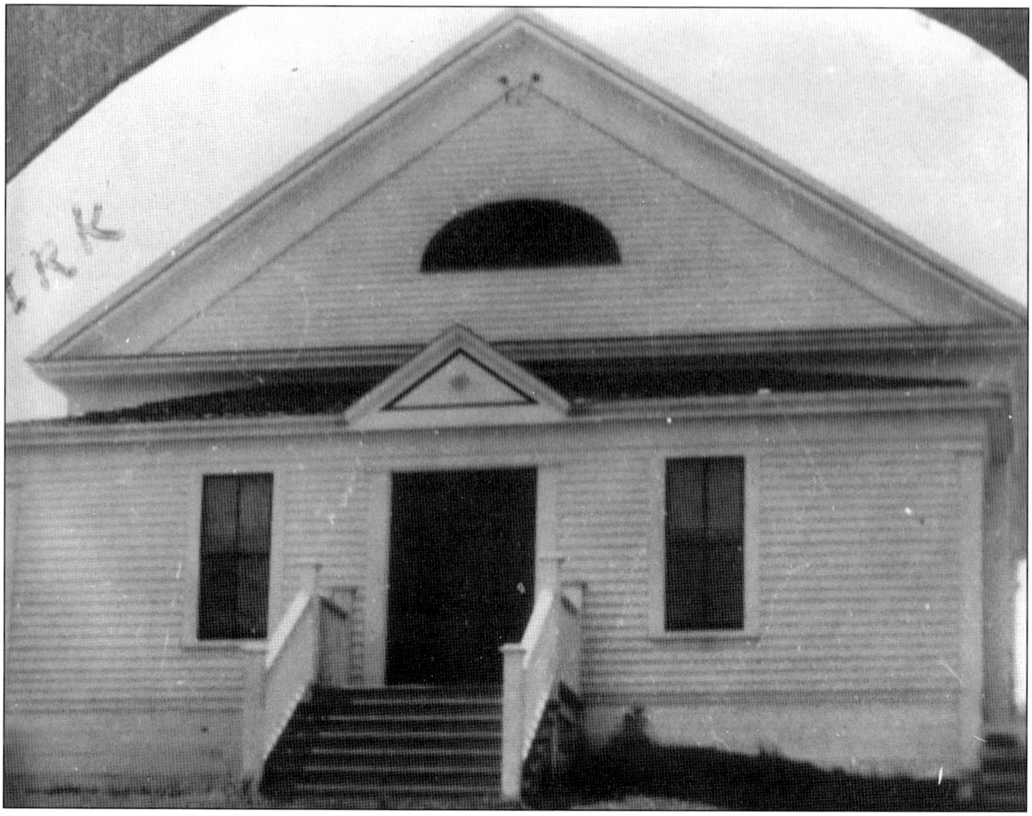

The "auld Kirk," at the edge of the falls' gorge is the oldest building used as a Presbyterian church in Canada. Lumber for the church was given by the first settler to the area, Peter Clinch, in 1790. In the churchyard is a memorial to Moses Shaw who died in 1805. It reads: "By fits and convulsions, my days were but seven. Christ died for sinners, and took me to heaven."

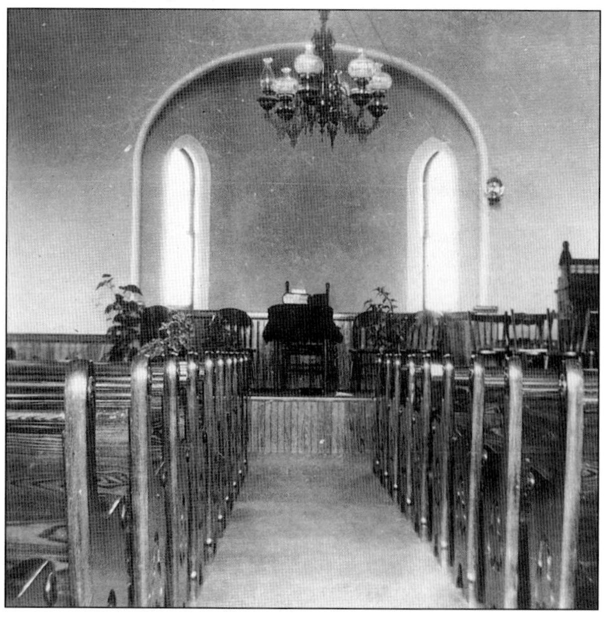

The United Baptist Church is shown above in the days of gas lamps, perhaps in the early 1920s. Electric Power was first available in St. George on a part-of-the-day basis soon after the pulp mill opened but was not on a full-time basis until 1922 when the power plant at Musquash was opened. (See page 92.)

The present United Baptist Church on Main Street was built in 1902–1906, and this postcard view is how it appeared soon after it was built. This church was the home church of Elizabeth Toy, which is why several images associated with the church appear in the following pages. Many of the events and activities of the United Baptist Church are representative of what went on in the religious and social life of the members of other church communities in St. George.

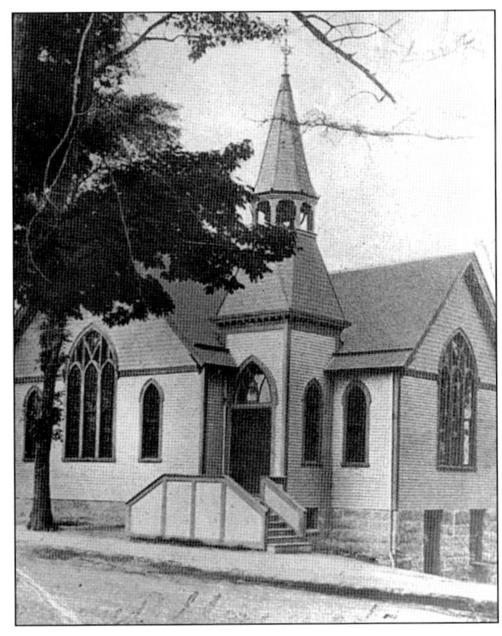

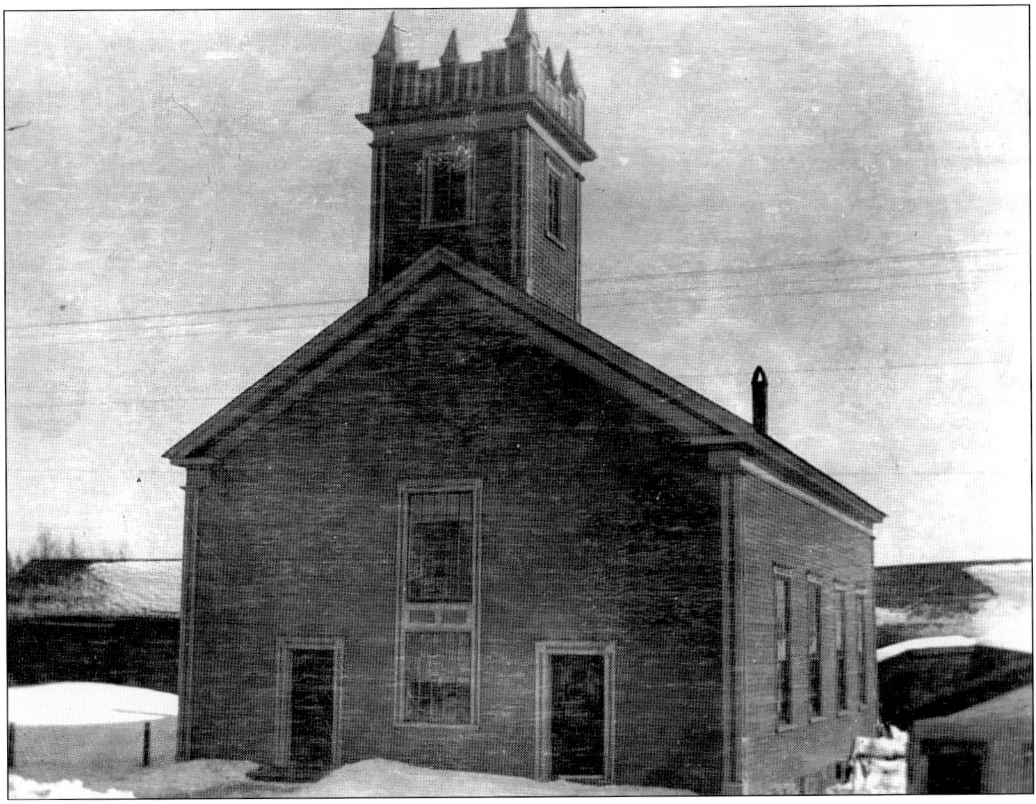

The original Baptist church was built on the south side of Main Street in the 1880s. In 1902, the church was rolled across the street and poked into a hole between two buildings. Later, it became Frauley's Furniture Store and is currently used as a Medical Clinic and Business New Brunswick Service centre.

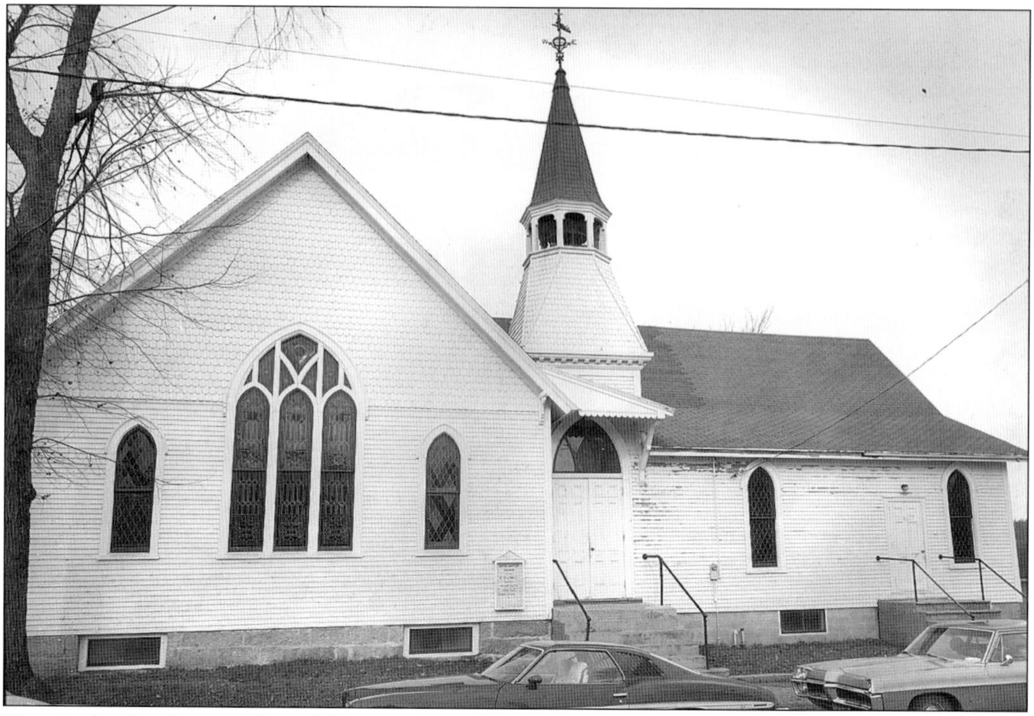

Here is the St. George United Baptist Church as it appeared after renovations in 1961. Looking at the previous photograph, it is plain to see that many changes were made by the carpenter Roy Spinney and workers Ray Grearson, Earl Leavitt, and George Henry. Unchanged though were memorial windows given by Senator Gillmor and Dr. C.C. Alexander.

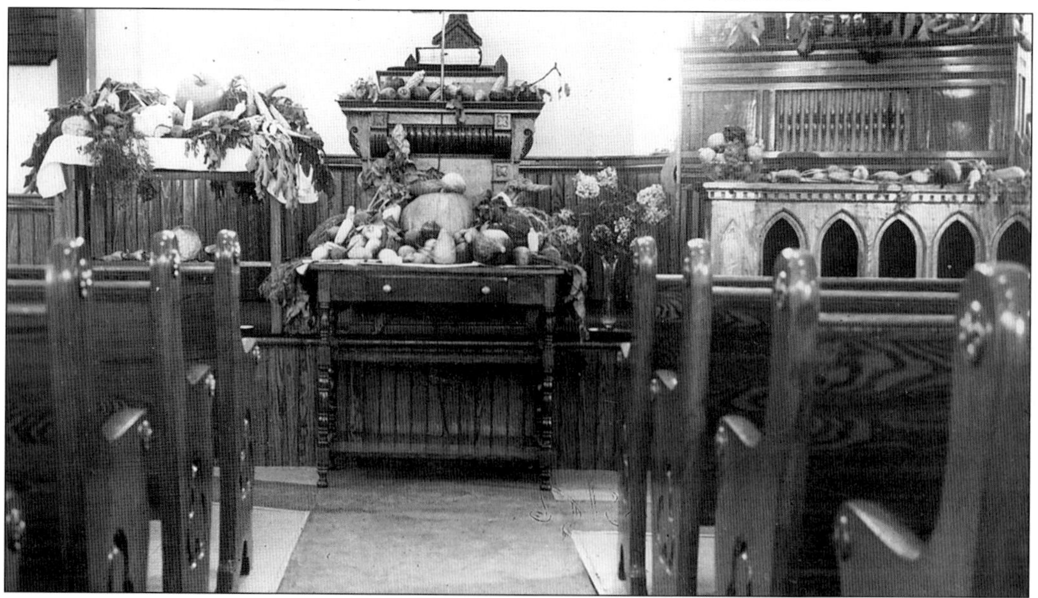

Shown here are the decorating efforts for a Thanksgiving service in the 1940s at the United Baptist Church. This tradition continues to this day. Today, Baptist churches decorate lavishly for Christmas, but in the early times, they did not do so, leaving that to their Anglican friends across the street.

Easter Sunday at the United Baptist Church on April 4, 1942, is captured here. Dick Levitt and Ronald Parks are all dressed up for their first day at Sunday school with their teacher, Elizabeth Toy.

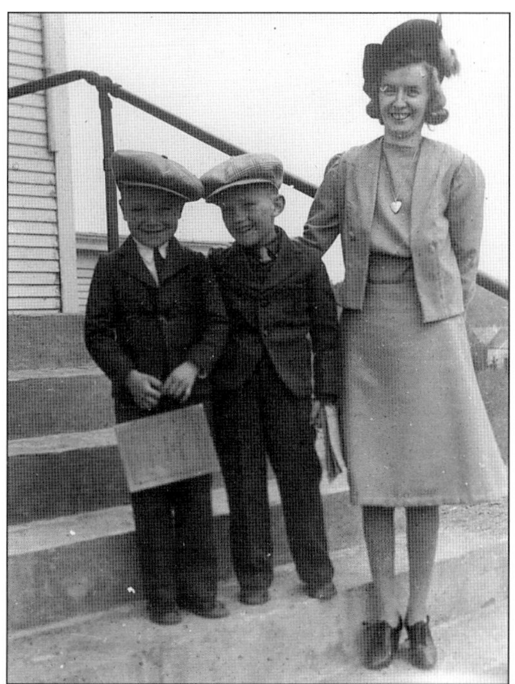

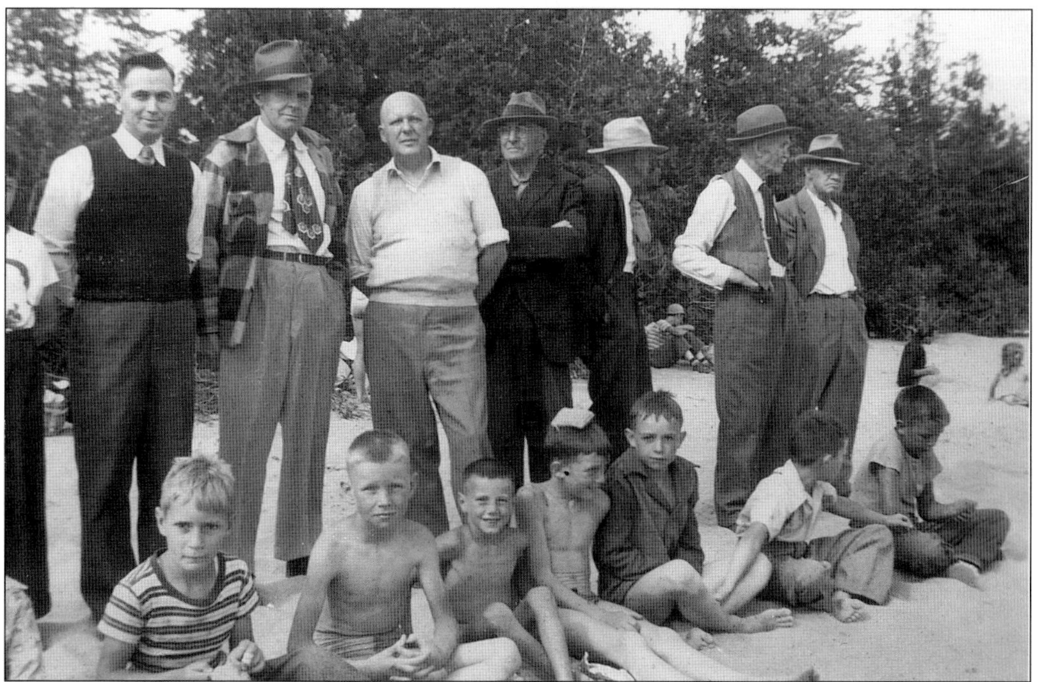

On August 8, 1954, the men and boys of the First Baptist Church enjoyed a Sunday school picnic at Canal Beach. Standing are, from left to right, Stanley Reid, Rev. E.G. Corey, Ray Grearson, Art Naylor, Henry Sherrard, Wall Stewart, H.V. Dewer, and Bill Wentworth. The seated boys include Eddie Cousins, Blair Meating, Jim Dunlap, Maynard Clinch, "Butch" Austin, and two unidentified boys. I remember my dad saying, "When I grew up in St. George, every boy in town became a Baptist when they held their picnic."

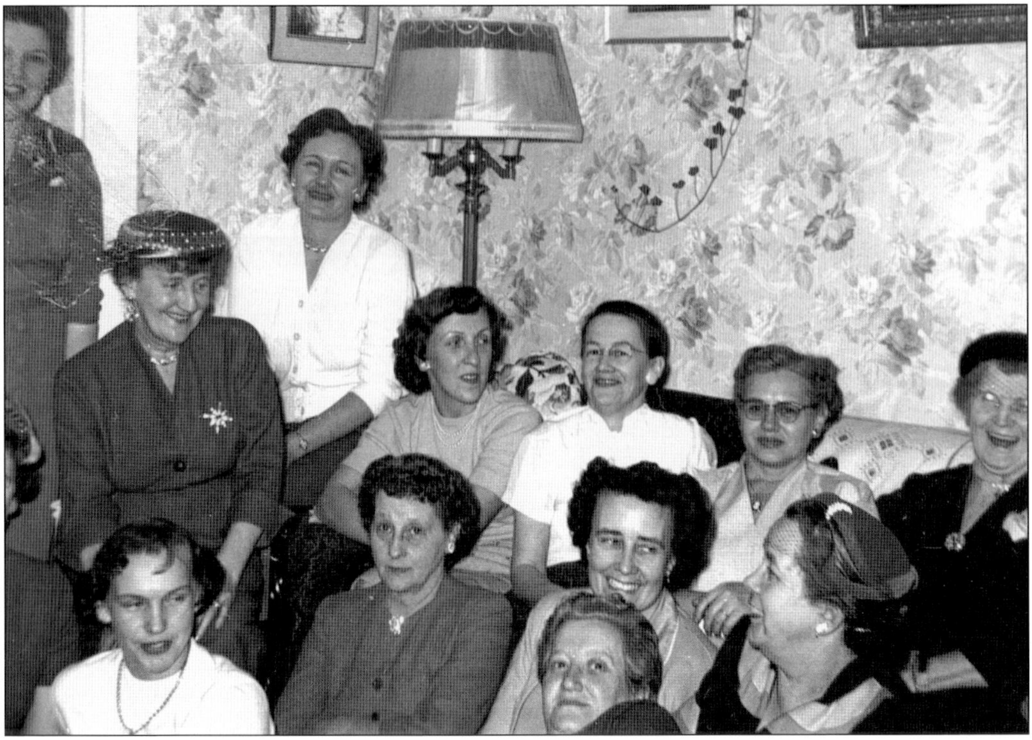

As noted earlier, the Girl Guides were active in St. George too and met in the Toy house for meetings, as Elizabeth herself was involved. This picture includes Mary Cook, Frances Trynor, Betty Spinney, Grace Simpson, Hazel Clinch, Frances Callaghan, Margaret Boudreau, Alice Doyle, Emma Gould, and Mae Scott on January 31, 1958, laying out plans for a guiding activity.

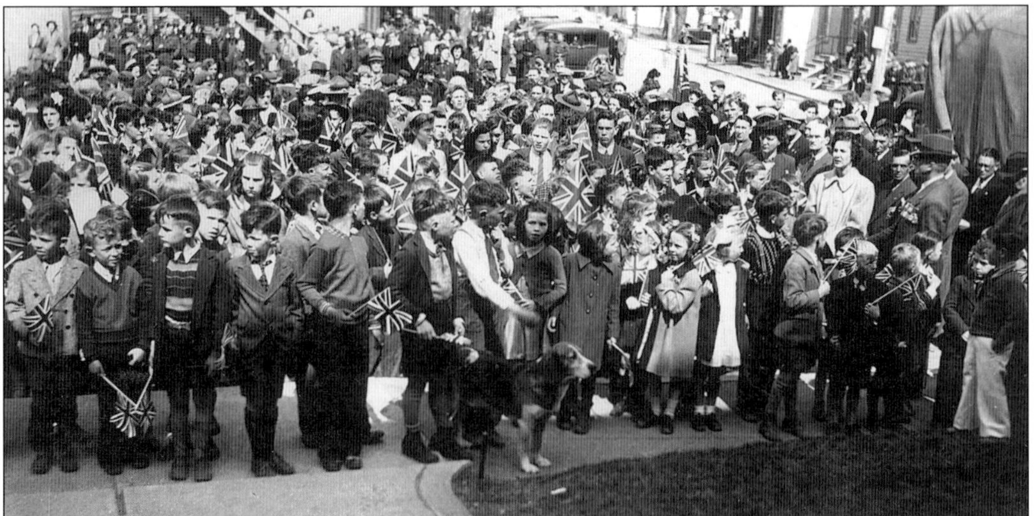

Whenever there was a public celebration, such as this Victory in Europe Day parade on May 8, 1945, you could count on members of the Cadet Corps, Boy Scouts, Girl Guides, the churches, and the schools to turn out en masse to add to the colour of the celebration.

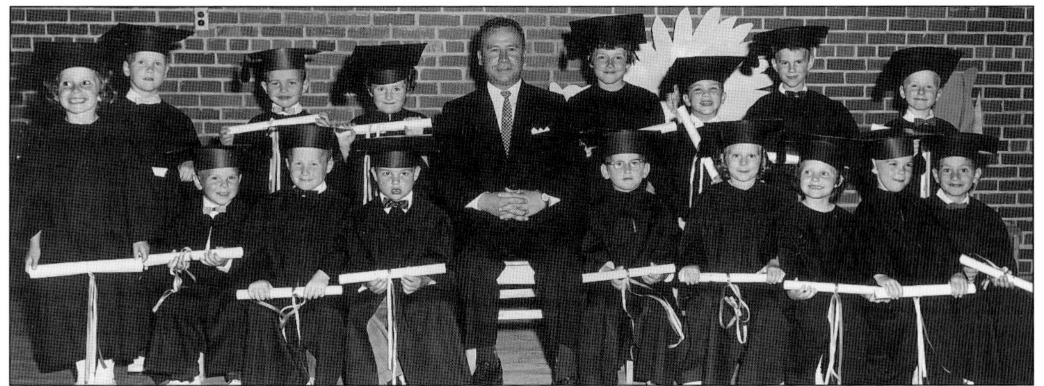

It was quite a coup when Louis J. Robichaud, newly elected premier of the province, came to speak at Florence Hegan's kindergarten graduation Class of 1962 at Eastern Charlotte Regional School. From left to right are the following: (front) Juliet Parks, Edward McGratten, Rodney Trynor, Donald Hill, the premier, Michael Henry, Sarah Smith, Susan Cairns, Heather Gillmor, and Paul McNichol; (back) Paul Harvey, Kenneth Savoie, Helen Stewart, Lynda Morton, Robert Wadlin, Alvin Adams, and James Gould.

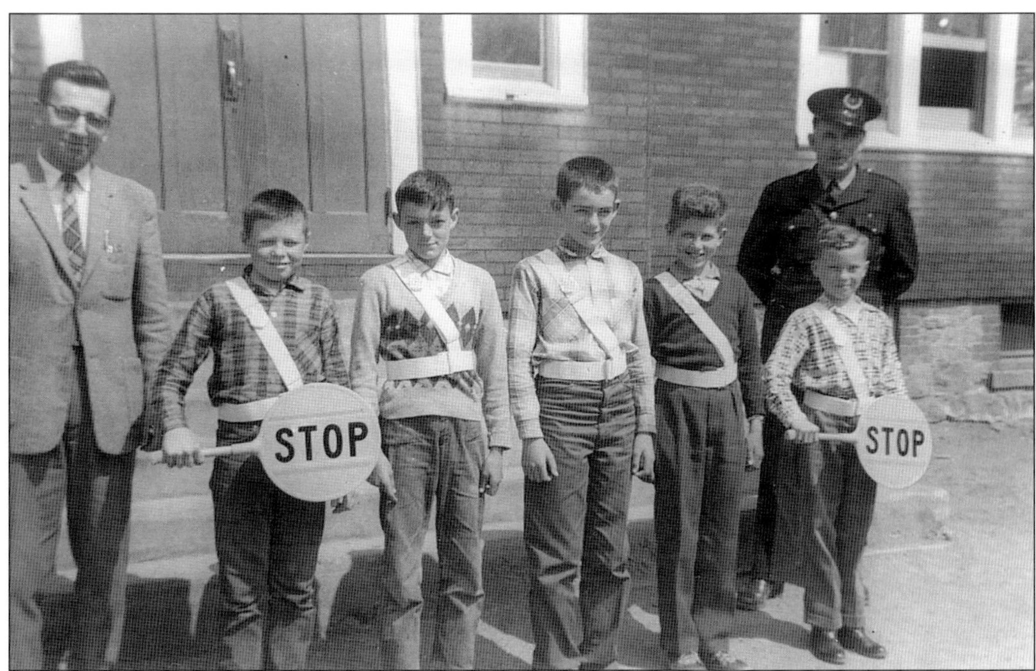

In order for students to reach school safely, the St. George Elementary School instituted a crossing guard program. Seen here is Donald A. Craig, the principal of the elementary school, with patrol leaders (from left to right) John Trynor, Michael Morton, James Chase, Robert Hines, and Robert Hicks. The policeman is Chief of Police Gordon McLaughlin.

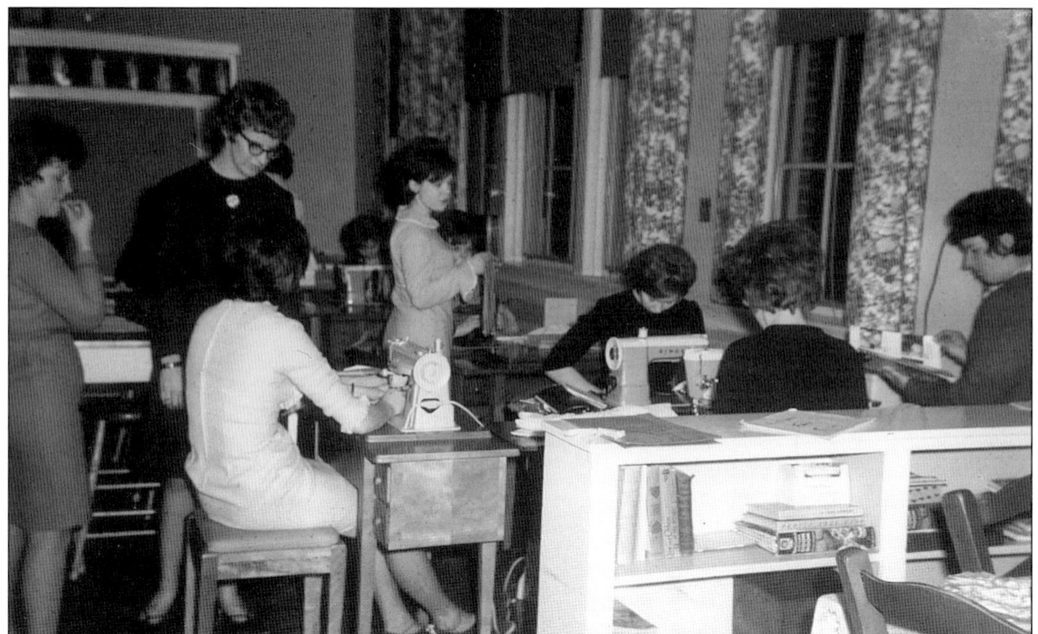

Education Week was a chance to show off the various courses that were available at the high school level in the district. In this case, we have a sewing class demonstration at the Eastern Charlotte Regional School. This was one of the many occasions Elizabeth Toy covered such events for newspapers but one of the few occasions when she did not note who the participants were.

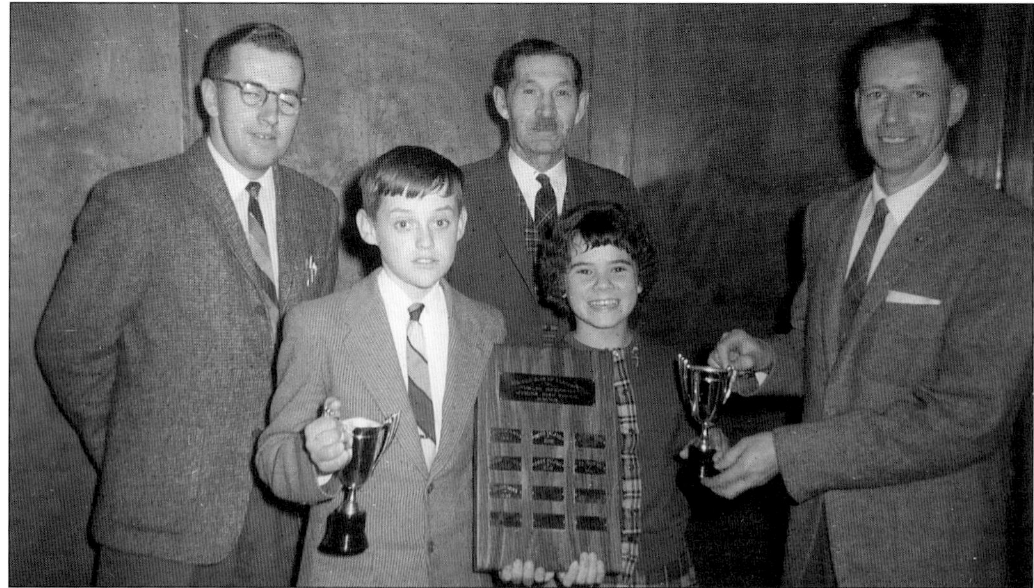

Education Week was also a chance to present prizes to winners of various contests, in this case, the Junior Oratorical Contest. At left is Donald A. Craig, who acted as chair of the event, with R.D. Caldwell Stewart, QC, who acted as chairman of the judges, standing behind the students. The winners are Ronald Saunders and Christine Graham of St. Andrews. Presenting their prizes and holding one of the cups is Hazen L Boyd.

Winter carnivals were a popular February tradition in Charlotte County in the 1950s and 1960s and included outdoor events like hockey challenges, snow sculpturing, and bed pushing contests. Indoors events included trampoline demonstrations, basketball competitions, and, as is seen below, beauty contests.

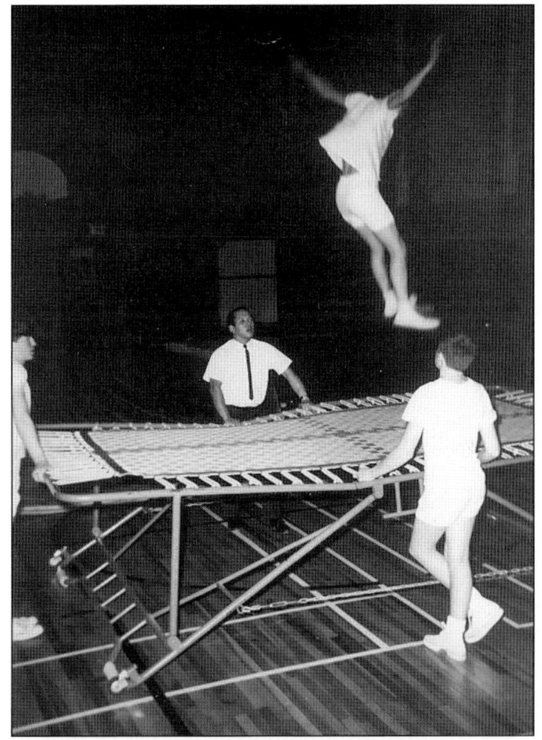

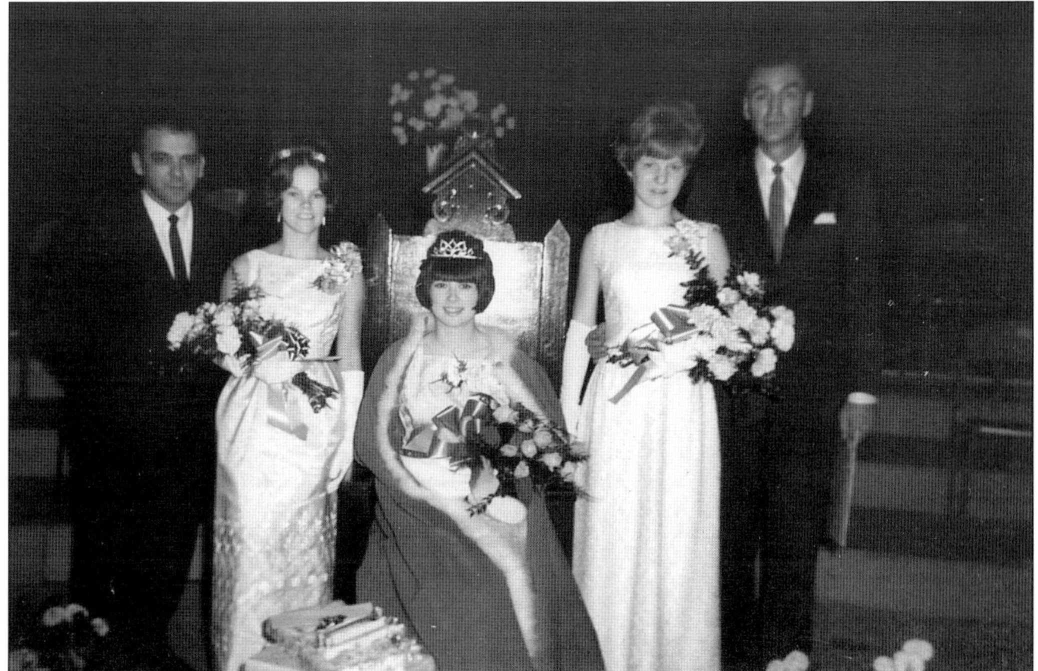

The Carnival Queen of 1968 was Lois Elaine Thorne, shown here with her second princess to her left, Jane Holly McLean, and her first princess to her right, Mary Patricia Armstong. The gentlemen are identified as Mr. Bernard (left) and Hal Sampel (right), the latter a popular radio personality from Saint John.

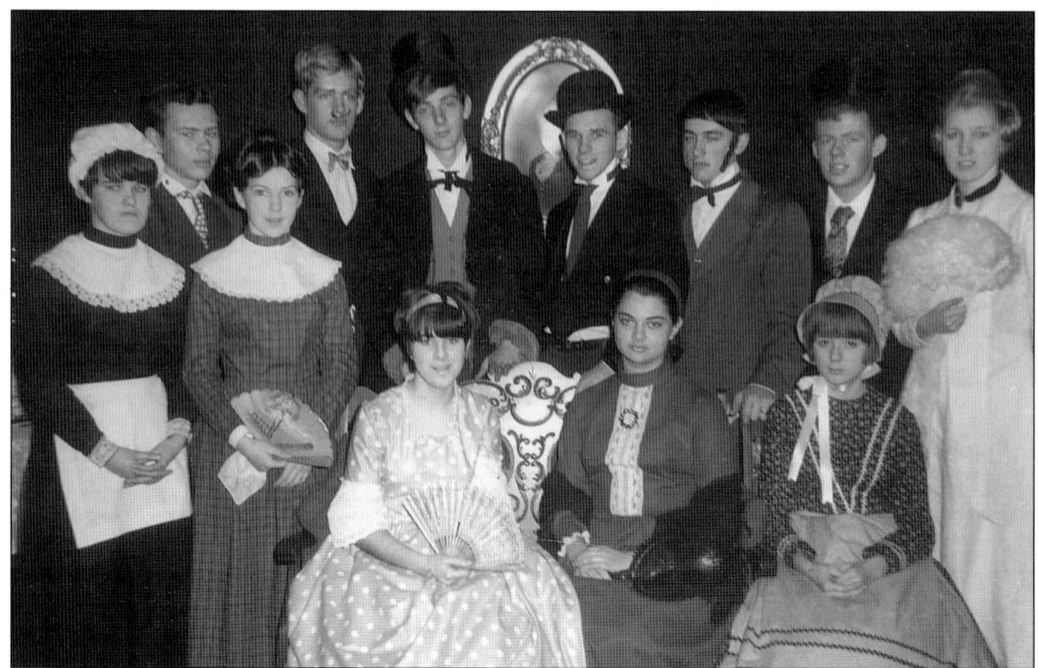

During Canada's centennial celebrations in 1967, students of the Eastern Charlotte Regional School undertook to portray the history of the country in skits and plays. In this scene, students are portraying George Brown, Charles Tupper, Sir John A MacDonald, George Etienne Cartier, New Brunswick's Leonard Tilley, and others. All were active in the formation of the county, and the students, it was hoped, would find role-playing more interesting than just reading about these historical figures.

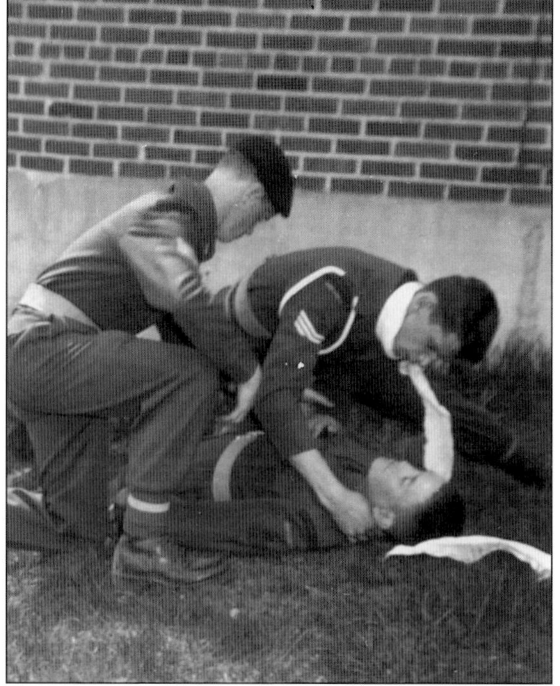

An important extramural activity was the Cadet Corps, which photographs in Elizabeth Toy's collection show had existed from the time just after World War I. They were still busy when she took this picture in 1962 with Cadet Everett Simpson (left) and Cadet Larry Hatt (right) coming to the assistance of "casualty" Cadet Larry Stanton.

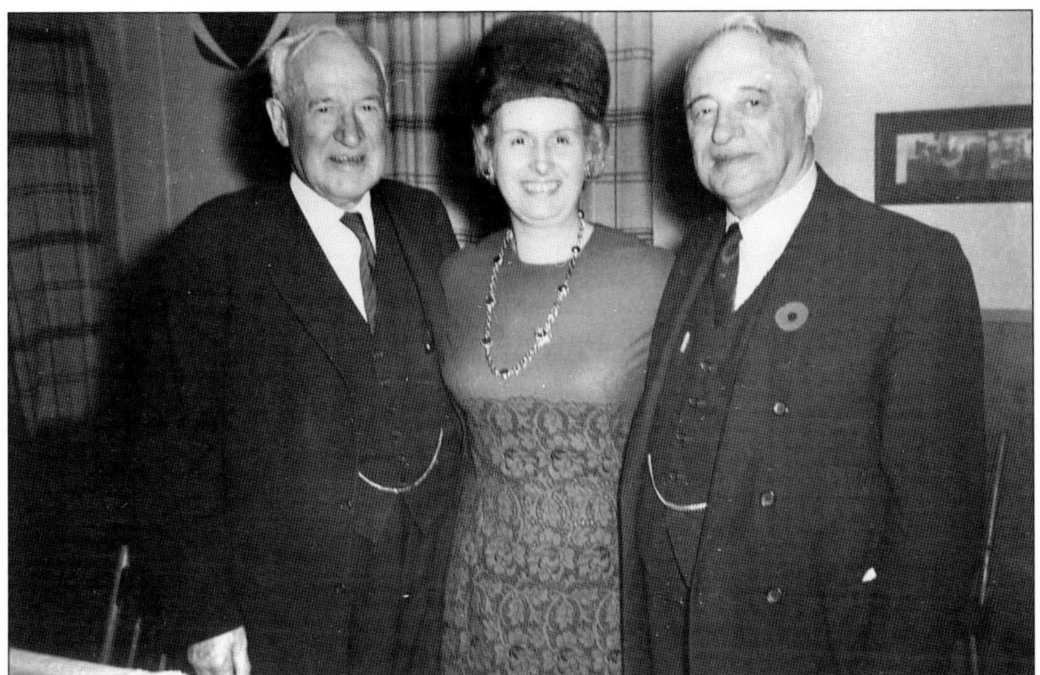

St. George residents took a series interest in the political world, and it was Elizabeth Toy's role to report the varied teas, rallies, and events impartially. Thus, in photograph above, (from left to right) Sen. Neil McLean, Margaret Rideout, and Dr. A.M.A. McLean, the principals at the Liberal reception at the Legion Memorial Hall in 1965, are pictured. A few days later, as seen below, the Conservatives used the same hall for an afternoon tea, and Elizabeth is back to take a photograph of Mrs. Maynard Sweeney (left) and Mrs. Hazen Magowan (right) presiding over the refreshments, while Helen Rubin (standing) is talking over the election. "She could do that with the best of them," Elizabeth has recalled.

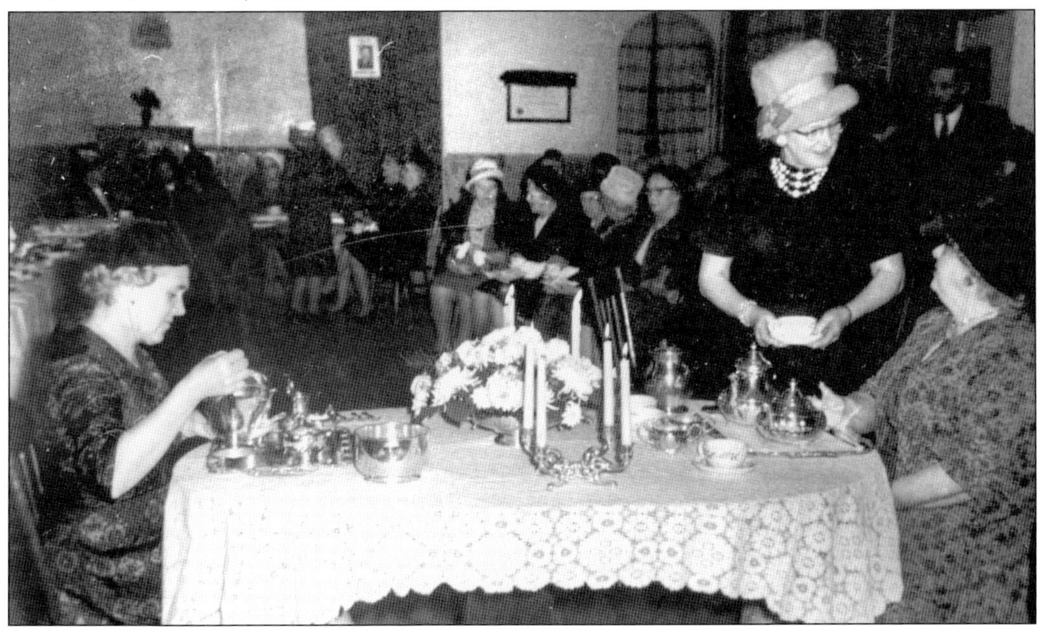

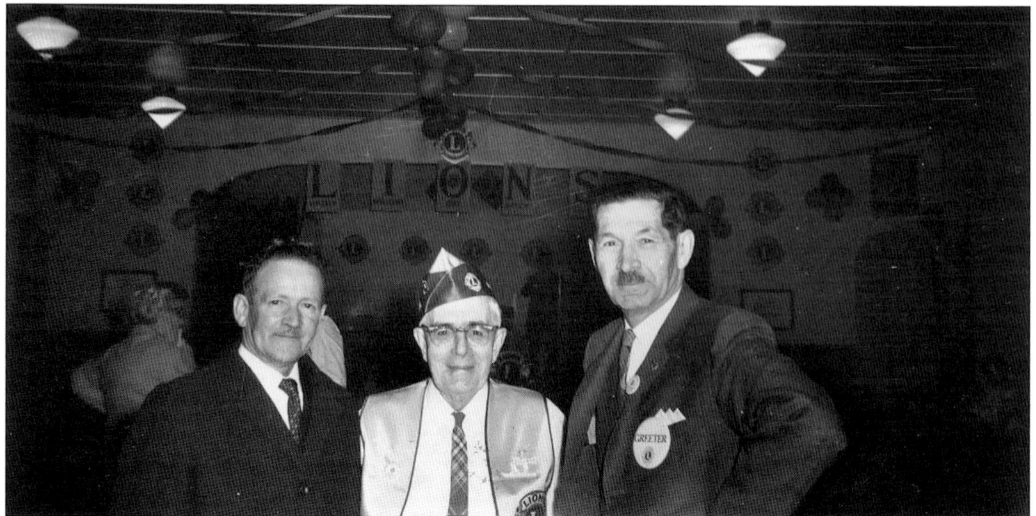

The community has supported many service clubs over the years. In 1965,Elizabeth Toy took this photograph of the Lions, just prior to a banquet at the Legion Hall. From left to right are Alfred Hawkins, Ralph J. Doyle, and R.D. Caldwell Stewart, QC, discussing the evening's program.

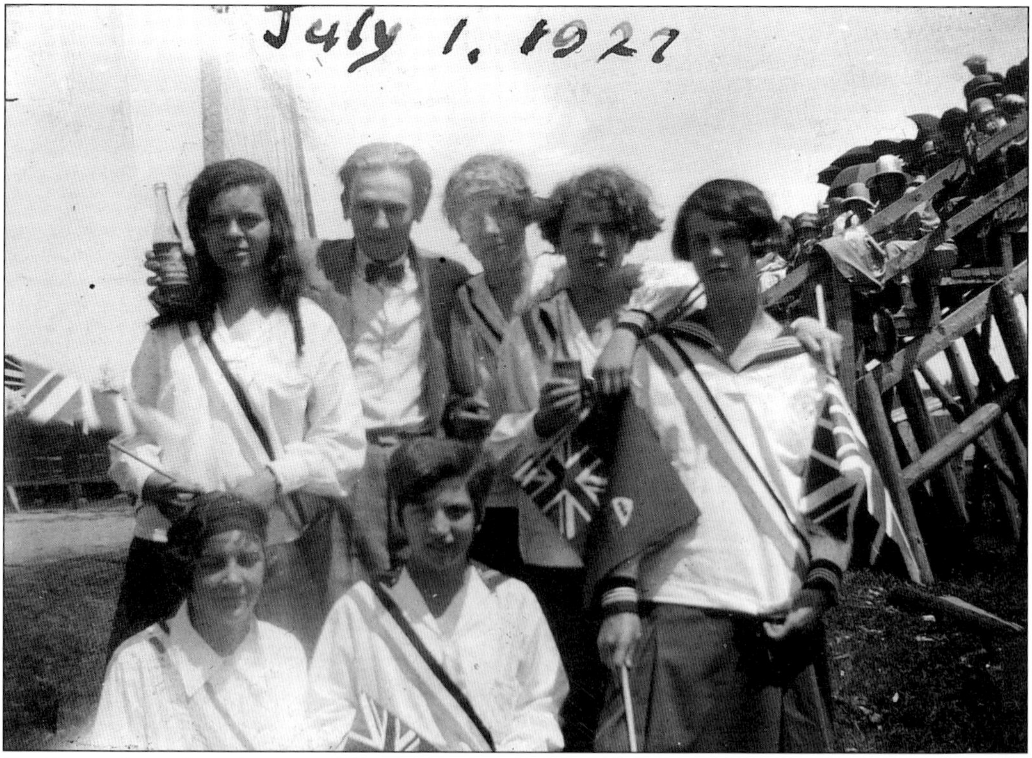

St. George has a long history of Canada Day—or Dominion Day as many of the older residents prefer—celebrations dating back to the 1920s. Pictured at the St. George ball field during the Dominion Day celebration of 1927 are, from left to right, as follows: (front) Eleanor Chaffey and Rose Brown; (back) Agnes Feeney, Harold Boyd, Lydie Campbell, Mary Lynch, and Monica Feeney.

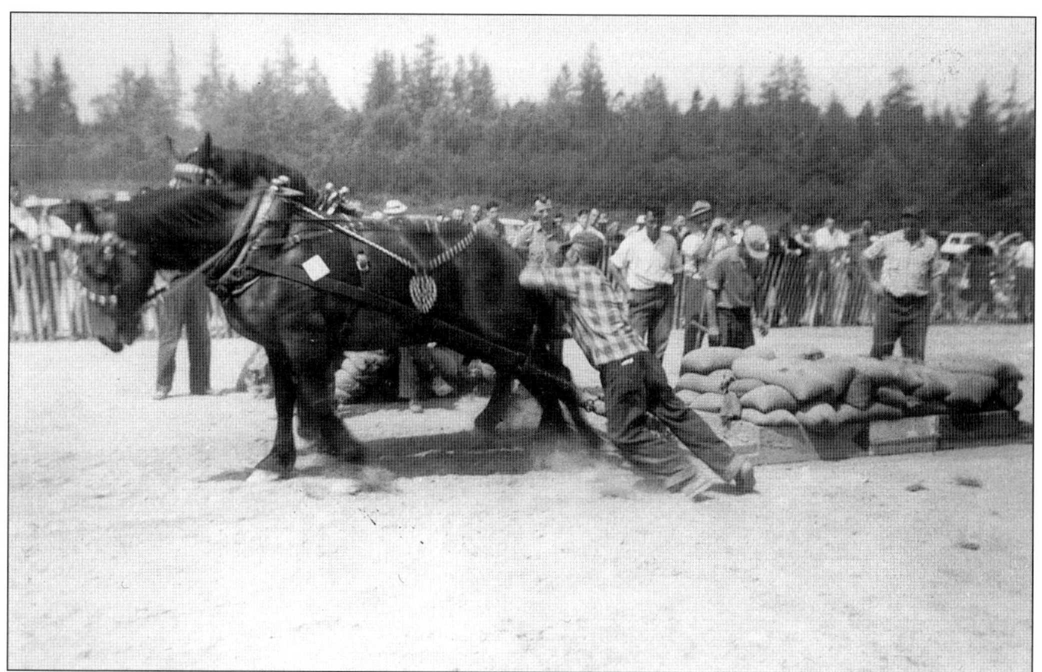

For St. George residents, celebration of Canada's birthday on the first was sometimes followed by taking a steamer to Eastport to join in the American celebration on the "glorious fourth." There, they might compare Yankee athletic competitions and band performances with those they had just enjoyed back home. Horse-pulling contests at the Legion field are shown in the upper photograph, while Bill Dalzell and the Caledonian Pipe Band of Saint John with 14 pipers is featured in the lower one.

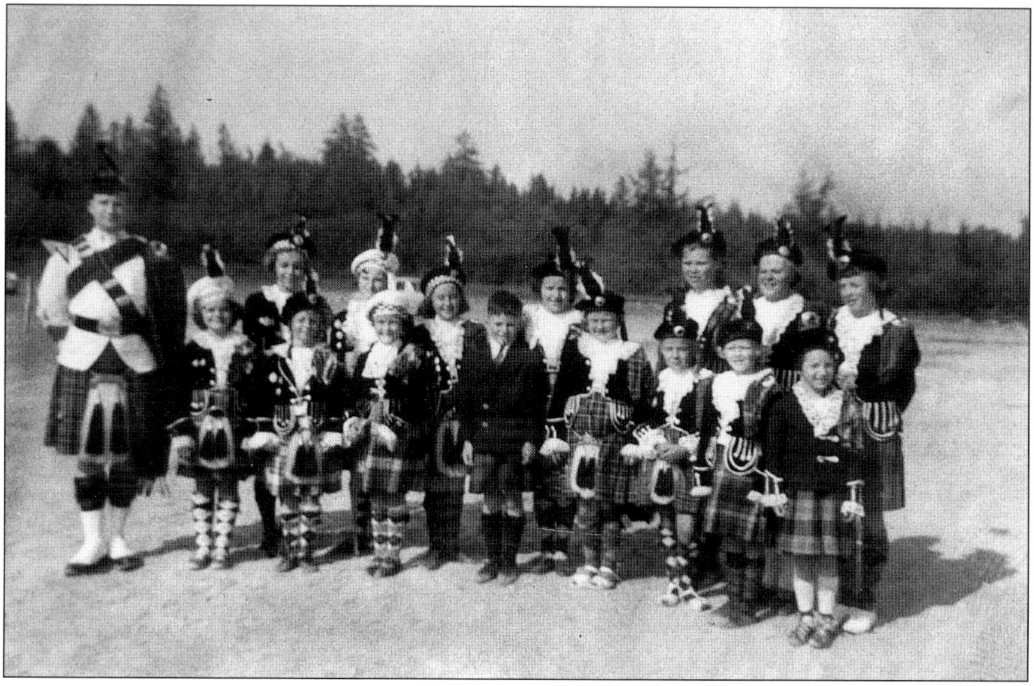

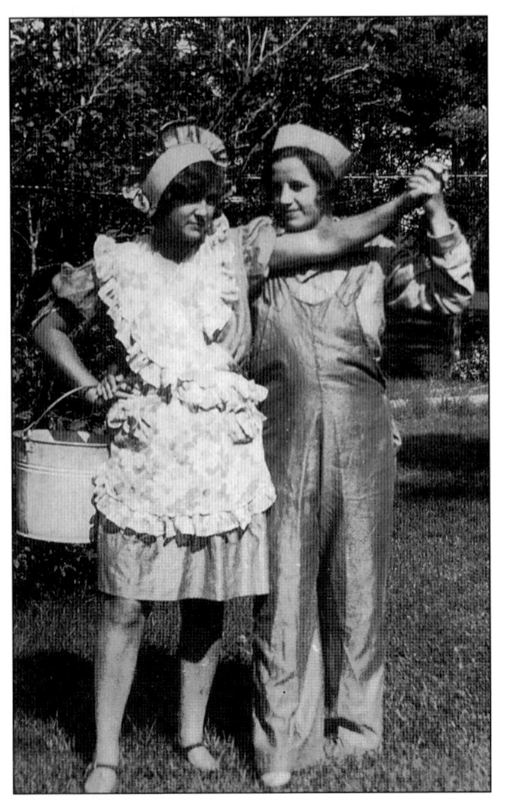

The best times are often those enjoyed right around the home. In the Toy backyard in 1931, "Pun" and "Es" are in college flappers costumes they have made so they can be part of a traveling play called *Out in the New Mown Hay*. "Pun" is Frances Toy and "Es" is Esther Goodeill. Twenty years later, below, Russell and Beth Waycott have just built a snowman in the same backyard. It seems to say that fun is fun. . . and perhaps fraternal, social, and religious activities transcend ages and community boundaries.

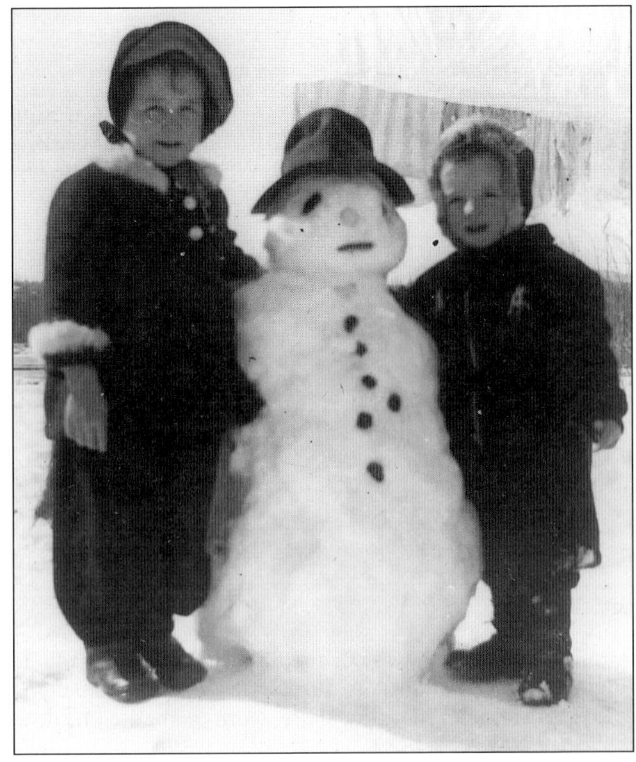

Five

Getting Around

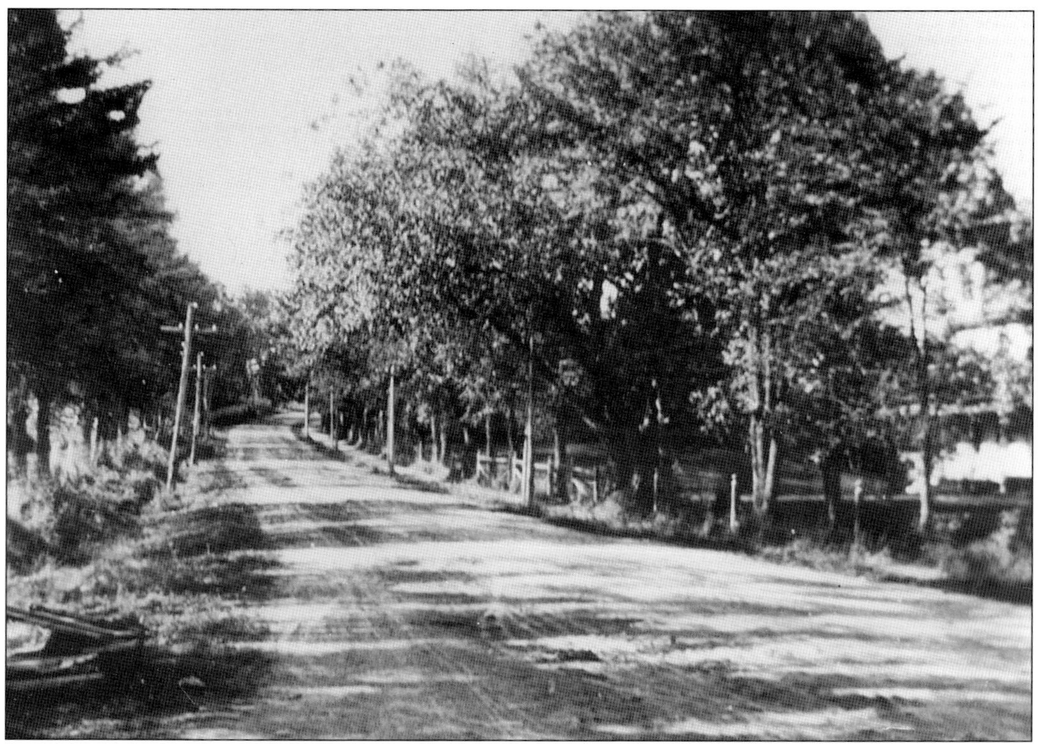

The first settlers on the Magaguadavic had little choice in ways of getting around. They could walk or take some water conveyance, like a canoe, rowboat, or sailing craft. Water travel was the preferred method for links with neighbours up and down the coast. It was some time before roads were built and before bridges were needed to span the rivers flowing into the Bay of Fundy. The first bridges were simple log structures, and later, sawn lumber, which was generally roofed over to form a covered bridge that lasted much longer than uncovered structures. It was early in the 20th century when steel structures were introduced. The horse was an indispensable method of travel, and initially, residents followed coastal footpaths that the natives had used for centuries. Many of these paths were later pushed back wide enough to let a wagon pass, and then stagecoaches began to run over them. It was a great improvement when the railway came to St. George in 1882, and the Grand Southern Railway made the conveyance of goods much easier up and down the coast. When motorcars came into use in the early part of the 20th century, better roads and stronger bridges were built. Within a few years, the direction of traffic changed too, for the province drove on the left till 1922. In this chapter, the methods of transportation, both pleasurable and practical, used by the residents of St. George to get around will be presented. The main highway along the coast ran right through St. George until the late 1960s, and this was the view that greeted the traveler entering or leaving town. This is the view looking east in the 1930s. It was officially known as Main Street; unofficially, many called it Elm Avenue. The trees, sadly, were gradually cut down as they became infested with Dutch elm disease in the 1960s.

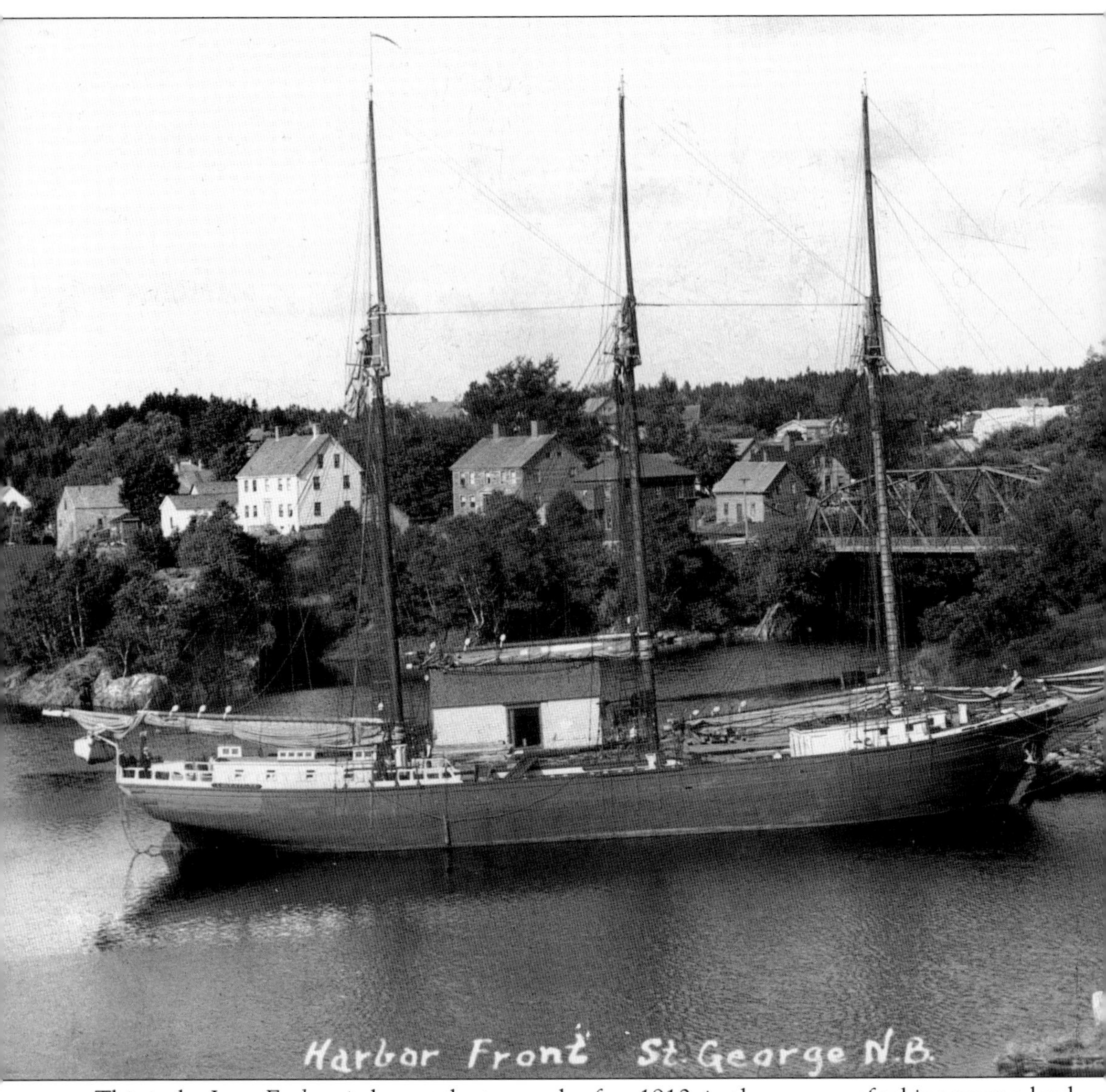

This is the *Lucy Evelyn* tied up at the town wharf, *c.* 1910, in the process of taking away a load of pulp from the recently opened St. George mill. In the background, the steel bridge or the lower bridge is in place, and the town Red Store Wharf shed can be seen on the left edge of the photograph. On the right of the road just beyond the bridge stood Crickard's Grocery Store, and to the left, the big white house is that of Frank Hibbard. These buildings are among the oldest in the community. Other ships that tied up over the years included the *Minas Princess*, the *Minas Prince*, the *Frederick H.*, the *Quaco Queen*, the *John R. Fell*, the *Ruth Robinson*, and the *R.R. Gavin*, as well as those pictured on the following pages.

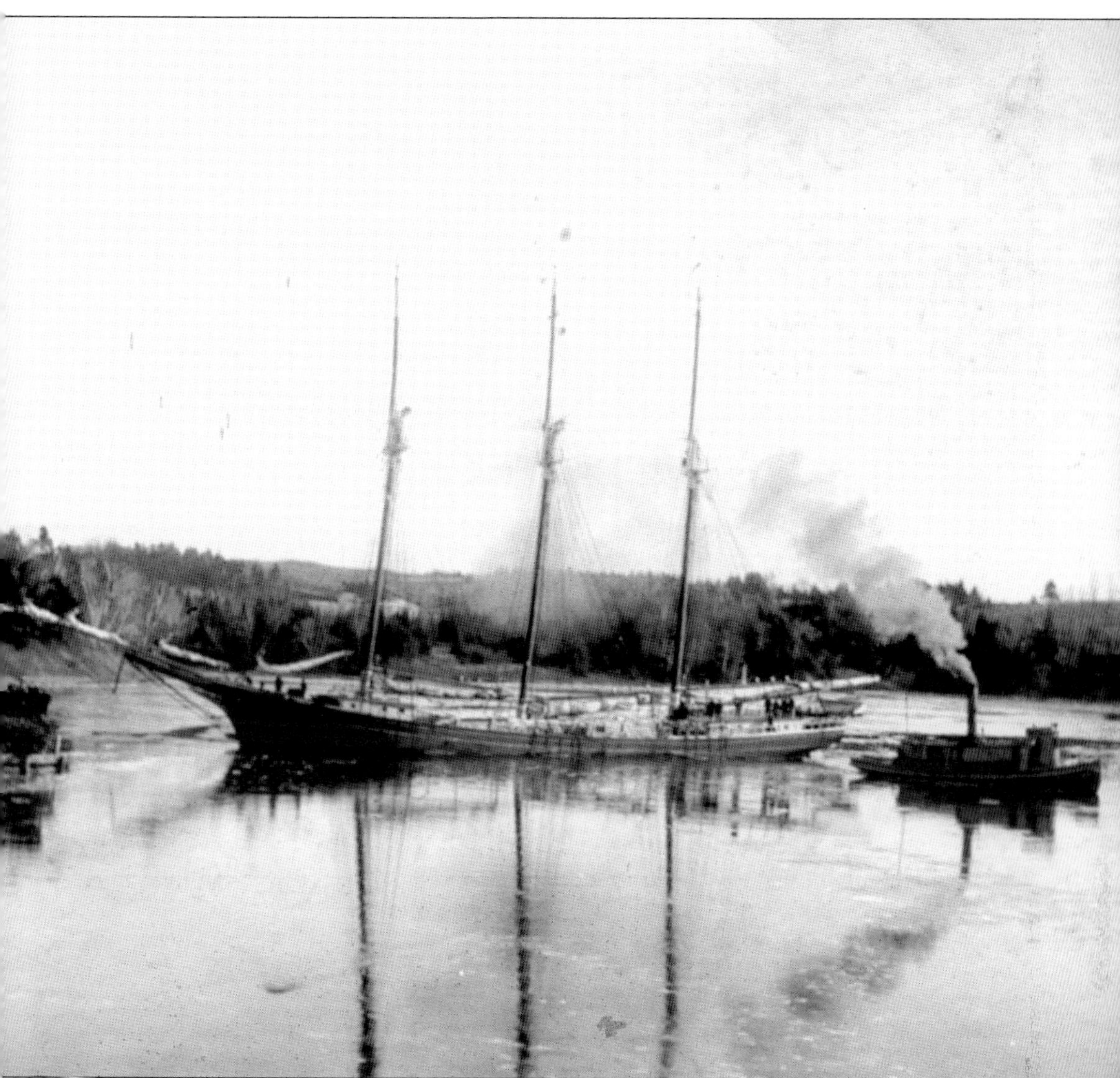

Note the cluster of men at the end of the public wharf in the St. George Basin. It is 1905 and an important occasion, as the schooner *George D. Edwards* is being pulled away with the first cargo of wet pulp from the St. George Pulp and Paper mill. She is bound for Norwalk, Connecticut, not far from Mystic, where she had been built only a few years earlier.

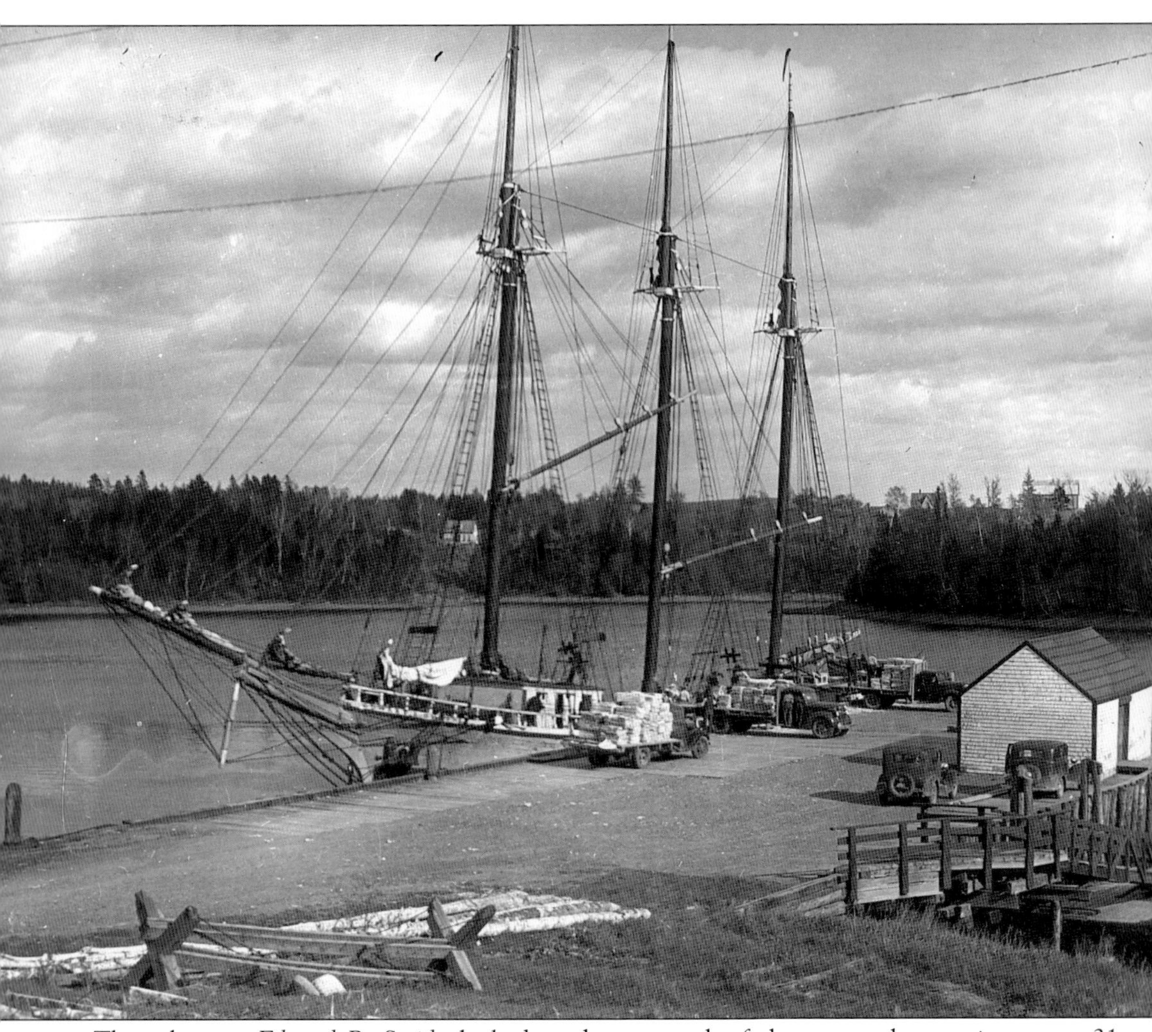

The schooner *Edward R. Smith* docked at the same wharf shown on the previous page 31 years later in 1936. Though driven off transatlantic routes by steel, steam-powered ships, the wind-powered coastal schooners were still able to profitably carry pulp from the St. George mill well into the middle of the 20th century and continued to do coastal work as far off as South America for other customers. Some still sail to this day as pleasure vessels and are great attractions.

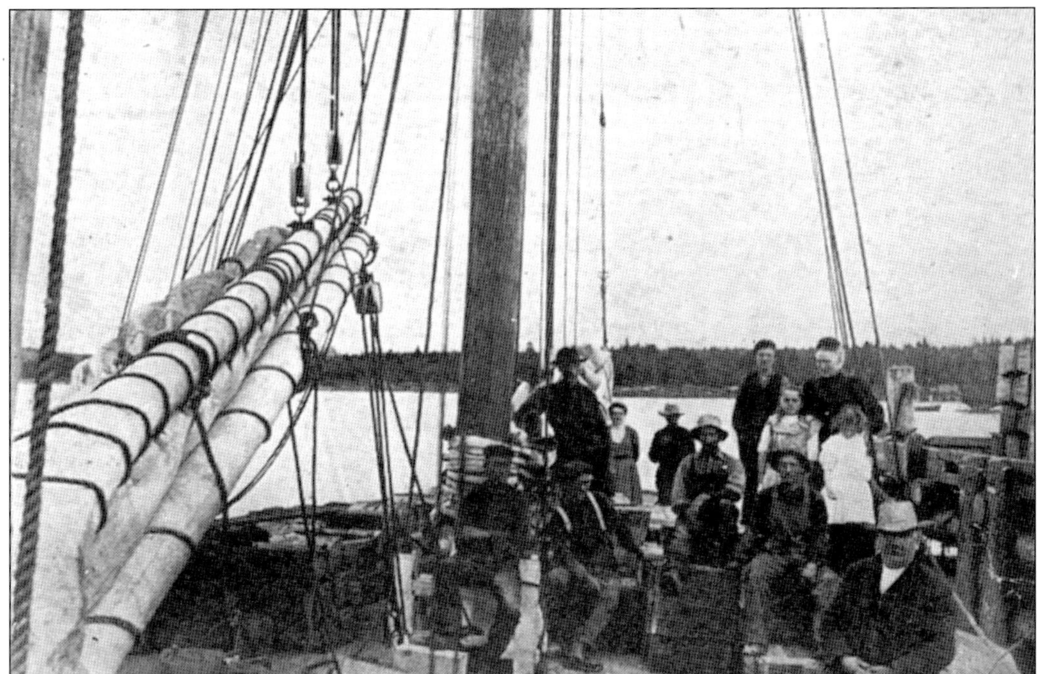

A deck scene on the schooner *Clara A. Benner* at Back Bay gives a look at what conditions may have been like onboard a schooner of the type that called on St. George. Obviously, this is a pleasure, not a work occasion, as we see women and children onboard. In the early days of Bay of Fundy schooners, it was considered bad luck to have women onboard, so none was ever allowed.

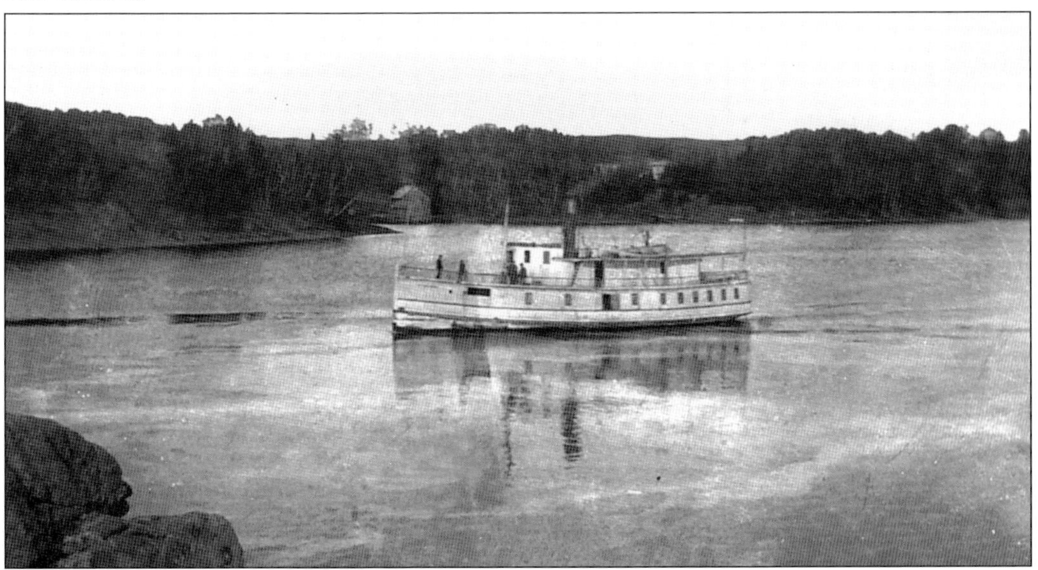

Passing Cannon Rock in St. George Basin, the 70-tonne *Viking Steamboat* owned by the Deer Island and Campobello Steamboat Company can be seen. It carried passengers and freight around the points of Passamaquoddy Bay and the neighbouring islands. Captains were Dan Richardson and later Frank Johnson. It sank at the wharf in St. Andrews in 1909 but was re-floated, and in 1916, it was finally retired, ending its days as a scow on the St. John River.

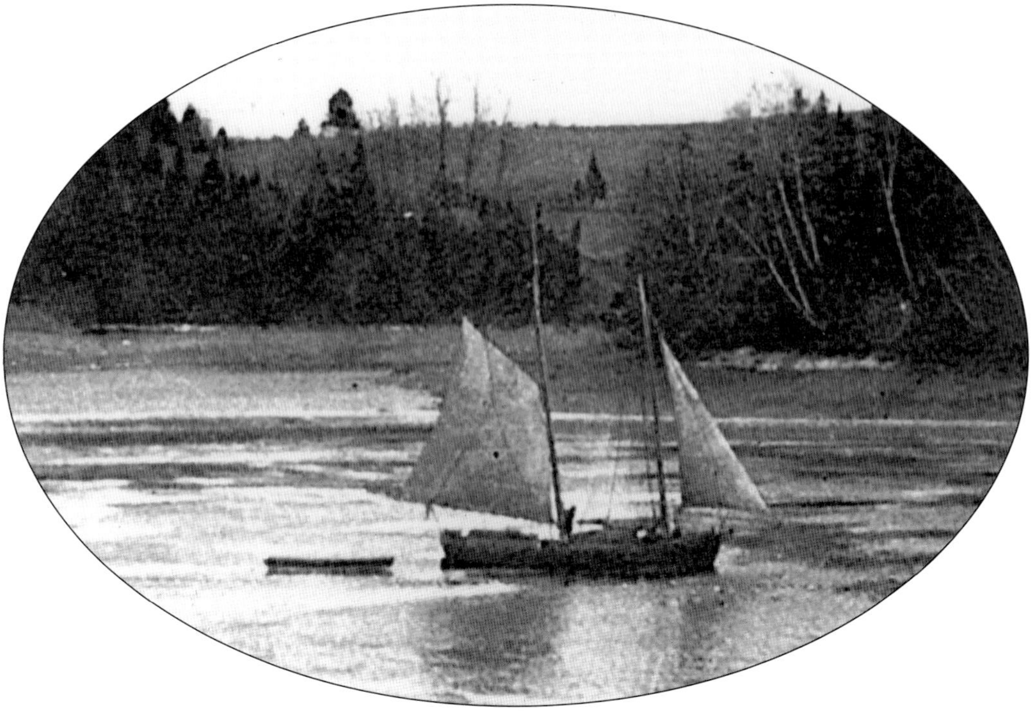

A sailboat in the St. George basin shows that this tidal zone was also used for recreational purposes. It would have taken a very skilled sailor to navigate in the area with its quickly changing currents and eddies combined with the wind sweeping down off the hillsides creating additional sailing challenges.

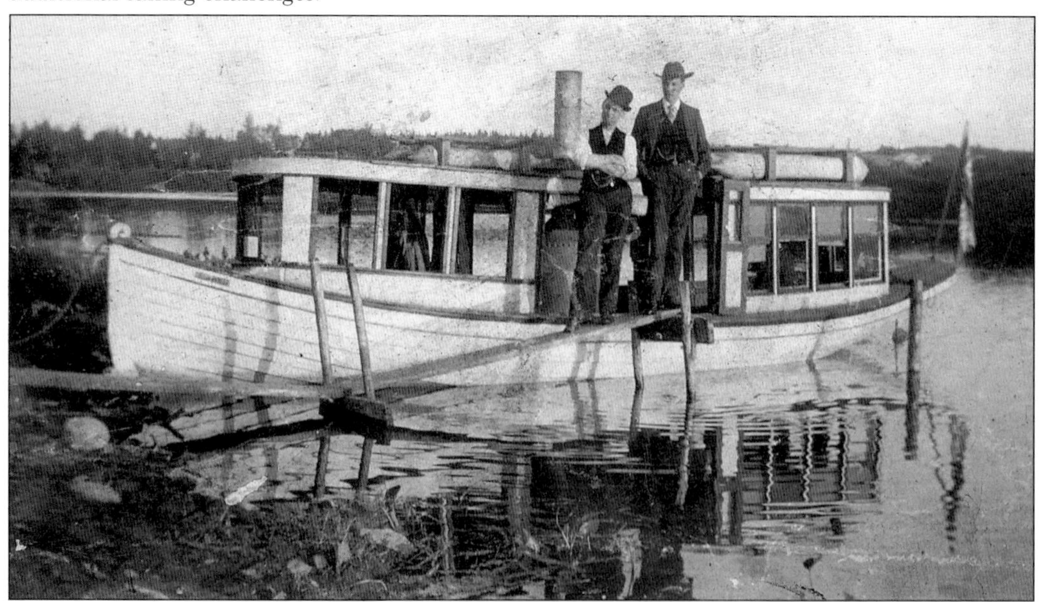

Pleasure boats were sometimes created from practical working vessels that had outlived their usefulness. With its glassed in area added, this vessel seems to have been fitted for passenger excursions and would have been comfortable even on a chilly or foggy day. Phoebe Toy took the photograph but did not identify the time, the men, or the vessel, which was unusual for her.

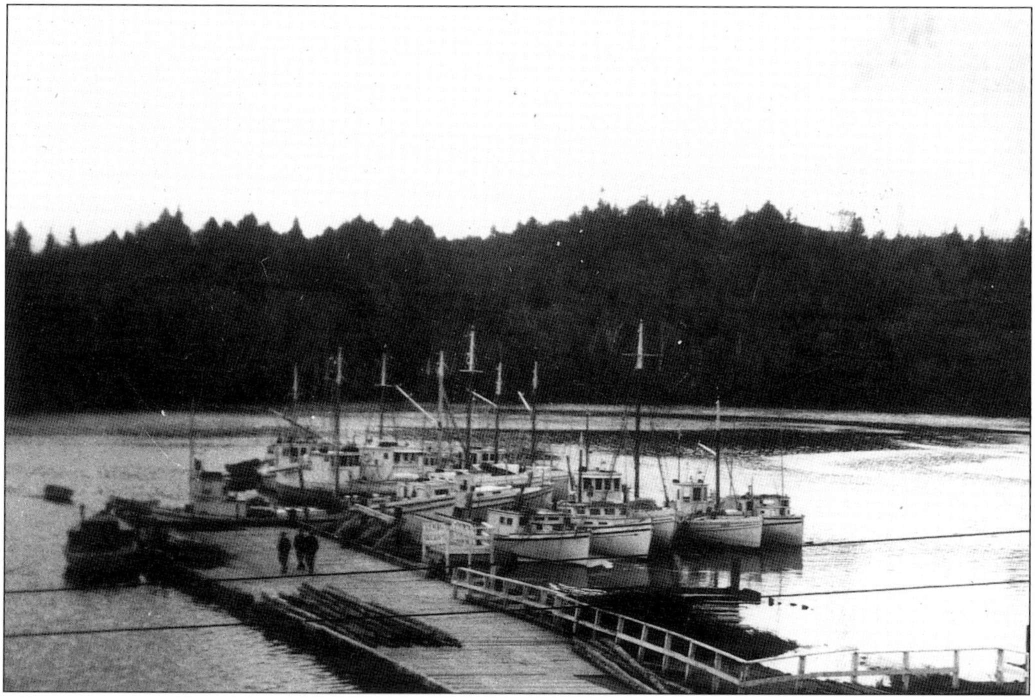

In October of 1952, Blacks Harbour herring seiners were pulled up side by side against the wharf, waiting to go out and make the catch. From time to time, a glut of herring would enter the estuary, and the vessels would chase in off the high sea and make the catch by netting off the mouth of the river in order to cluster the fish, trapping them in their nets.

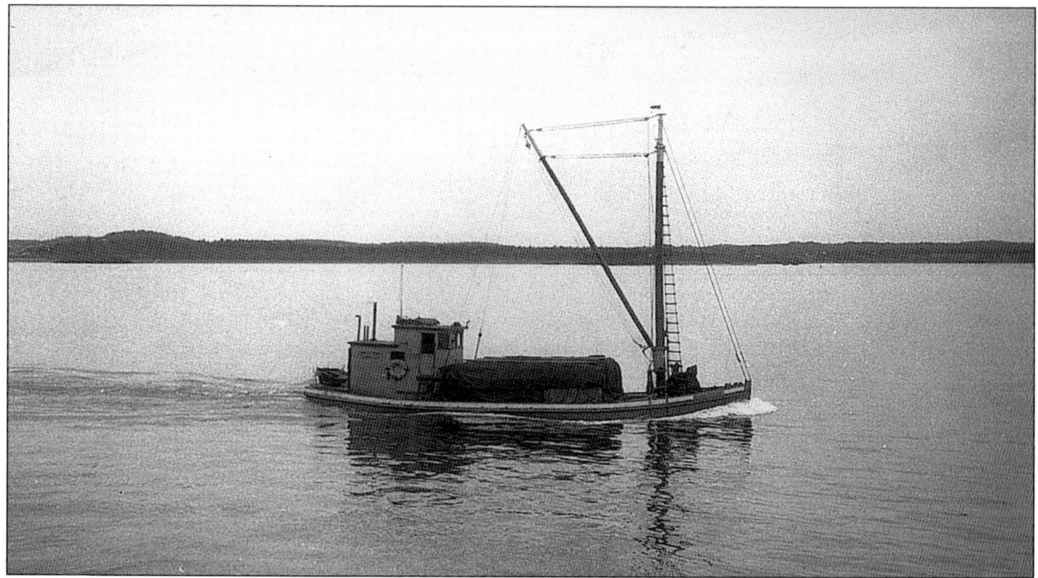

It is obvious from observing the waterline that this herring seiner is heavily loaded. The cargo, covered with the canvas on the deck, is a heavy one, and it is good the day is calm. The seiner is headed out across Passamaquoddy Bay, maybe delivering sardines or materials for packing them to one of the U.S. canneries at Eastport or the largest cannery in the world at Blacks Harbour.

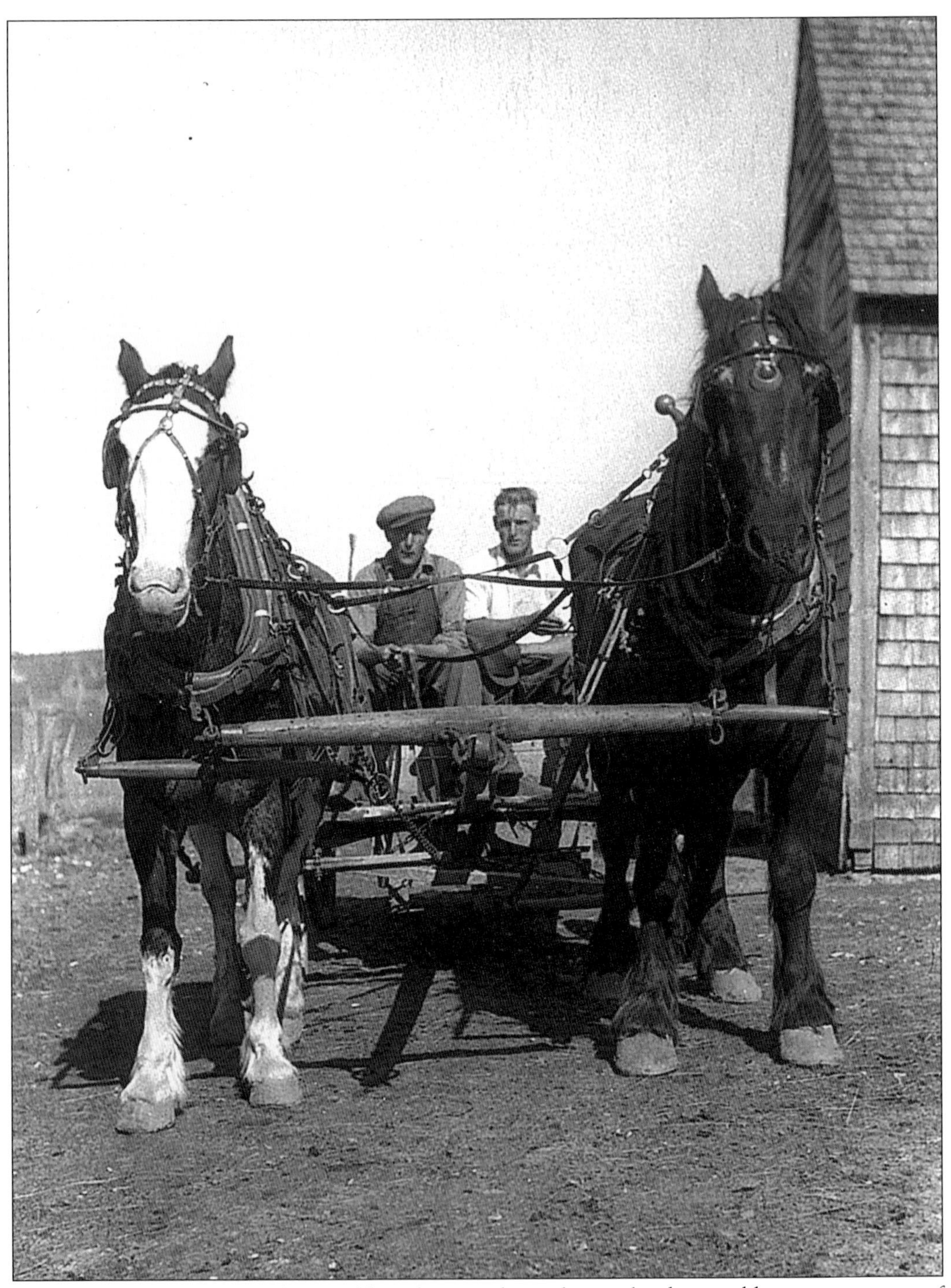

A pair of horses was an indispensable aide to early settlers in hauling stubborn stumps out of the land, helping with planting, and carrying commodities to the homestead. In winter, the pair could be hooked to a sleigh or wagon to go to church or to take a pretty girl out for an evening ride. This unusual white-faced horse may have been half of Stanley Spinney's team, according to some St. George residents.

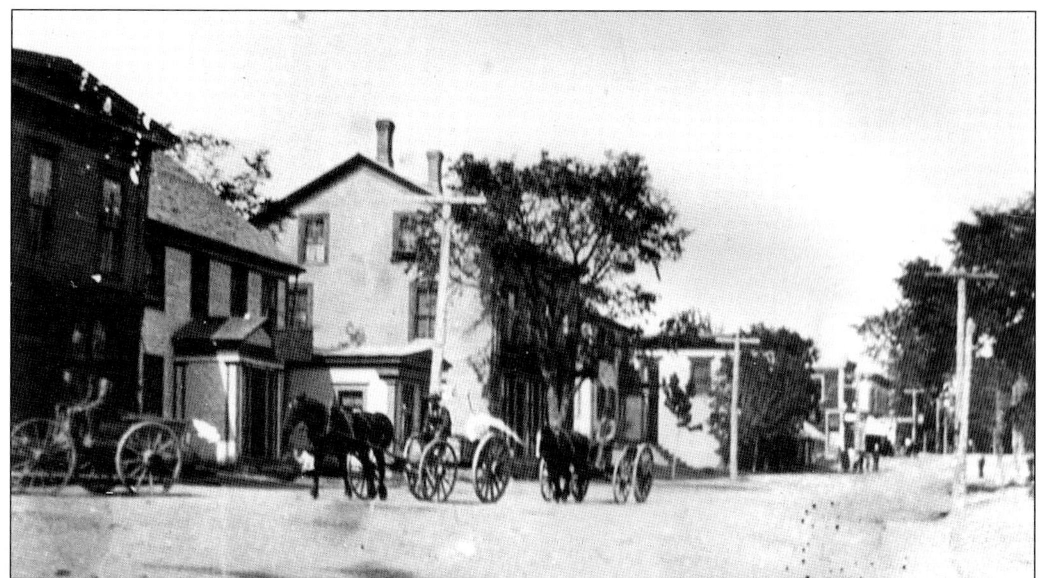

The dust of summer and the mud and ruts of spring are but memories in this scene as wagons dispense gravel onto St. George's Main Street. When this picture was taken, *c.* 1915, it was common for the government to close roads for days in the spring. In August of 1939, paving of Route One was completed except for a six-kilometre stretch through St. George where work was needed due to culverts that had heaved the previous winter.

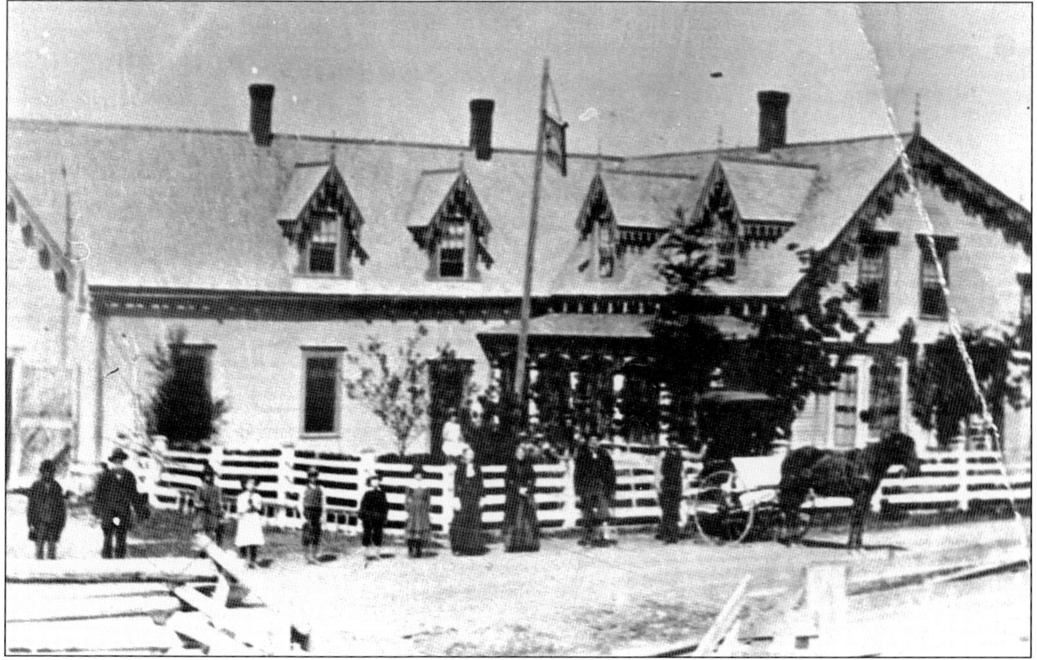

Travelers needed convenient hotel accommodations as they journeyed the roads from town to town. This is Tom and Eveline Goss's stagecoach house of the 1880s, located on Riverview Avenue. They also operated a funeral home at the same location. Three teams, like the one in the photograph, waited at the railway station to take visitors to the area's hotels. By 1910, there were other accommodations, including the Carleton House, Victoria House, and Boyd's Hotel.

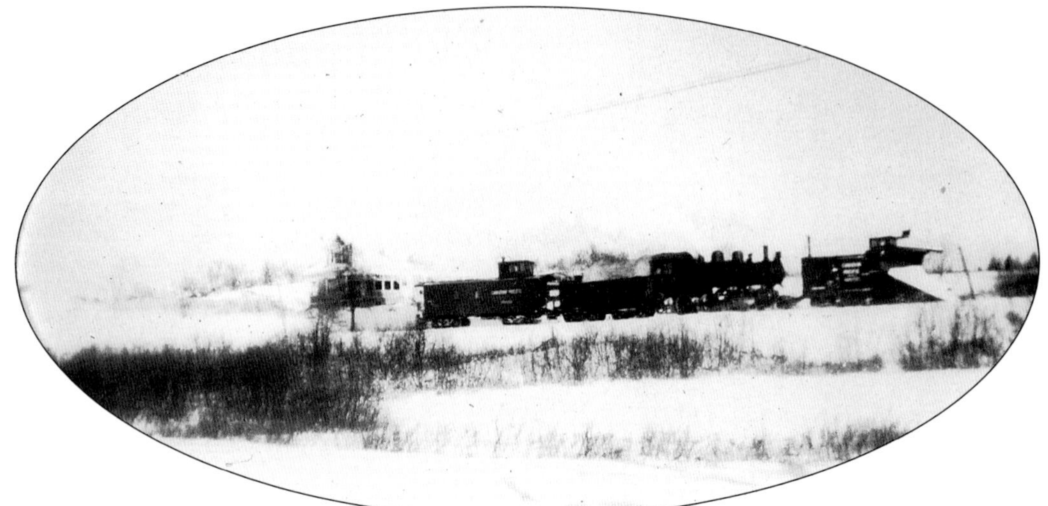

It took a sustained effort over many years for Col. J. M. Greene to convince politicians and the public that a 132-kilometre rail line along the rocky Bay of Fundy coast was possible. A rally was held in St. George in 1873 to support his hopes, but it was not until January 4, 1882, that the line was finally opened. A trainload traveled to St. Stephen that day and enjoyed a lavish feast at the Cotton Mill. (See page 110.) On the return trip, 300 gathered at the St. George Temperance Hall for a round of speeches and toasts to the new line. They were then led to the station shown below by the St. George Band, and their torch-lit parade passed under a huge spruce arch constructed over the tracks. (Courtesy PA, 18-238A.)

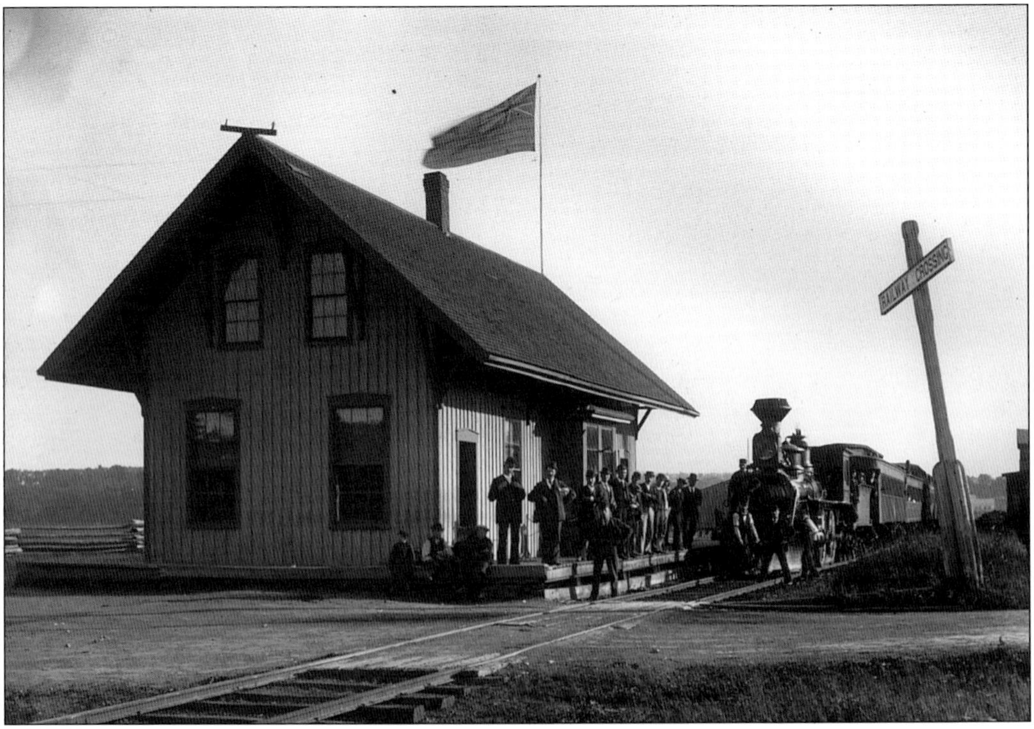

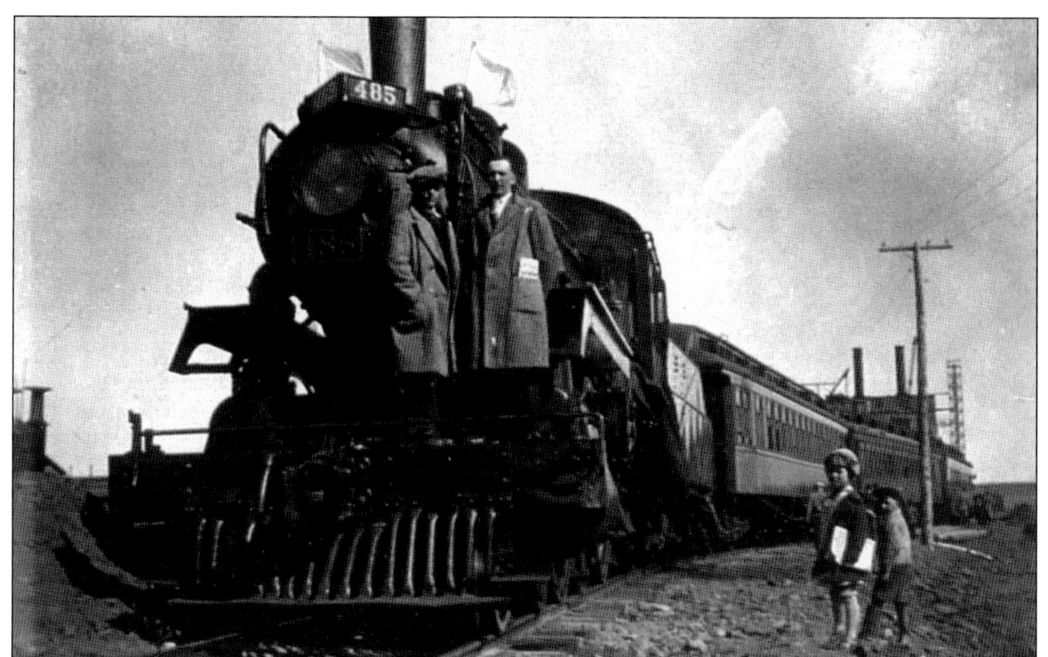

When Edwin Toy took this photograph in 1931, the Shore Line through his town of St. George had been reduced to three visits a week. In 1935, it stopped running the entire line to St. Stephen, and instead began to offer daily service to St. George, which ended in 1955. It was used for freight as far as Lepreau until the late 1970s; by the 1990s, all the track of the line that had cost a million dollars to build in 1880 was gone.

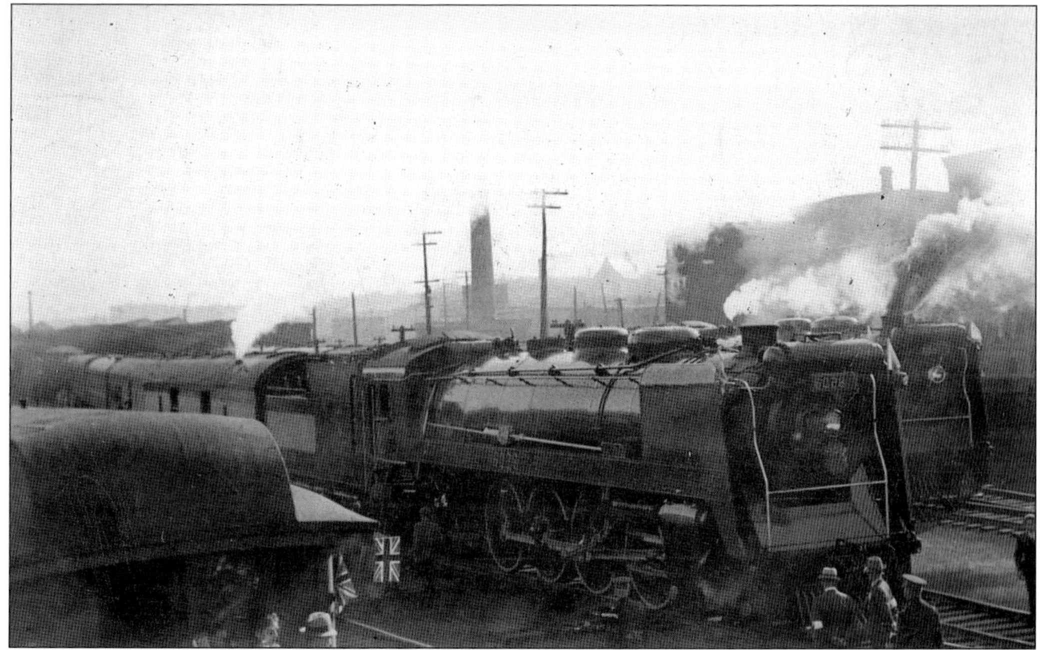

In 1939, Elizabeth Toy traveled to Saint John and took this picture of the *Royal Train* at Union Station. It was hauling King George VI and his wife, Elizabeth (the Queen Mother who died in 2002), on a cross-Canada trip. They were the first reigning monarchs to ever visit Canada.

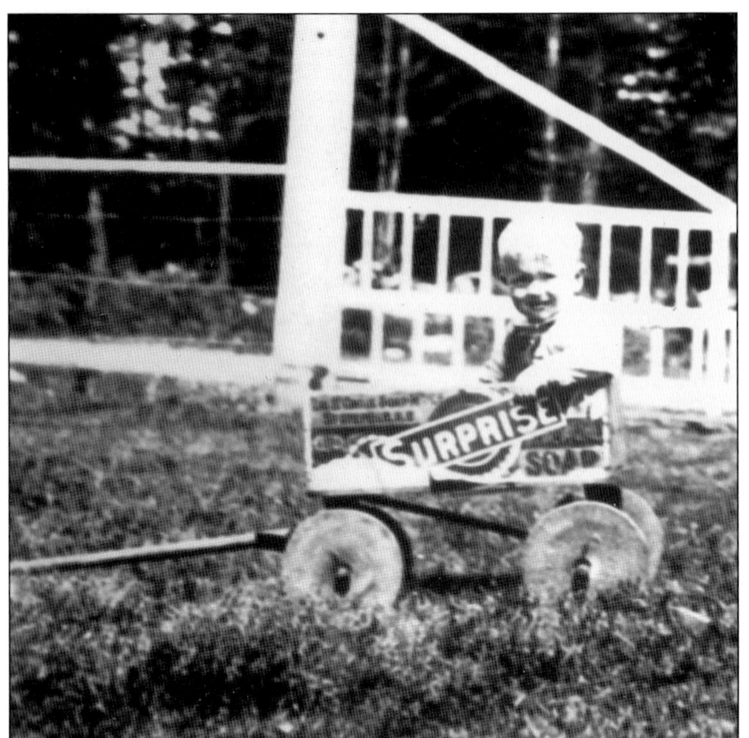

Not all ways of getting around need be serious, as shown in this *c.* 1925 photograph of New River's Lloyd Mealey in a cart built for him out of a wooden box that once held Surprise Soap. This was an important Charlotte County industry that operated in St. Stephen from 1878 until 1947 and, at times, produced about 50 tons of soap each week; thus, there were lots of leftover boxes for boys like Lloyd to enjoy. (Courtesy Lloyd Mealey.)

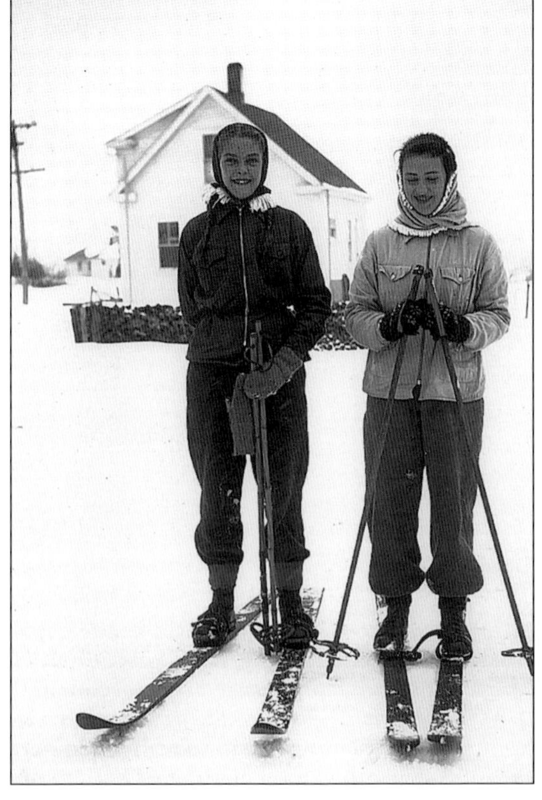

In the early days of motor vehicles, snowshoes and skis were a much more reliable way to get around in the winter months, especially during the winter of the "big snow" in 1923 when over two metres of snow fell on St. George. Deep-snow winters continued to occur in unpredictable patterns, so girls such as Roberta Spinney (left) and her friend Ann Smith (right) always kept an old pair of skies handy just in case.

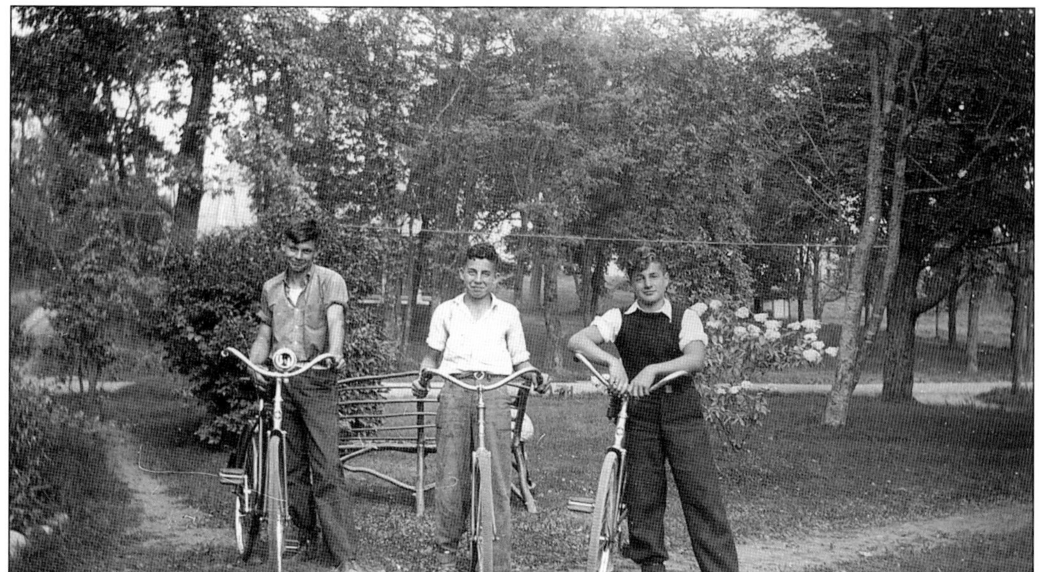

It was the introduction of the bicycle with its pneumatic or safety tire that laid the way for much of the later mechanical developments of the first automobiles to hit the roads. These boys are enjoying a ride on Sept 10, 1937, in the St. George area. From left to right are John Williamson, Eugene Toy, and Donald Stewart.

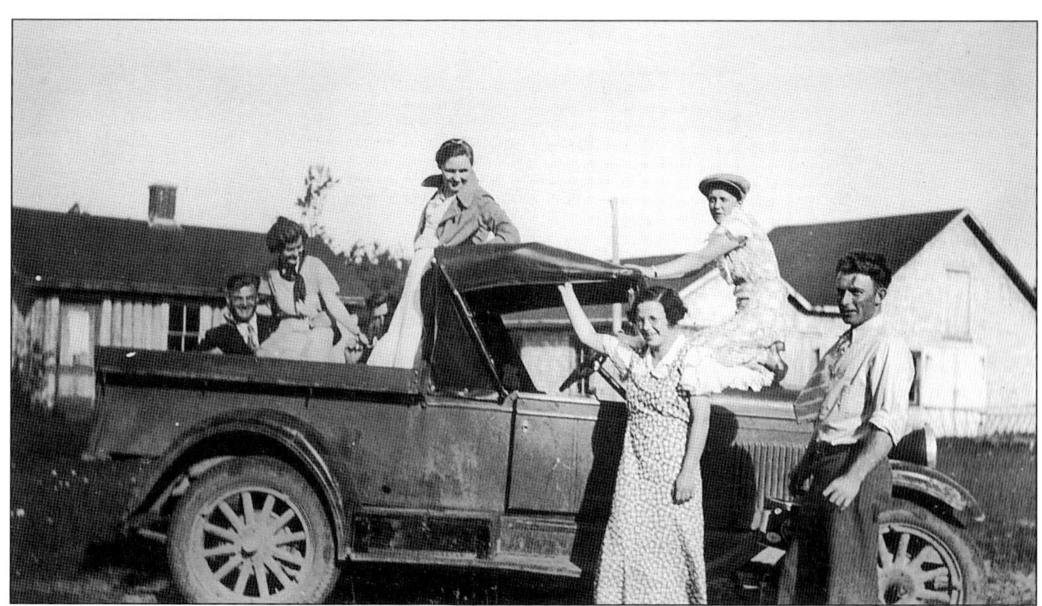

Motor vehicle travel was such an adventure in the early times. Who would bother today to take a shot of an outing just a few kilometres from home, but when this group of Elizabeth's friends went from St. George to MacDoughall Lake for a picnic, on July 8, 1933, they thought it an occasion that called for a photograph.

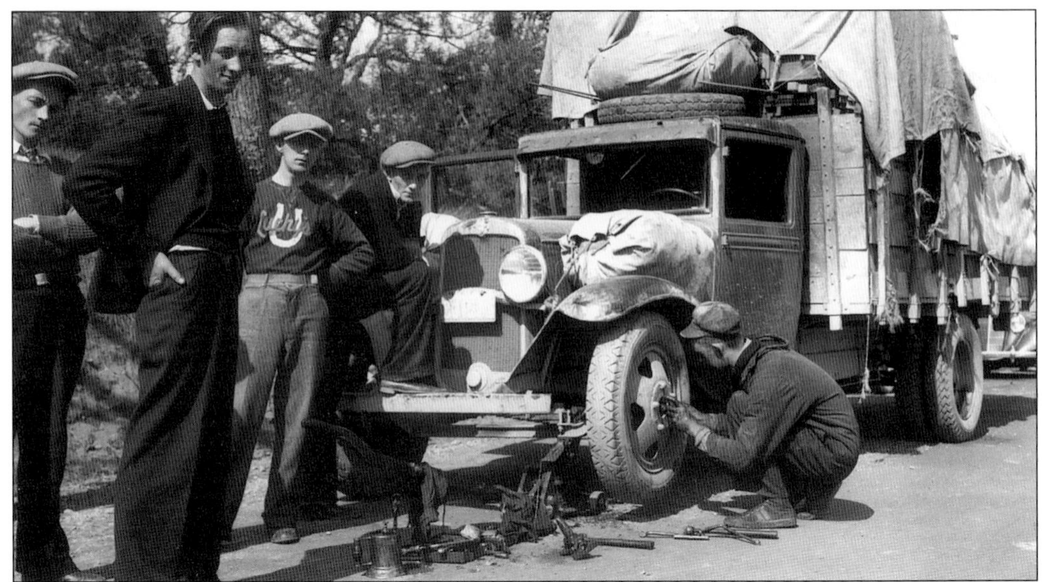

In 1908, the *St. Croix Courier* described the Pocologan road east of St. George as having "bald ledges" that were "impossible to get over," and noted there was no guard rail to prevent "going into the sea." Though conditions did improve, roads continued to be hard on vehicles and break downs on the side of the road were common as is the case here in a photograph shot by A.V.F. Duffy of Sydney Waycott's truck in 1935.

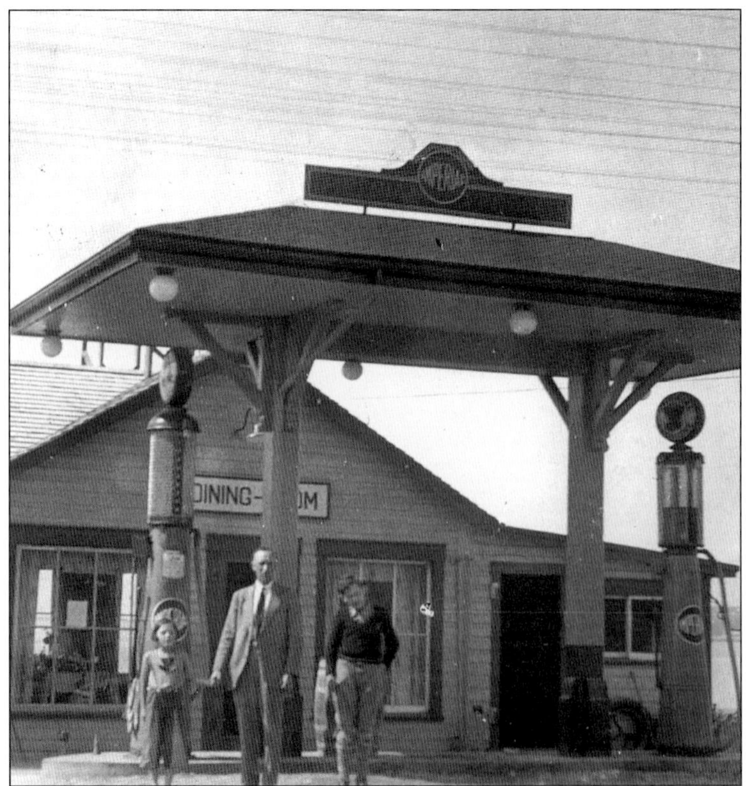

By the early 1940s, an Imperial Station, where gas, repairs, and dining were available, was established on the road at Pocologan, as seen in this photograph. Alice Garner provided this photograph from her early days in the area when her grandmother ran the Bayview Cabins.

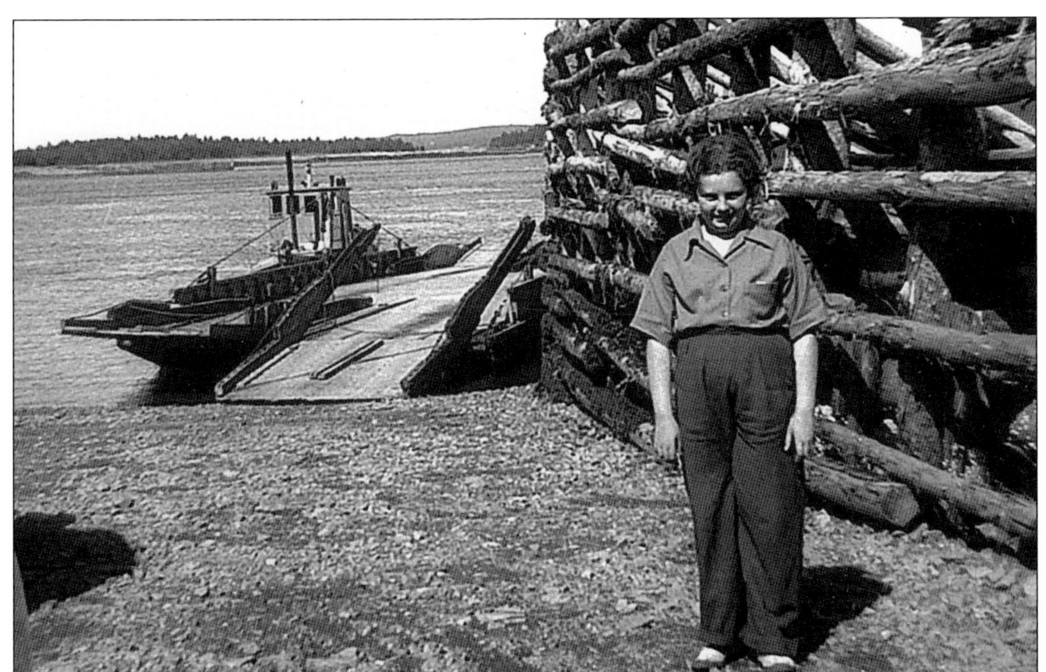

Before the advent of motor vehicles, passengers traveling to the offshore islands took one of the cruisers or steamers that would provide foot passage. Once vehicles became more common, scows were pressed into service to carry vehicles between the mainland and the islands. In 1930, about 1,000 cars (eight at a time in hourly trips) used the service in the three summer months on a pay-as-you-go ferry service (similar to the lower photograph). In 1934, the government of New Brunswick made this a free service, as is still the case today. In both views, the ferry service is from L'Etete to Deer Island; the lower photograph is from *c.* 1960, with Jean Helen Toy in foreground.

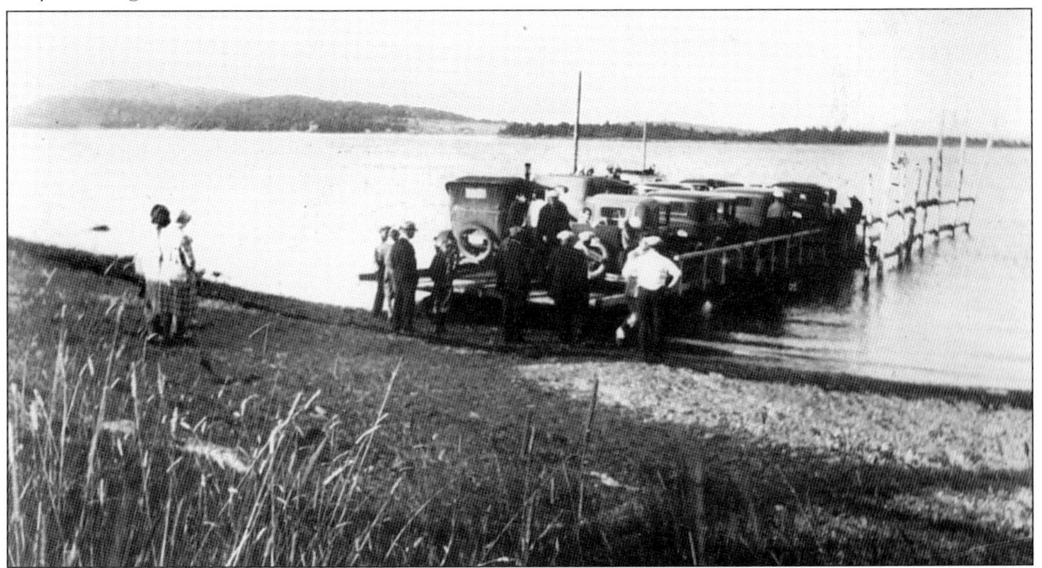

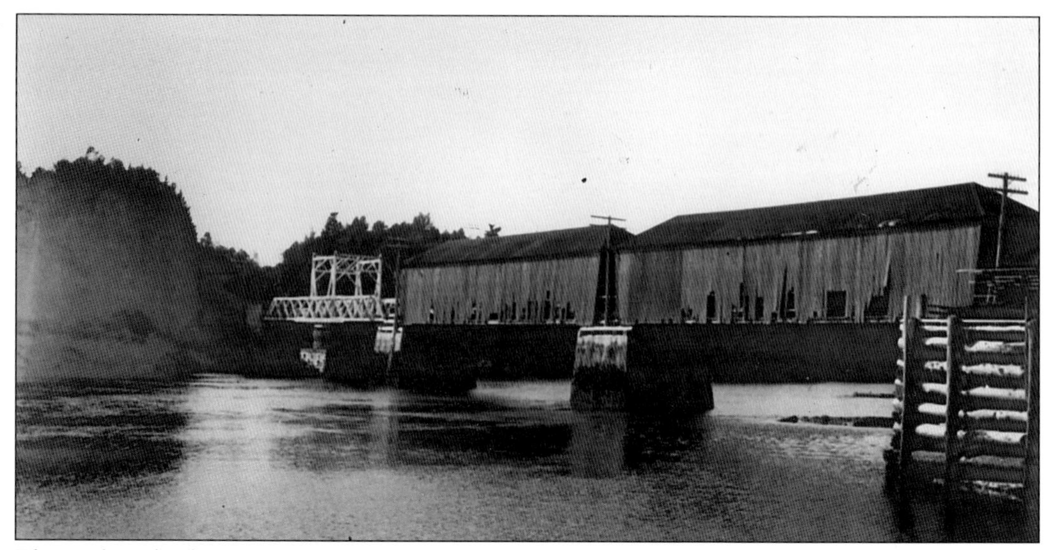

The earliest bridges were often covered. In this 1921 photograph by A.V.F. Duffy, a covered bridge that crossed the Digdequash is shown. In 1938, tenders were called for a steel bridge to replace the covered bridge, which was no longer considered safe, and Saint John Shipbuilding was the successful bidder at $65,000. Thus another covered bridge disappeared. About 60 covered bridges remained in New Brunswick in 2002, with 8 of them not far from St. George.

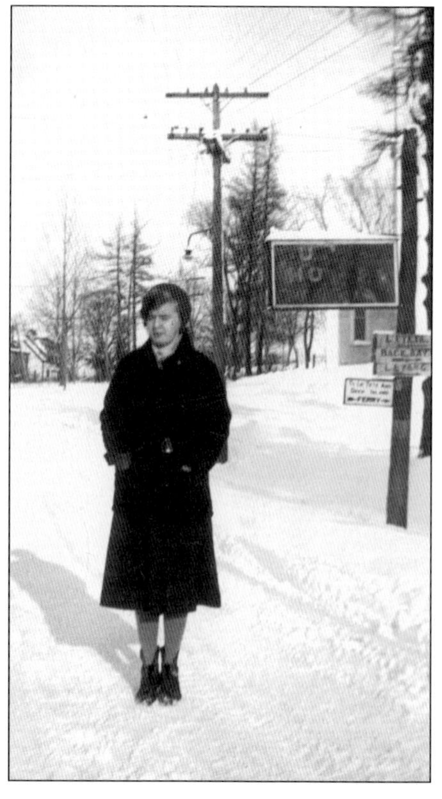

Look closely to the right-hand side of this photograph, and attached to the pole is the kind of roadside signs that would have directed the St. George traveler to L'Etete, Back Bay, L'Etang, and the L'Etete Ferry to Deer Island. Just above it is the sign for the Murray House, which was featured on page 42.

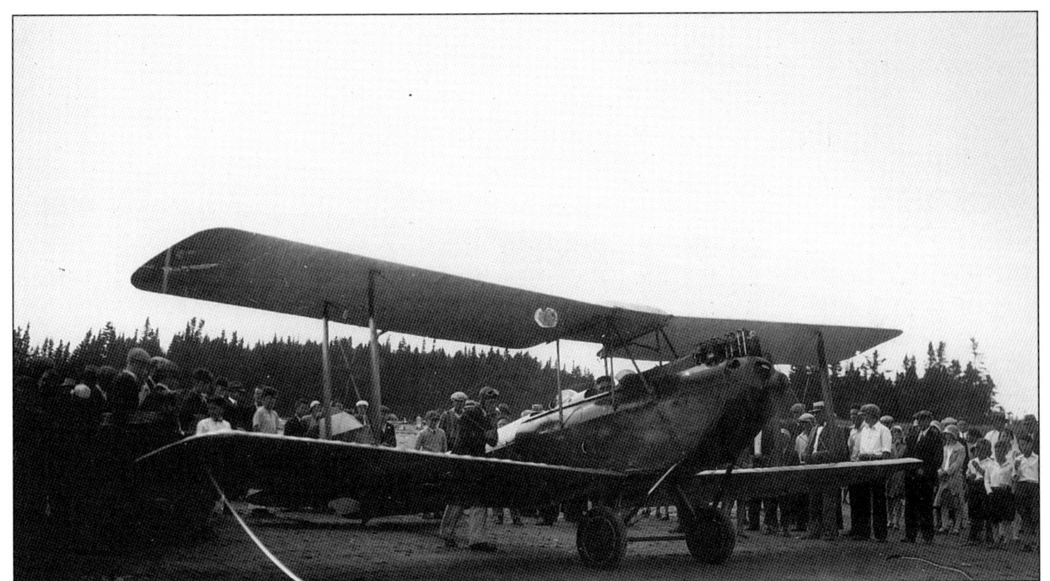

A.V.F. Duffy took this photograph of "Tom Carr's Moth" at New River Beach in 1927. Carr was taking picnickers on $5.00 flights over the beach. Five years later, transatlantic flyer James Mollison flew past the beach on his way to New York, ran out of fuel, and landed at Pennfield. (See page 124 for more of that story.)

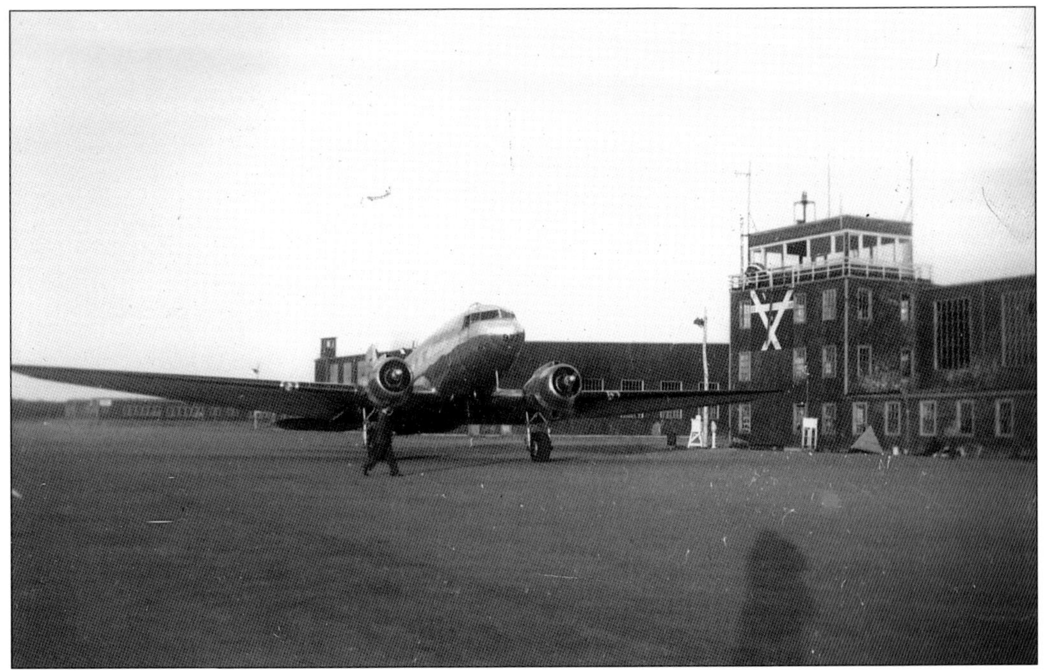

The Pennfield airstrip was developed during World War II as a training ground amidst great secrecy. There are few reports or photographs from the war years. After the war, the strip became the southern New Brunswick base for Trans Canada Airlines. The inaugural flight from the field was made on April 15, 1947, with a plane following a route from North Sydney to Moncton, Pennfield, and finally, on to Boston.

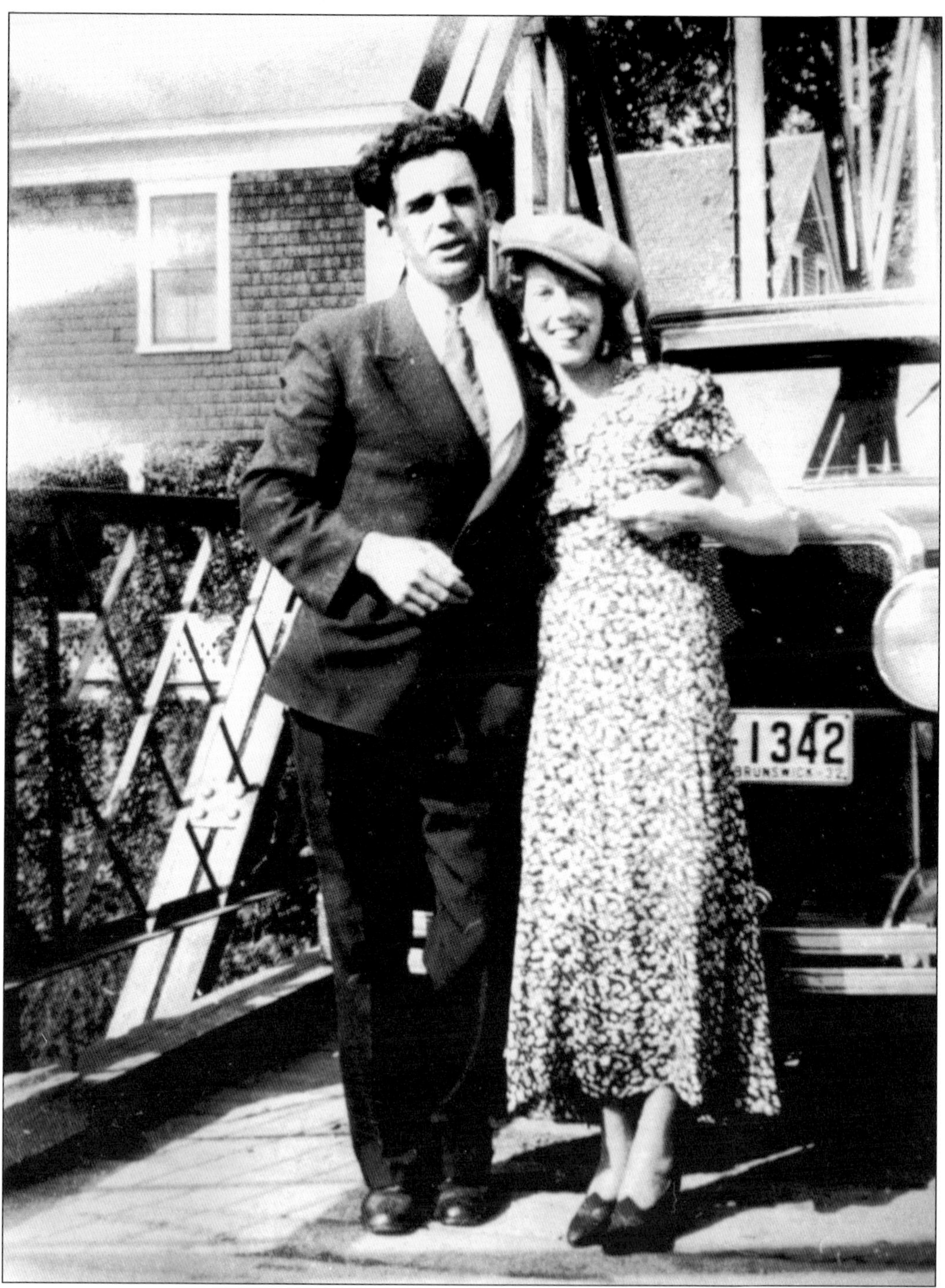

This photograph depicts St. George's first taxi operator, Cecil Doyle at the lower bridge over the Magaguadavic. Not only did he use his vehicle for conveying the town's residents to their appointments, even as far off as Saint John, but also, when his work was done, found it convenient for courting. Here he is seen with his wife-to-be, Margaret Hatfield, in the summer of 1932, and he was still talking about those early days in town when he was over 100 years old.

Six

A Peek at Some People

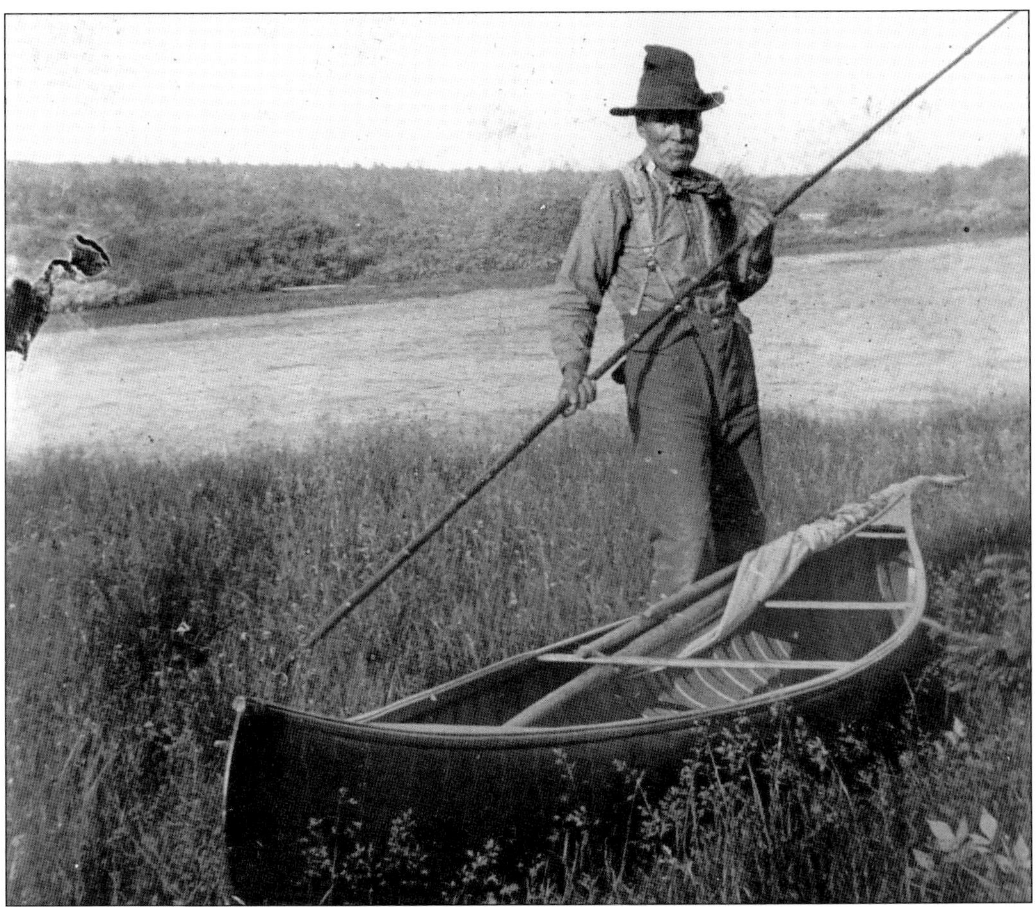

Who are those people and what are they up to? This is a question that is often unanswerable in many an old-time scrapbook or photograph album where the compiler has not recorded the date, the event, or the people. But a reporter, by the nature of their work, must not only be a keen observer but also a careful chronologist. Elizabeth Toy's collection reflects her years writing for four local papers. Two were published on a weekly basis, the *St. Croix Courier* of St. Stephen on the Canadian side and Eastport's *Quoddy Tides* on the American side. In addition, she wrote for the *Daily Gleaner* of Fredericton and for the provincially circulated *Telegraph Journal* of Saint John for many years, paid always by the column-inch. Amazingly, she did this without driving herself but rather by depending on taxi service or neighbours to reach her stories. Among her 2,000-plus photographs are many of interesting people doing interesting things; a sample is offered in the following pages. We begin with Louie Francis or, as he was usually called, "Louie the Indian" standing in the tall grass at Indian Point on the Magaguadavic. He has come to town in a birch-bark canoe that he made loaded with ash axe handles and baskets to sell. The merchants were always glad to have his items for their stores.

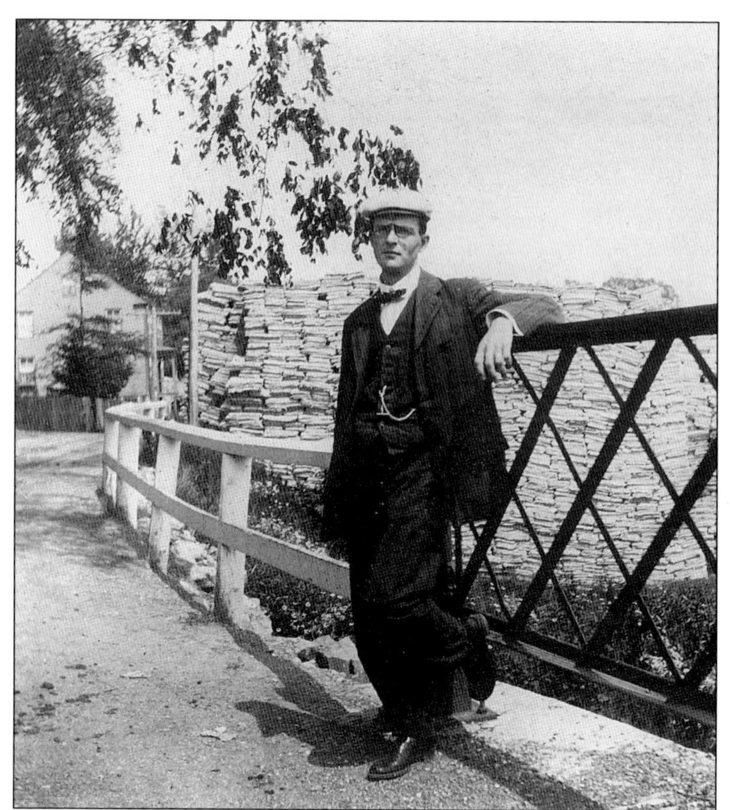

Elizabeth Toy's mom, Phoebe, took this photograph of her dad, Alvah, probably c. 1905, three years after he came to St. George to serve as the accountant for the new pulp mill. Phoebe developed her own film at the time. Behind Alvah, piles of wet pulp are waiting to be loaded into a schooner. Below is Bill Spinney in 1935 lifting a 100-pound bundle of St. George wet pulp.

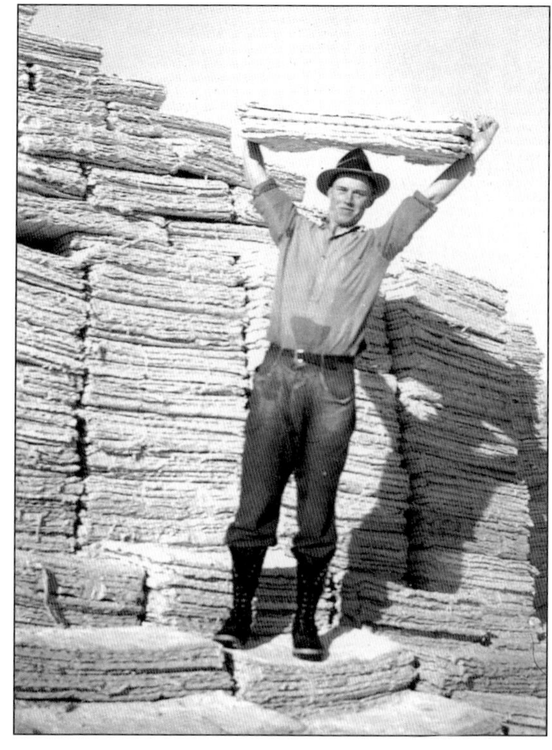

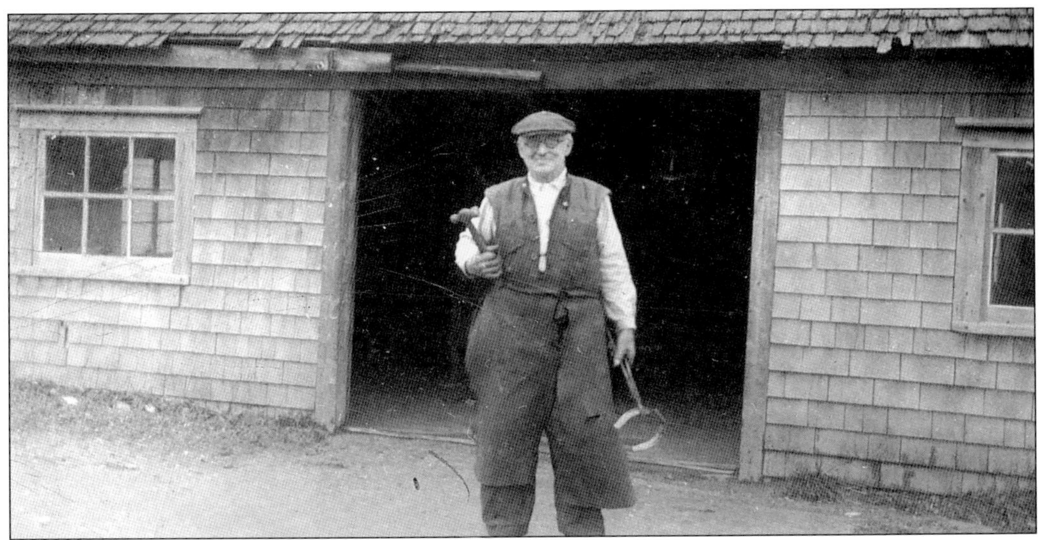

An important man in the days of the horse and wagon was the blacksmith. This is James C. Chase, and he was skilled not only in shoeing but also in repairing various pieces of equipment used in the pulp mill and the granite sheds. He often invented pieces of gear needed to make a machine function better or more safely. He was born in 1863 and lived until 1953, witnessing both industries in their peak years.

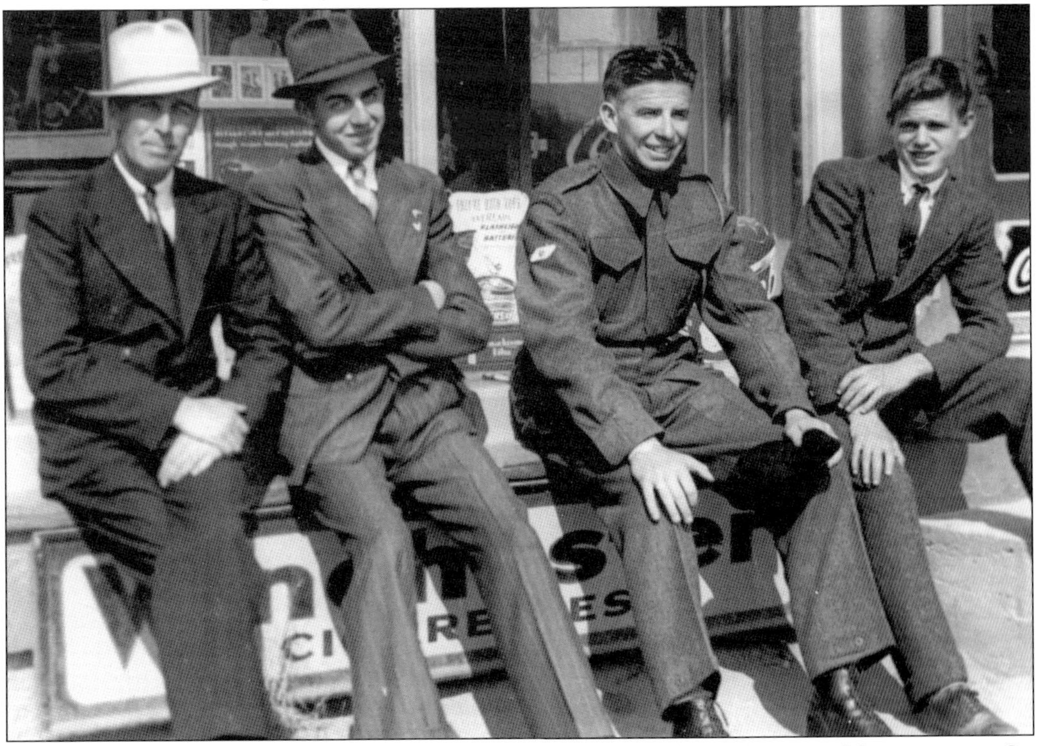

The lad in the uniform is Lawrence Stewart. He has joined the forces and has come to St. George on Sunday afternoon, September 28, 1941, to meet with some of his buddies and chitchat about what is going on in his life. They are in front of Boyd's Store on Main Street. From left to right are Manfred Henry, Eugene Toy, Lawrence Stewart, and Murray Patterson.

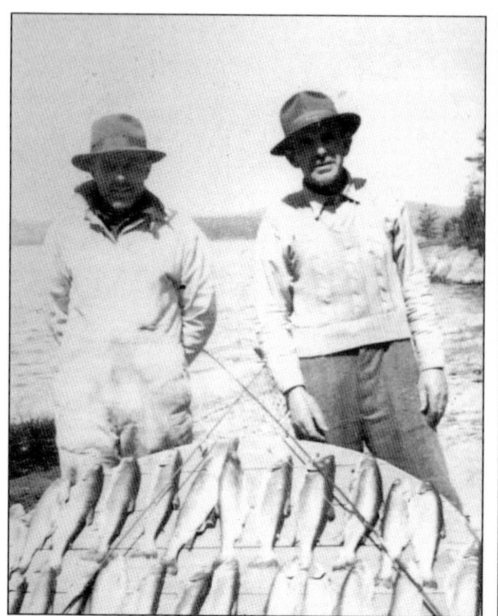

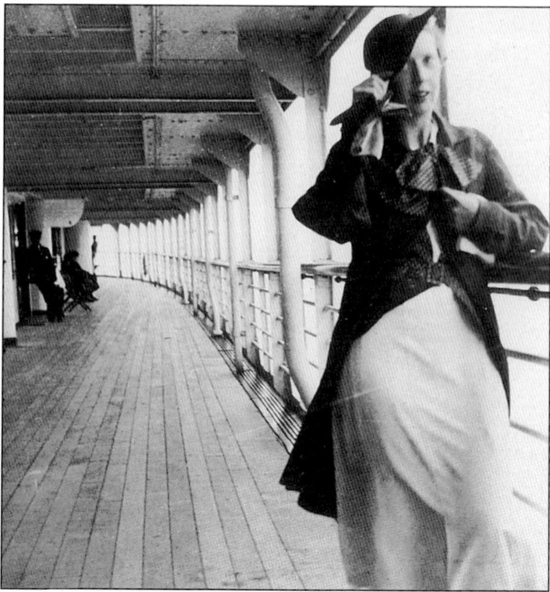

There is always time for relaxation, and different folks have different ways to enjoy their leisure time. In the top left picture is Herb Parks and Cecil Doyle with a fine mess of trout they have caught from Lake Utopia. To the right is Dot Wilson in August 1935 on the Boston boat, no doubt heading for Filene's Bargain Basement and the wonders of the big city. Below are two couples that were good friends: (from left to right) Alvah Toy and Phoebe Toy, and Pearl Campbell and William Campbell. Both men worked at the pulp mill.

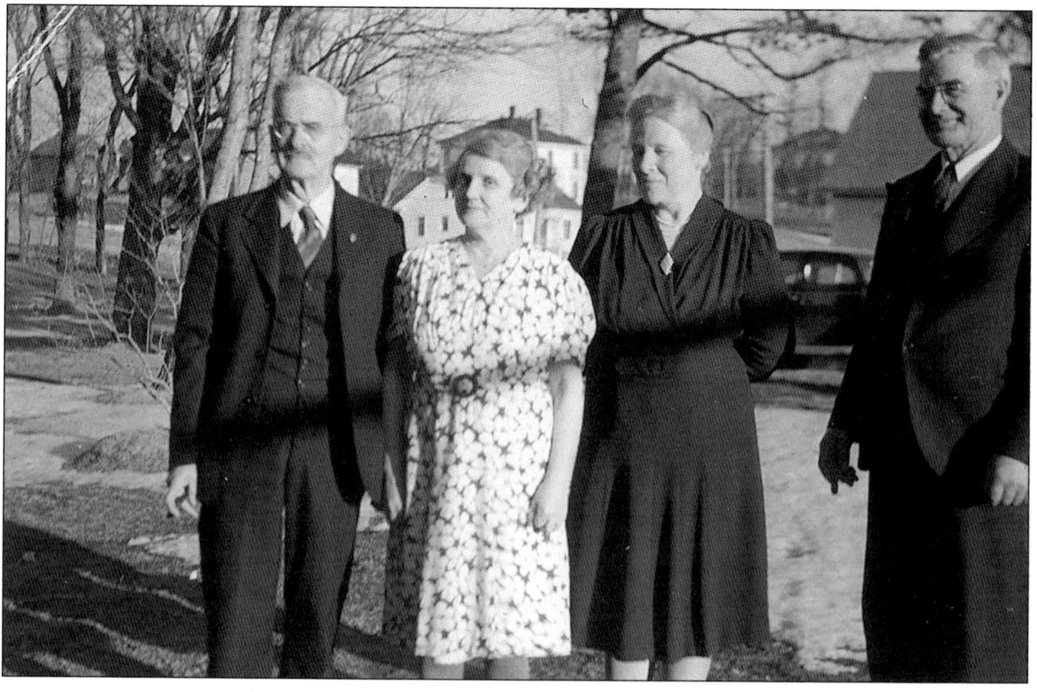

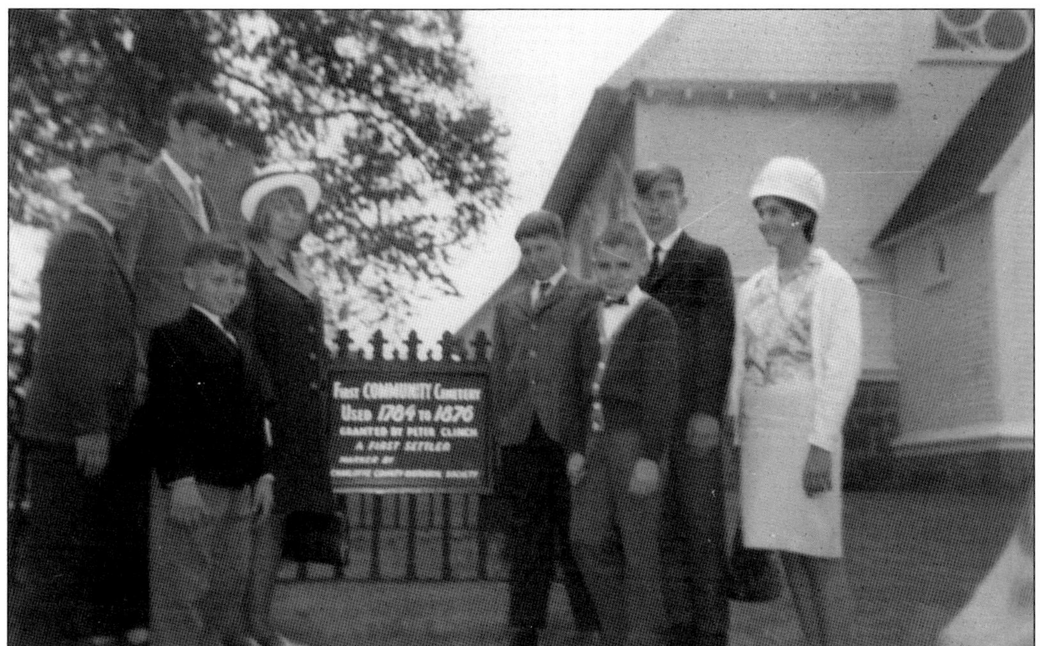

In June of 1966, the descendants of Peter Clinch gathered at St. Mark's Cemetery to pay tribute to their illustrious ancestor as the Charlotte County Historical Society had arranged a new grave-site plaque marker. From left to right are as follows: (front row) an unknown fellow, Susan McLean, Ian McLean, and Thomas McLean; (back row) Robert M. Clinch, Mark Clinch, Billy Campbell, and Stephanie Campbell.

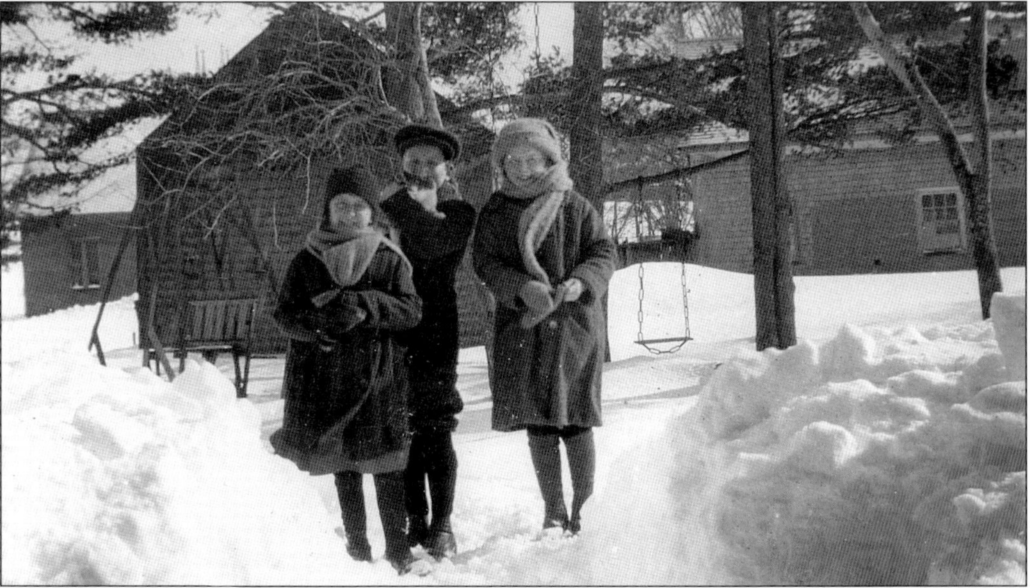

Edwin, Elizabeth, and Frances Toy stand atop a huge snowdrift with Hugh Meating's barn on Riverview Avenue in the background. It is the winter of 1923, which was remembered as the winter of big snows and deep cold. In fact, it was so cold that several Deer Island residents walked across the seldom-frozen saltwater of Passamaquoddy Bay to St. Andrews on February 23. The heavy snow led to the great floods of April pictured in Chapter Two.

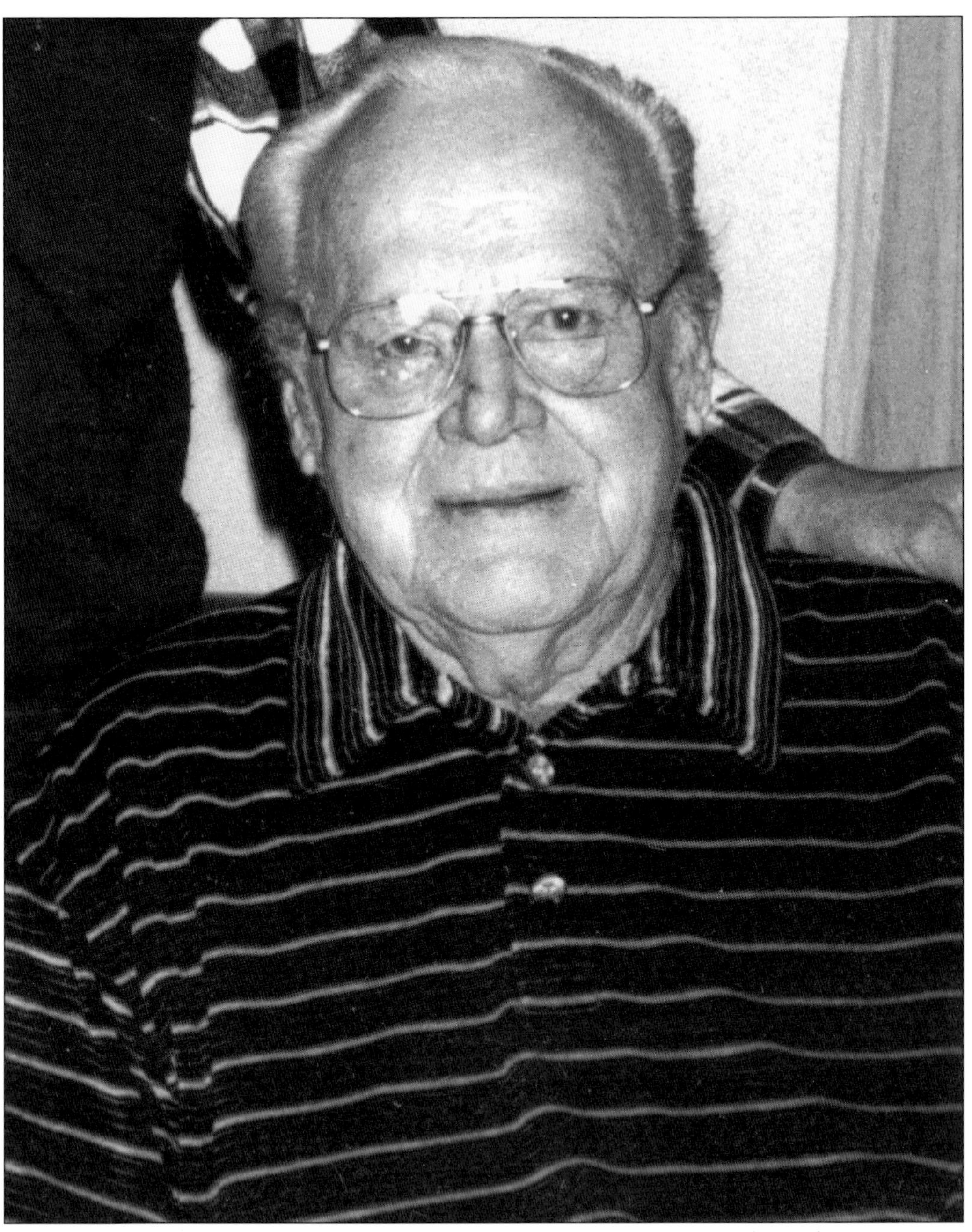

Steve Campbell is the author of "Come Back With Me," "Come Back With Me Again," and "Remember When," his memories of St. George from the 1920s to the 1990s. One of those memories appeared in the *St. Croix Courier* on January 14, 1926, three years after this photograph was taken, and tells of an incident when he lost control of his sled on Back Hill, crashed head on into another, and was thrown eight metres.

Seven

Along the Shore and Among the Islands

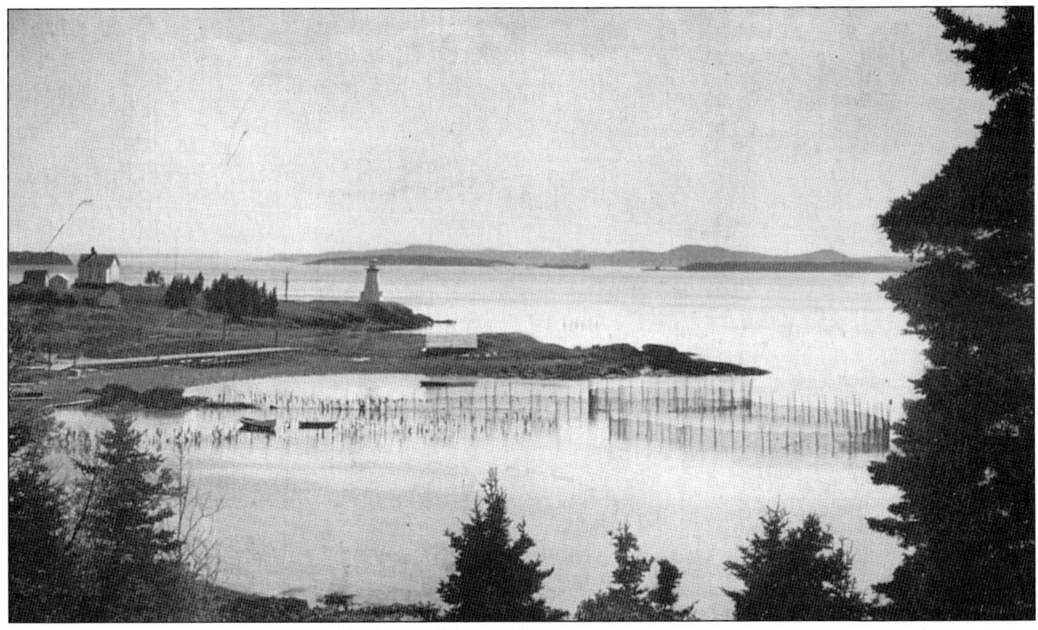

The crenated Bay of Fundy coastline from Musquash to Milltown provides not only a scenic vista but also sites that are rich with stories based on both folklore and historic incidents to be explored in this chapter. In this particular image, the location is about halfway along the shore between Saint John and St. Stephen at the Green Point Light, just 10 kilometres south of St. George. It is not far from where the car ferry travels to Deer Island, which is linked to Campobello Island by ferry in the summer but only accessible by driving through Maine in the winter. Further offshore, the largest of the islands, Grand Manan, can be easily seen from the other islands but not easily reached, for it is necessary to travel through Blacks Harbour to take the car ferry to that island. In times past, boats linked all three islands with the mainland much more conveniently than is the case today. With the weir in the foreground, the lighthouse in the background, and the offshore islands Deer and Campobello on the horizon, this postcard photograph by Climo Studios of Saint John is a fine representative shot to begin the seventh chapter, which explores St. George's neighbours along the Charlotte County shore.

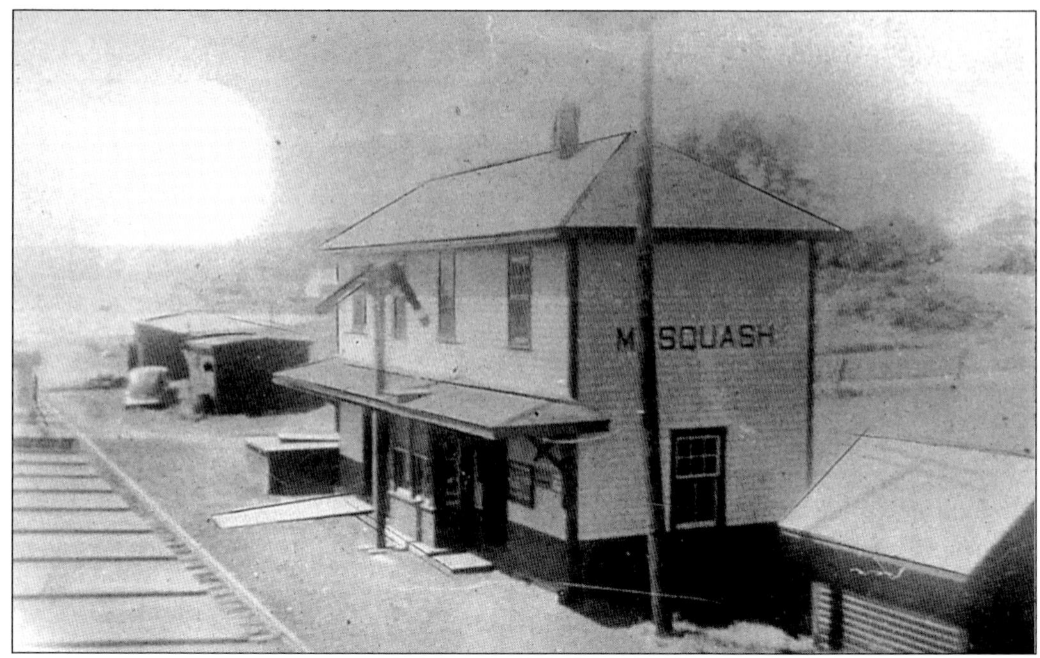

The Musquash railway station was 55 minutes from Saint John on the Grand Southern Line to St. George. Of the eight stops on the two-and-three-quarter-hour run, this is the only photograph that exists of a station house. It was taken by railroad buff Dyson Thomas in the 1940s. Musquash was originally known as Clinch's Mills and was a thriving community until it was devastated by fire in 1903 and then hit by a flood in 1923.

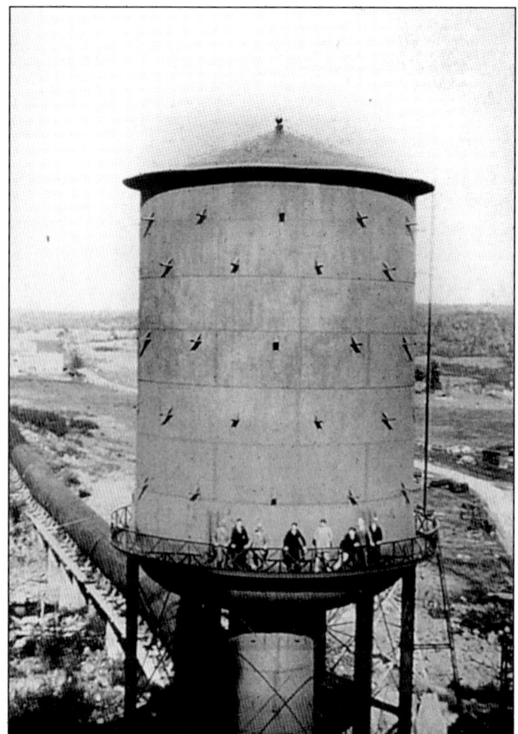

In 1920, the New Brunswick government formed an Electric Power Commission, and by 1922, they had built the province's first hydroelectric generating station at Musquash to compete with private plants that were charging very high rates. Power from Musquash arrived in St. George in 1922, just weeks before it arrived in Saint John. In 1929, Eugene Toy visited the site as part of his studies at the University of New Brunswick and took the picture of his fellow students on the plant's water tower.

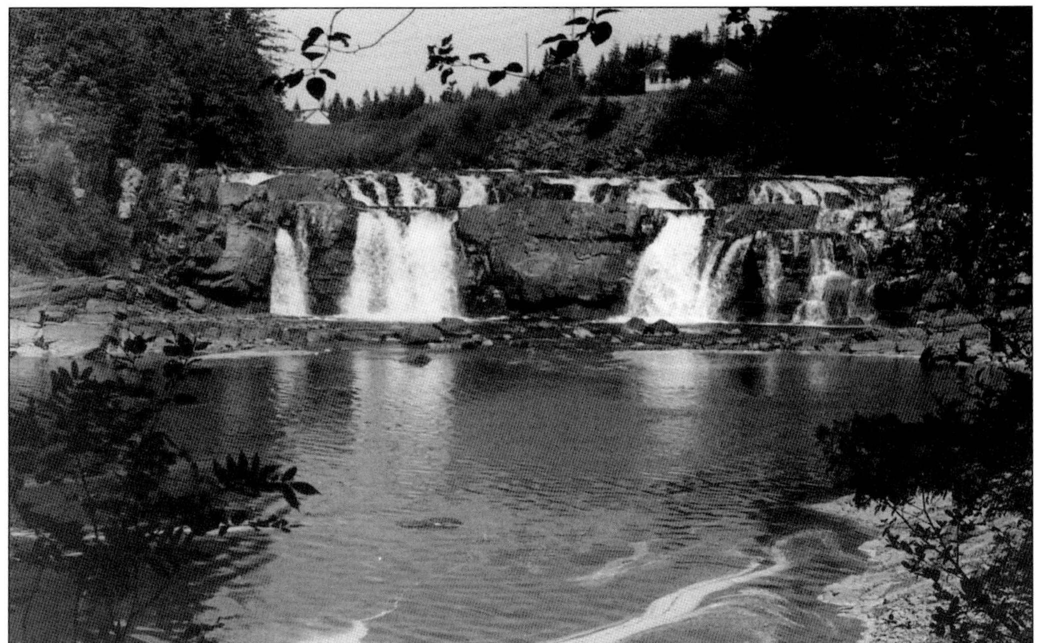

The Lepreau River flows into the Bay of Fundy just west of the Charlotte County line. It is the only waterfall on the Charlotte County shoreline that is comparable with the Magaguadavic's Rainbow Falls. Lepreau Falls and the surrounding park seem bucolic today but once supported several sawmills; the site was considered in 1920 for the electric power plant that was built at Musquash and later for a pulp mill. (Courtesy Goss.)

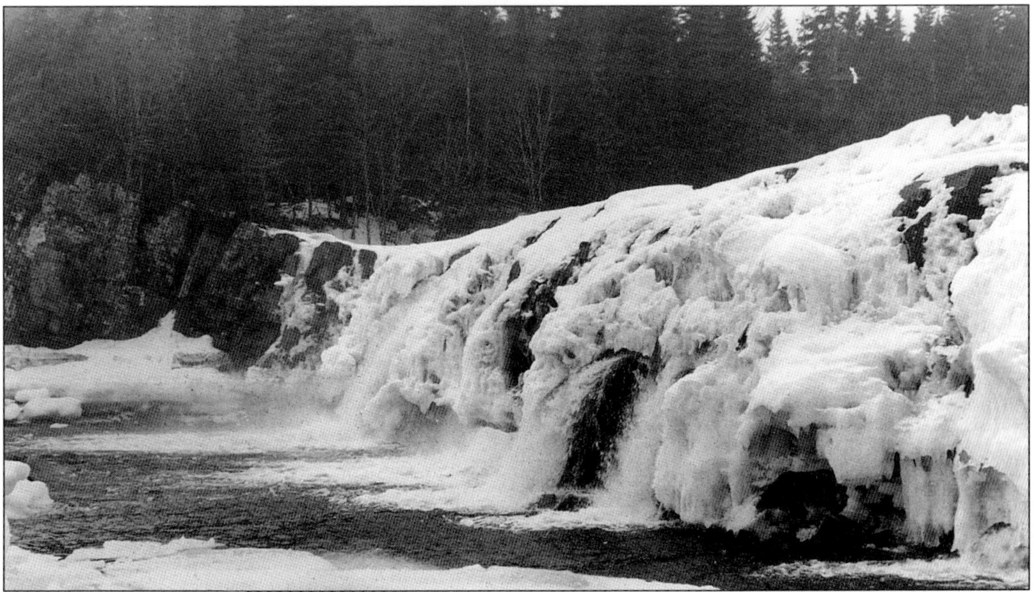

Lepreau Falls frozen in winter presents an even quieter scene. But if one listens carefully, the echoes of long ago may boom through the stillness, and the voice of Kilby Reynolds, the man who dared to build the Reversing Falls Bridge in Saint John in 1853 after three previous attempts had failed, might be heard calling out to his workers to increase their production in the huge mill he had built alongside the falls.

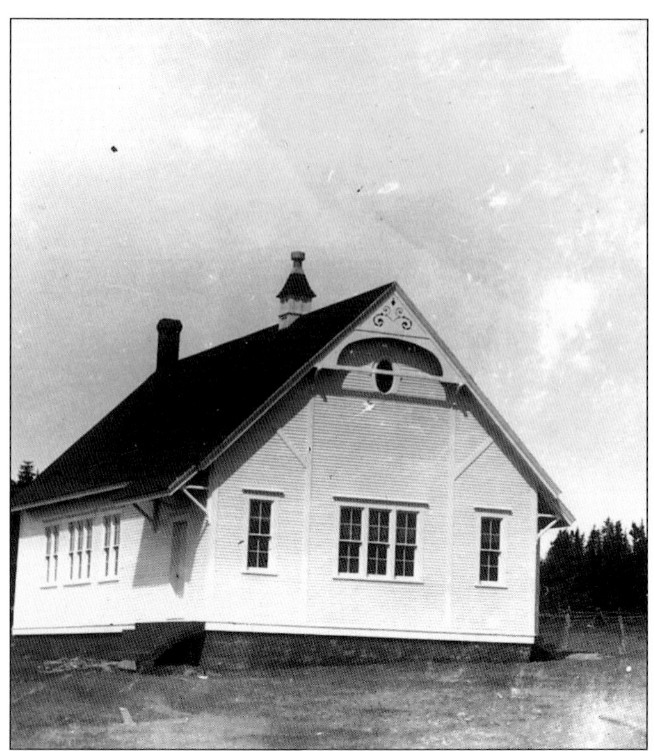

The Maces Bay School is shown here in this 1921 photograph by A.V.F. Duffy, which he took while on one of his down-the-coast motorcycle trips. Solidly built, with fancy fretwork and rooftop cupola, it was typical of coastal community schools. Today, it serves as a senior citizens meeting centre.

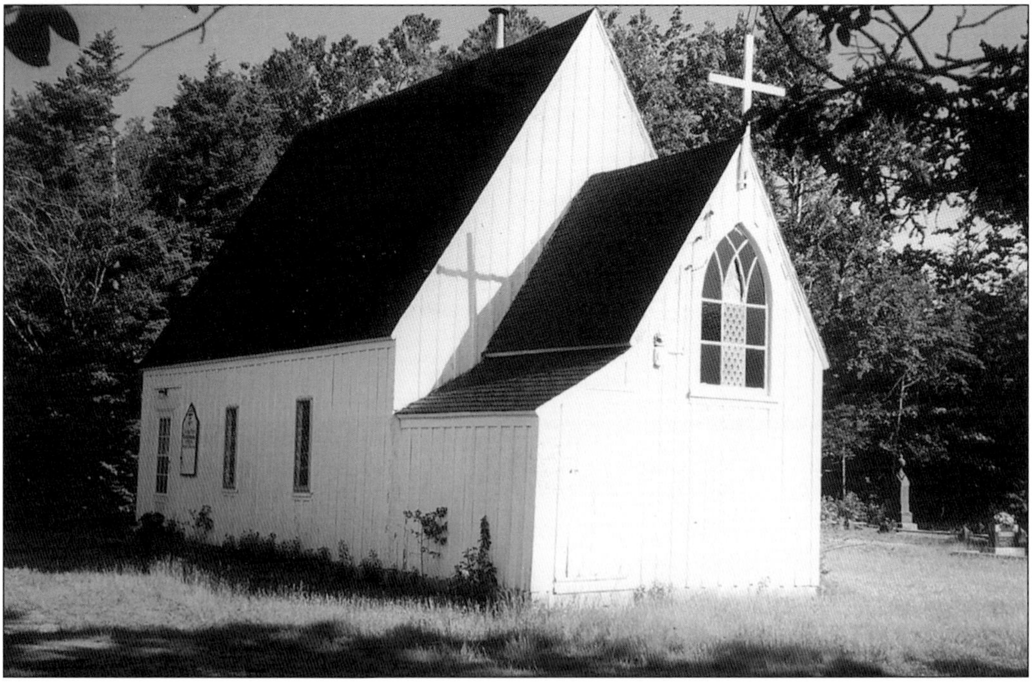

The church of the Transfiguration, Anglican (Episcopal is also noted on its sign for American visitors), was built in 1889 and still serves the parishioners of Bethel. It is typical of small churches of varying faiths that served the scattered communities in the days of horse and buggy but are in danger of disappearing in today's more mobile society. (Courtesy Goss.)

Bridges were important structures on the roads that joined the communities, not to the degree of schools and churches but essential to reach either of them for sure. This bridge had a centre hump, and daredevil drivers loved racing up the inclines as it lifted their cars off the road for a short fly. The bridge crossed the Little Lepreau Basin and connected Maces Bay to Lepreau. (Courtesy June Malloy-Prebble, who never did the daredevil trip!)

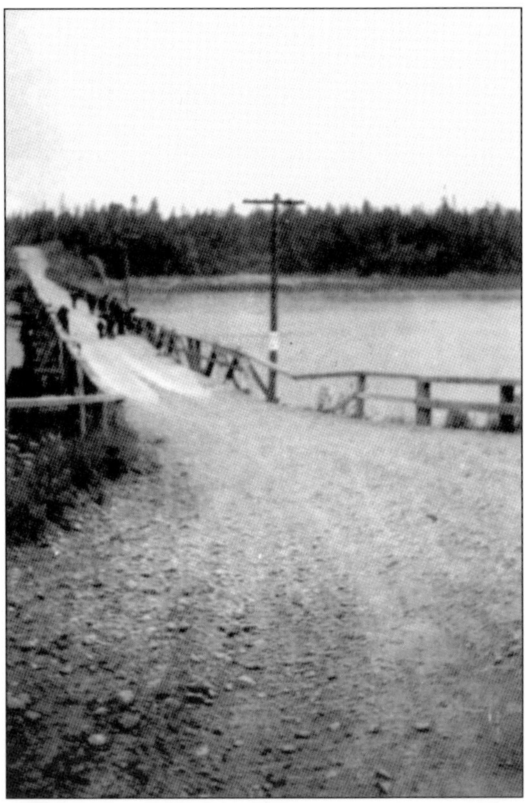

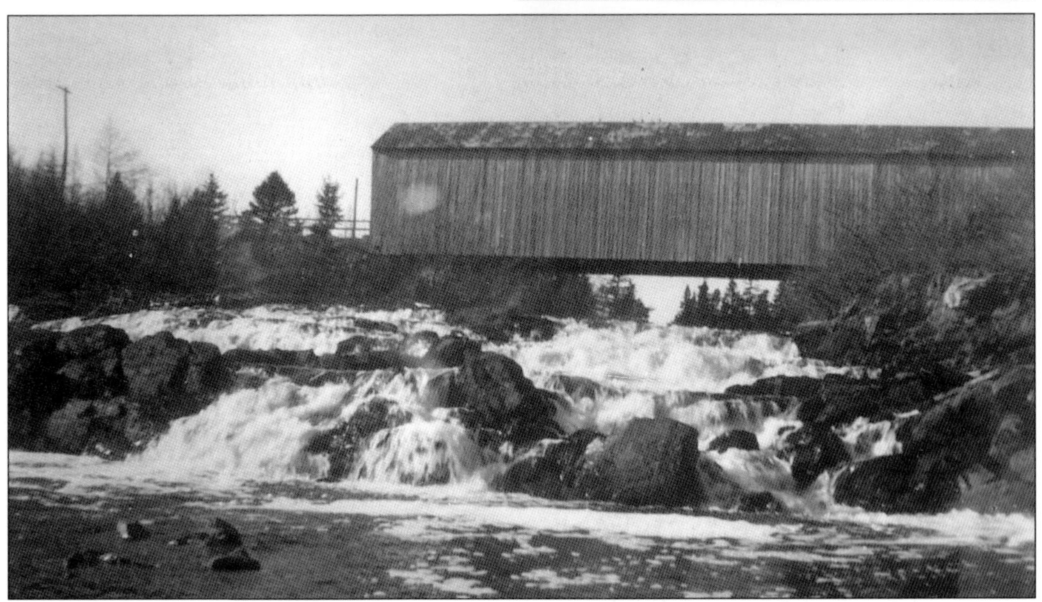

The Little Lepreau covered bridge is another June Malloy-Prebble photograph from the 1940s and is typical of covered bridges built over the rivers or streams at places like Musquash, Seely's Cove, and Digdequash. Being narrow, many of them were removed as vehicles got bigger and highways were widened. Others were burned in acts of vandalism, often at Halloween. This one survives off Route 790, though it is not used for car traffic.

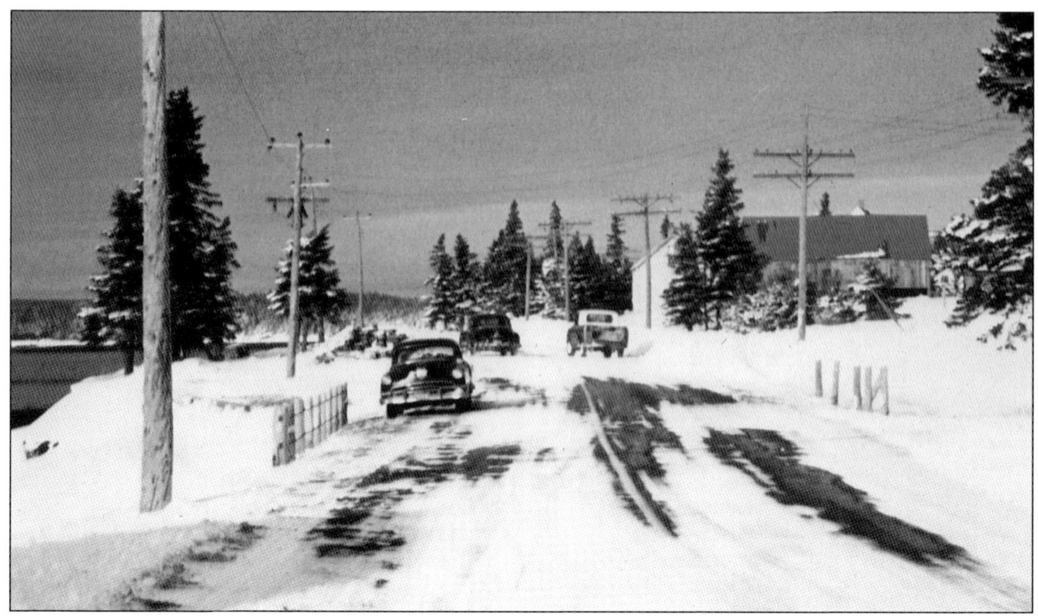

This photograph of Maces Bay was taken on Dec 23, 1962, as evidence of the death of Dr Whiteside of the Provincial Hospital staff. On back, it notes that Stuart Bonnefant and Herman Denton found Dr. Whiteside's car on this snowy highway overlooking the rocks of Maces Bay. News reports say he drowned when overcome by the tides while hunting ducks. The photograph also illustrates a typical winter road along the Charlotte coast. (Courtesy Centracare.)

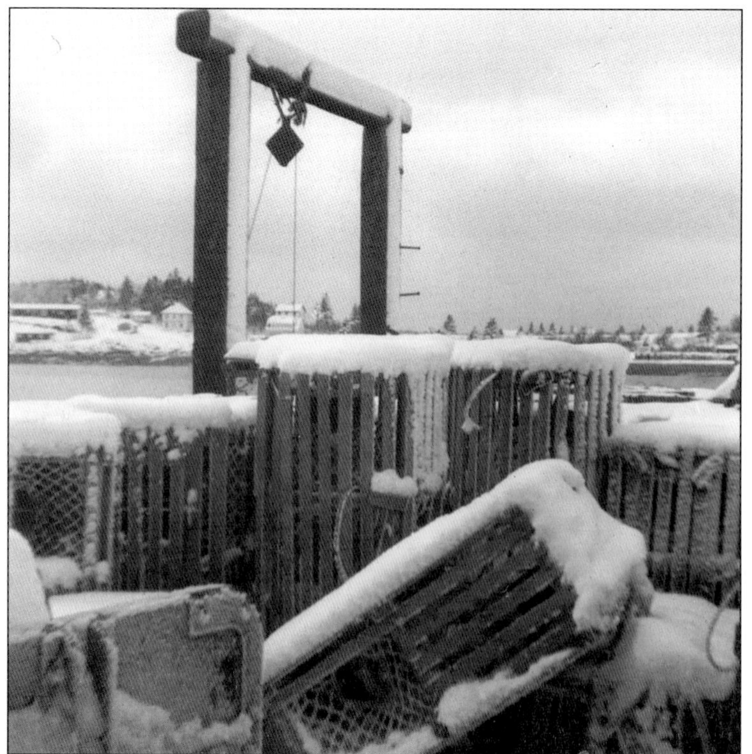

This image of lobster traps stacked up for the winter was taken at the Chance Harbour wharf in 1976. It could be anywhere along the Bay of Fundy coast in the era when traps were still all-wood construction. Today, most fishermen appreciate the advantages of the wire trap. They also appreciate the cash they get for worn out wooden traps like these, as such traps have become prized collectors' items by inland tourists looking for a seaside souvenir. (Courtesy Goss.)

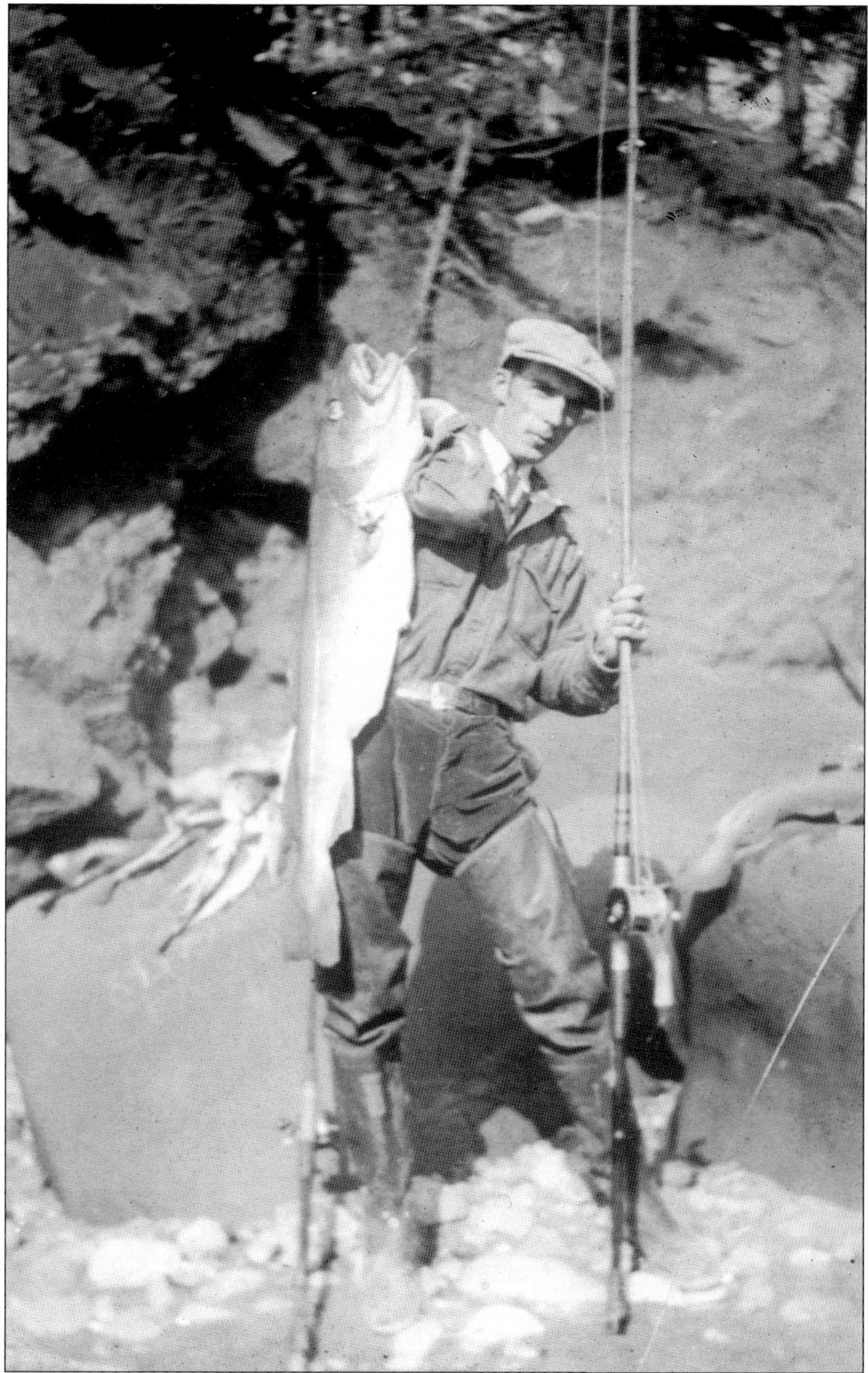

Do not tell Harry S. Deaner Jr., a friend of Morris Conde of Pocologan, that surf casting is not normally done in the tidal zone of the Bay of Fundy. He came from New York where it is a normal way to fish and caught this 40-pound cod at Point Lepreau by rod and reel in August of 1931 to prove the technique worked in New Brunswick too. (Courtesy Alice (Conde) Garner.)

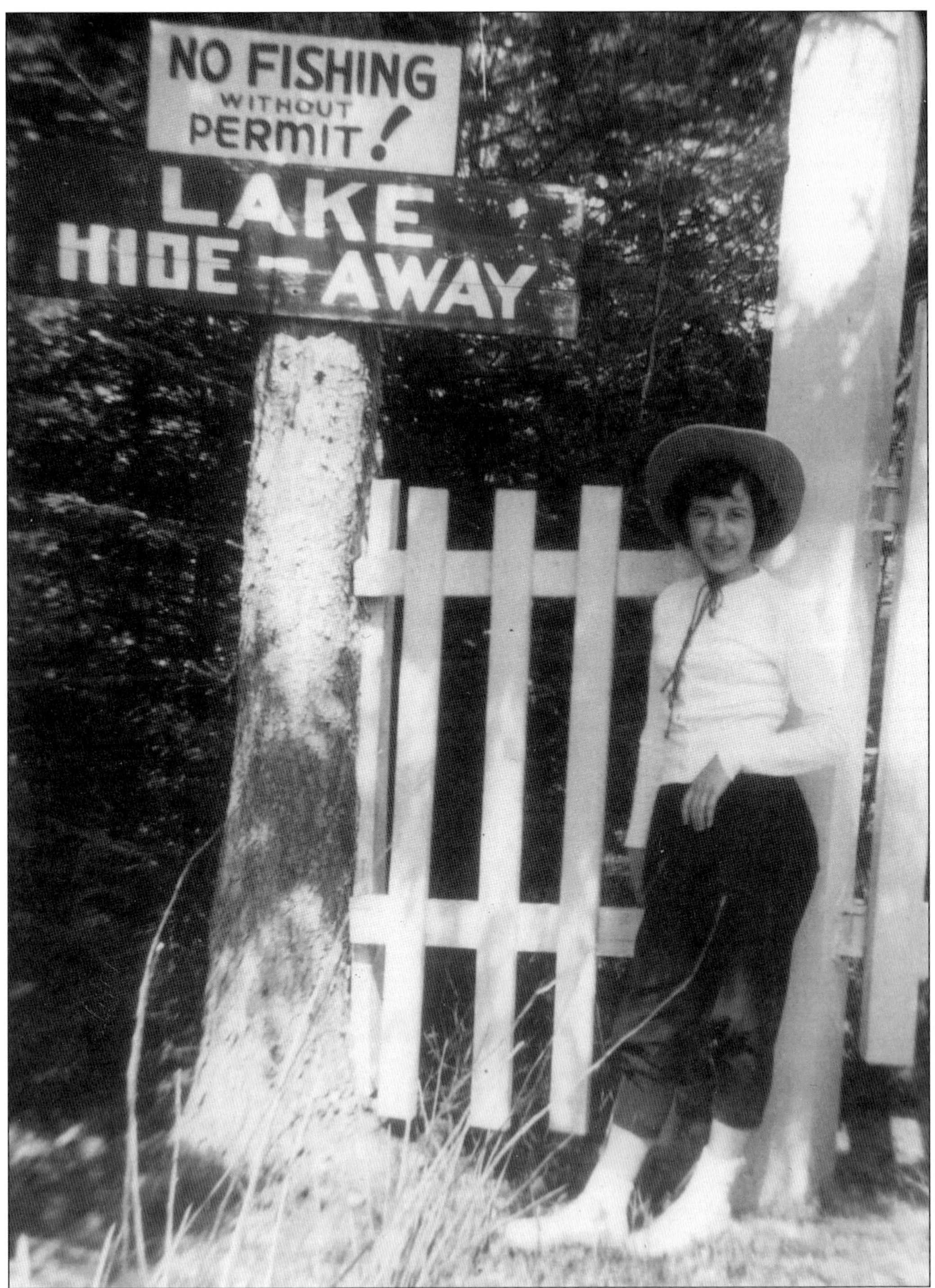

There were lots of opportunities for inland fishing in Charlotte County too, as Rosie Malloy points out at the roadside at Lepreau. Lake Hide-Away was off the Jos March Road, and June Malloy-Prebble, who provided the photograph, remembers it as a "beautiful spot with canoes and a camp." It was owned by Charles Wilson in 1957 when the photograph was taken.

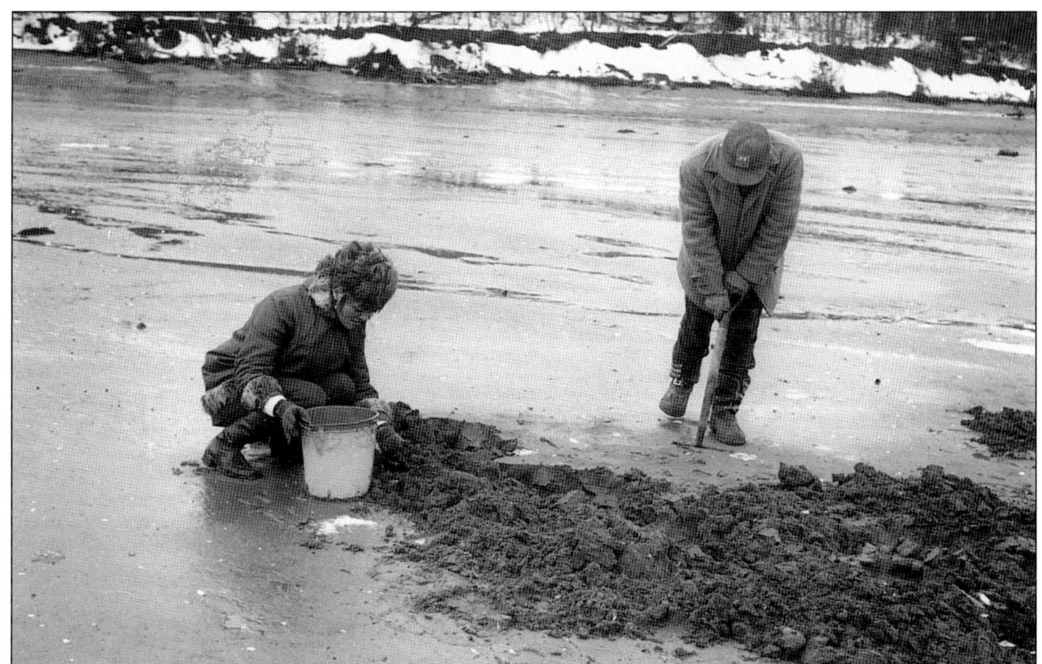

Clamming at Pocologan, and many other flats along the Bay of Fundy, was a popular recreational activity as well as a way of picking up some income during hard times when pulp mills or sawmills were adjusting inventory and closed. It was reported in the *St. Croix Courier* in April of 1952 that there were more than 1,000 acres of clamming flats being worked from Oak Bay to Lepreau.

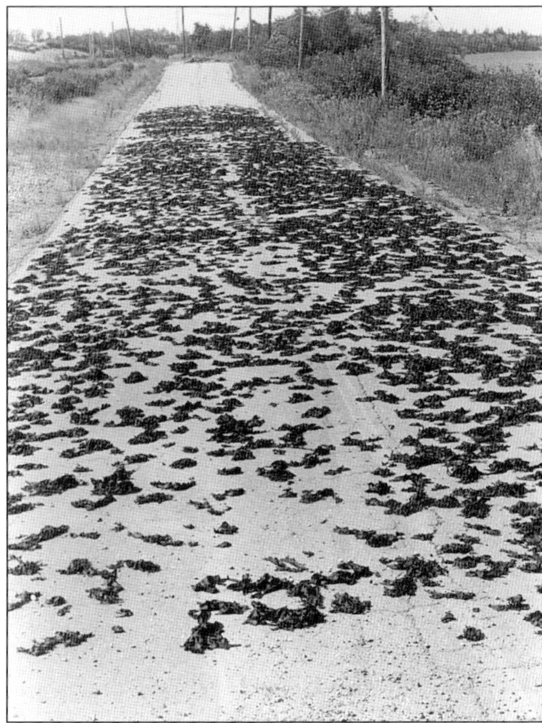

As Route One along the coast was improved, many a piece of the old highway became abandoned. The asphalt surfaces became a favored place to dry dulse (and nets for the fishermen) as it would be undisturbed and, being black, get the most heat from the sometimes scattered sunshine. (Courtesy Goss.)

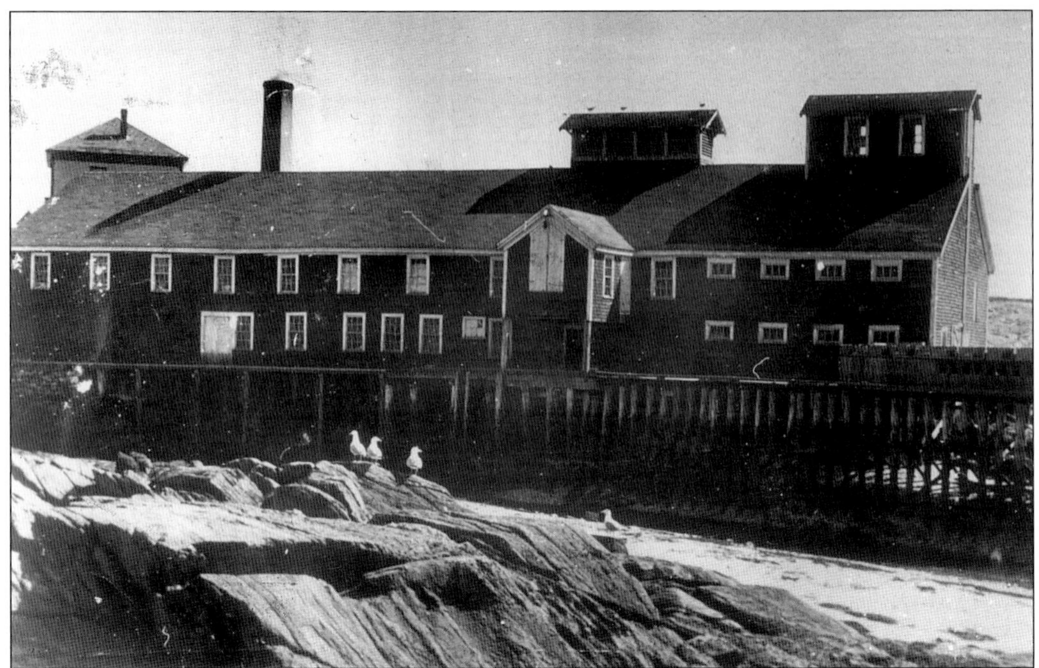

One of the bigger factories in which clams were processed was the Shaw and Ellis plant which stood on the rocks in Pocologan Basin at Loch's Brook. The plant employed 40 to 60 workers, and bought clams from diggers all along the coast. Their bestseller was the Indian Chief brand of clams that was shipped around the world. As clam stocks declined, the plant closed and was torn down in 1967. (Courtesy Lloyd Mealey.)

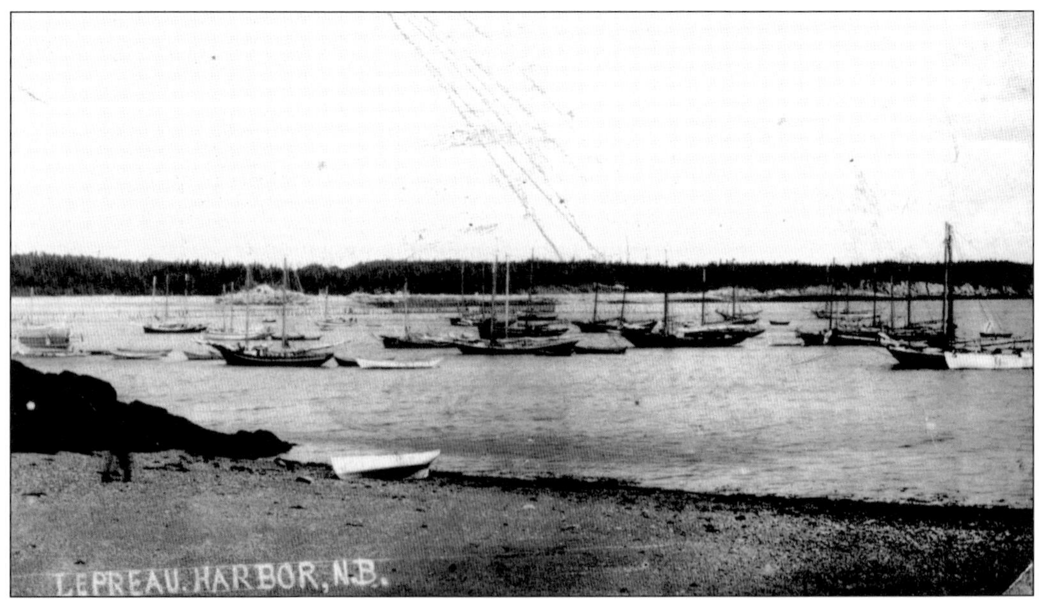

Lepreau Harbor, and indeed almost every sheltered harbour along the coast, would have both fishing vessels and weirs as a way of capturing the fish for the sardine-packing plants. The biggest Canadian one was operated in Blacks Harbour, but fishermen could also sell at several towns along the coast of Maine.

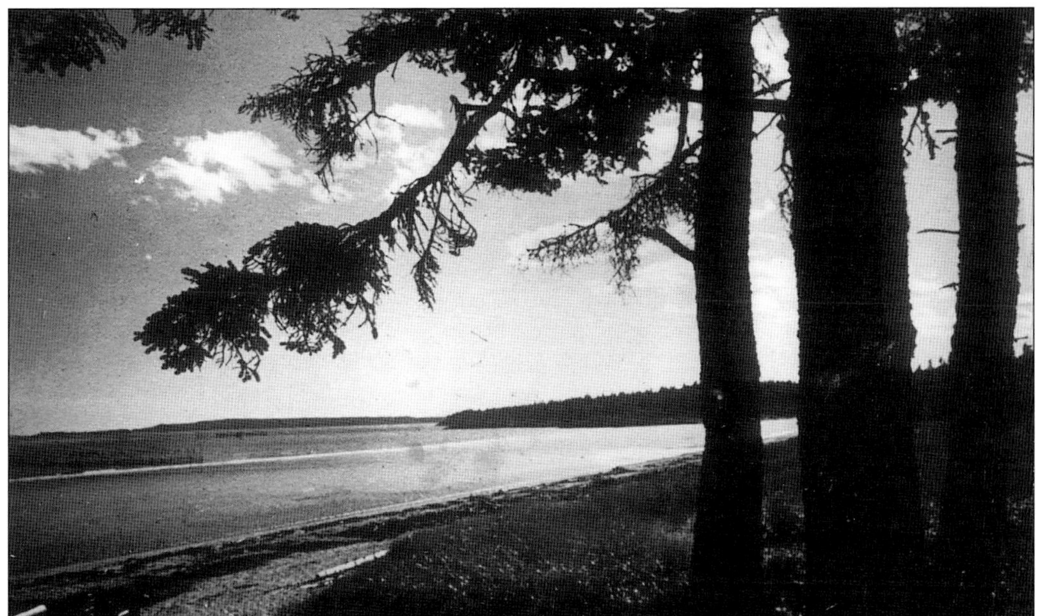

Here is a view looking west at New River Beach. In 1930, this area was one of four New Brunswick locations considered for New Brunswick's first national park. It ultimately opened in 1948 farther east and up the coast at Alma. The beauty of the kilometre-plus long stretch of white sand was not sufficient to overcome the fact that to build the national park at New River would have disrupted many more people than to do so in the wilderness of Albert County.

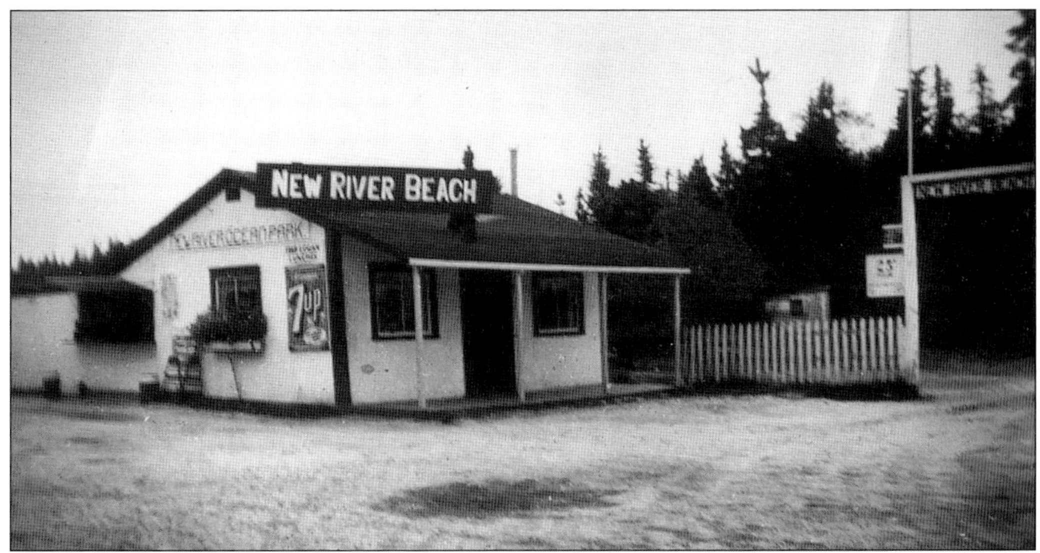

Visitors have been enjoying New River Beach since the railway opened a station at New River, nine kilometres inland, in 1882. In the 1940s, Lloyd Mealey, when courting his wife to be, Gracie, loved to take her to Jack Knight's canteen and provided this photograph. When they married and settled in the area, they swam there almost every summer day. It became a public park in 1960 when Marjorie Knight sold it to the province.

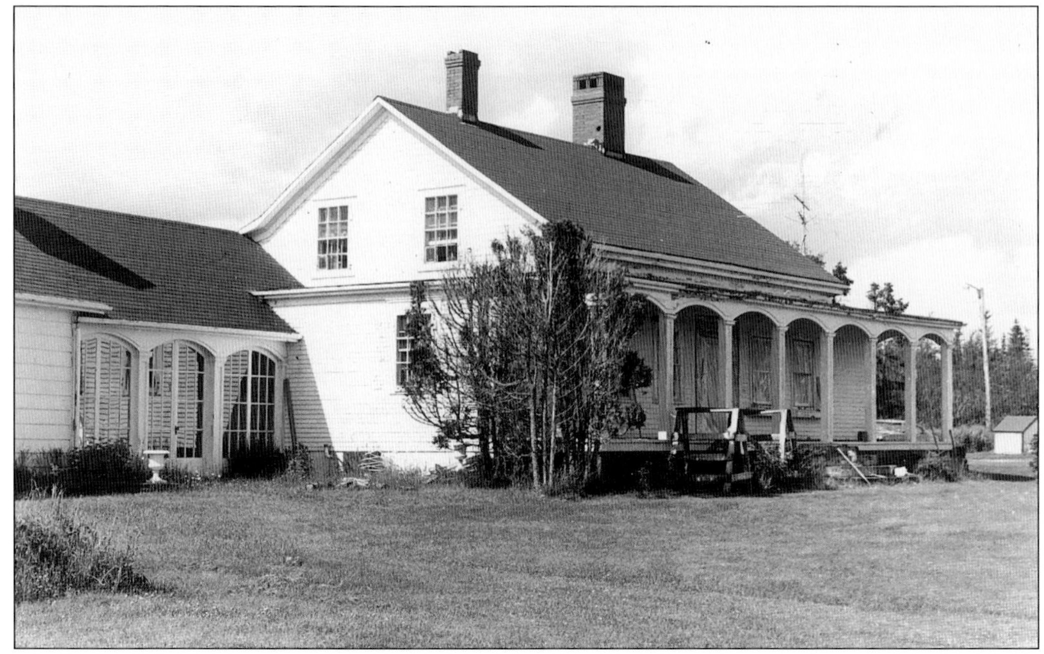

The Knight property overlooking New River Beach is where the bodies of 10 of 11 seamen were laid out after they had drowned in the Saxby Gale, in which the *Barque Genii* sunk on October 4, 1869. One man's body, John Roix, was found weeks later off Barnaby Head, and the spot is now known as Dead Man's Cove, as his ghost is seen there from time to time calling to hikers enjoying the trail.

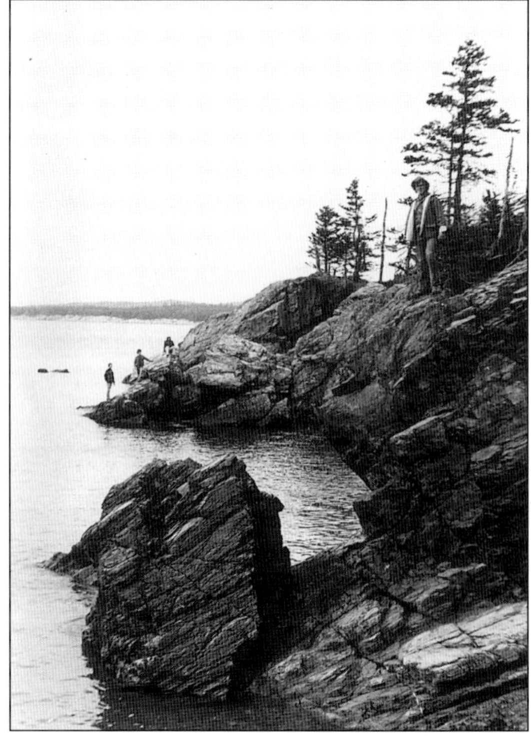

Adjacent to the east end of New River Beach is the beautiful Barnaby Head nature trail where the rocks overlooking Maces Bay provide dramatic drops to the ocean and great places for exploring. That is Michael Phillips on the top of the rocks and some of his St. George's Scout Troop patrol members closer to the water. (Courtesy Goss.)

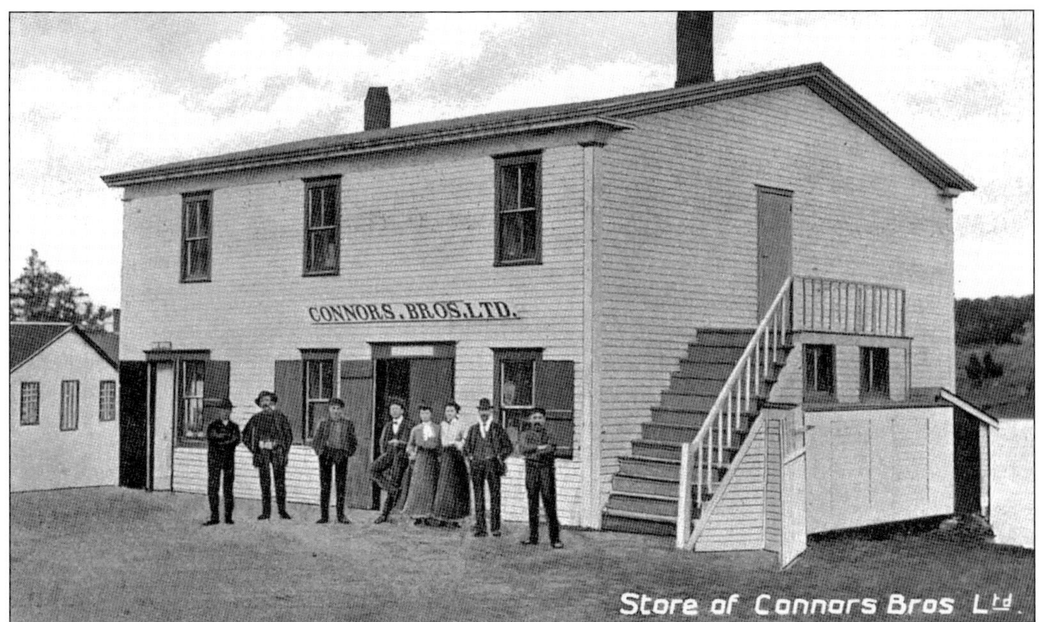

Pictured is the Connors Brothers Ltd. store at Blacks Harbour. At the time this postcard was made, Connors Brothers was well on its way to becoming the largest sardine-packing plant in the world, eclipsing American plants along the Maine coast. Standing in front of the company store in 1903 are, from left to right, Frank Thompson, Pat Connors, Neil Thompson, Stafford Morrison, Laura Murry, Mae Connors, George Justason, and one unidentified man.

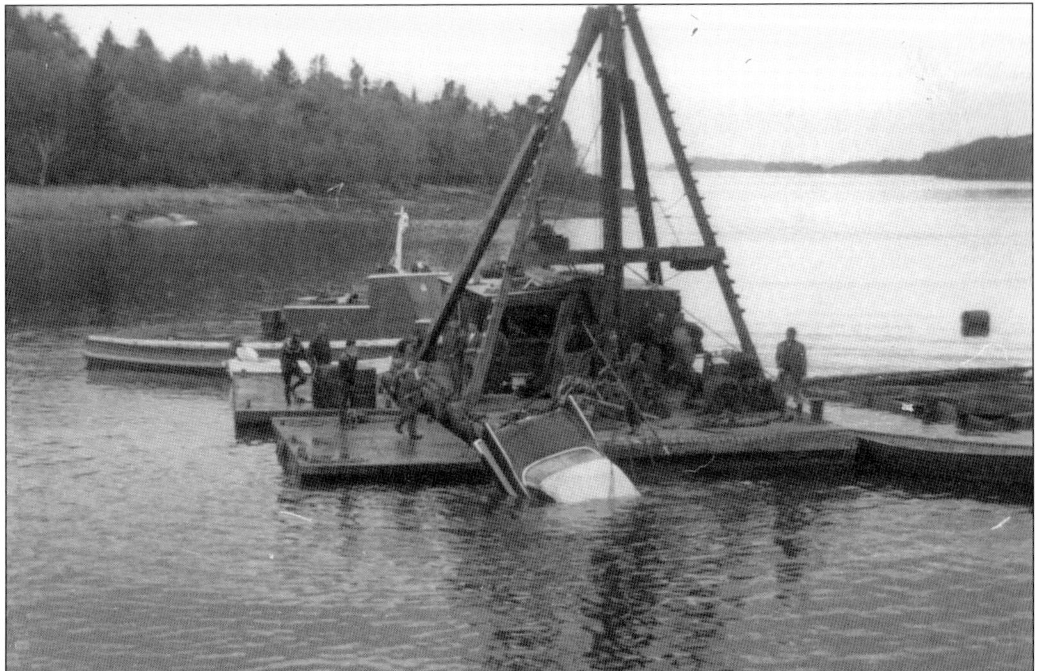

In September 1964, the Blacks Harbour government wharf collapsed and 17 cars tumbled into the bay. Though all were recovered, the saltwater soaking made them unusable. Amazingly, no one was hurt.

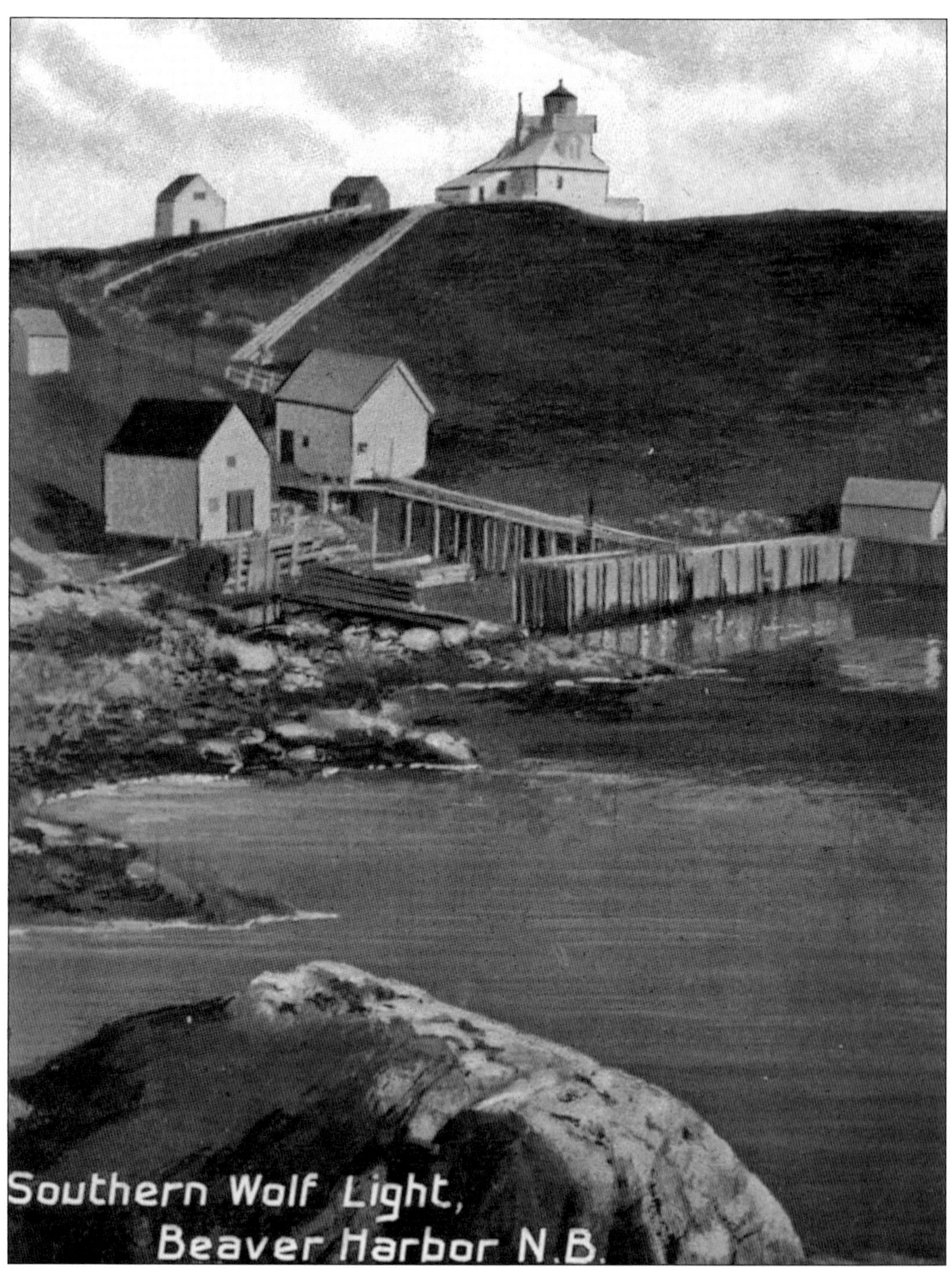

The second lighthouse in Canada was established on Partridge Island off Saint John Harbour, and soon the Bay of Fundy was well stocked with lighthouses to guide mariners along the rugged coast, home of the highest tides in the world. The Machias Seal Island lighthouse on the border between Canada's Charlotte County and Maine's Washington County remains the only manned lighthouse due to an ongoing dispute as to whether it is American or Canadian territory.

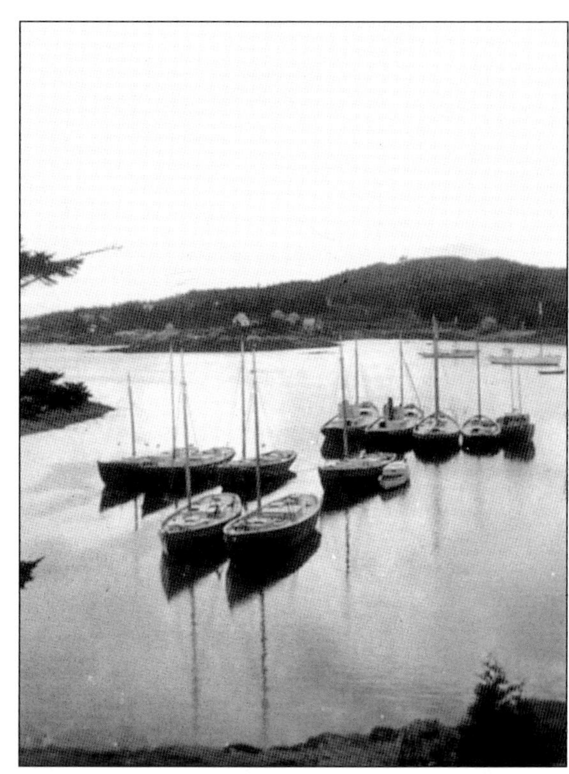

In the photograph to the right are sardine boats photographed in Lord's Cove by Elizabeth Toy during a visit to Deer Island on September 12, 1930. In the photograph below is the lady she spent the day with, Helen Adams (right). Helen's son John Gilman sent the photograph to Elizabeth for consideration in this book, as he had heard his mom speak of Elizabeth often. Soon after the visit, the island became more accessible to cars with the start up of a regular ferry crossing from L'Etete. The island boasts unspoiled beauty at almost every turn and is home of the world's largest lobster pond and the world's second largest whirlpool.

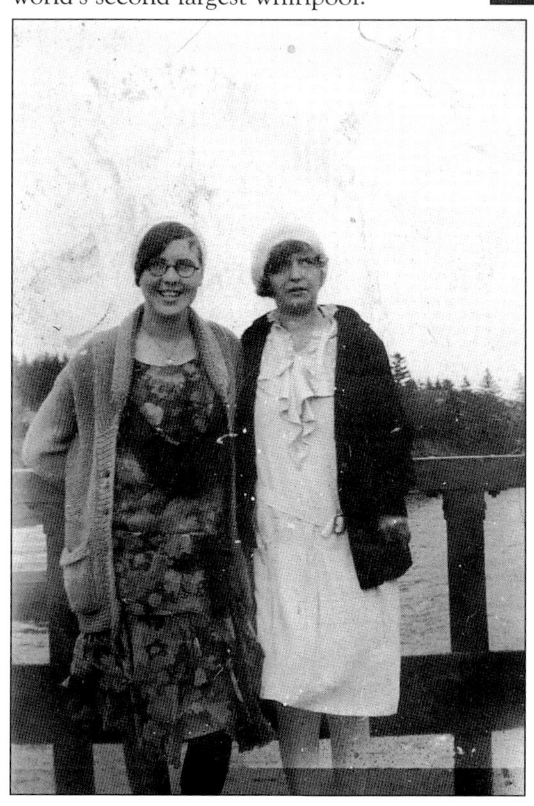

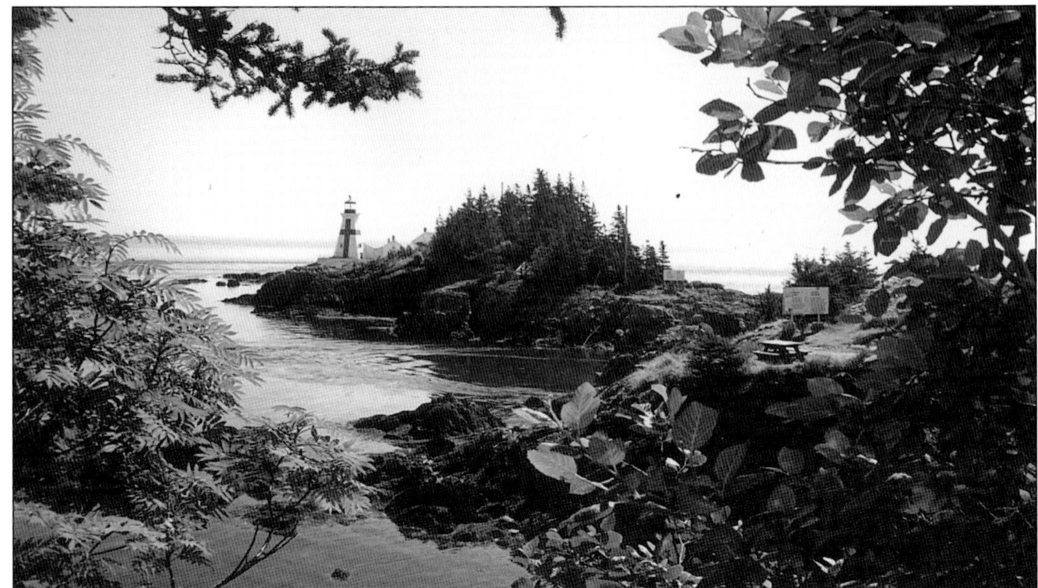

Though recent photographs, these two sites are landmarks on Campobello Island that have been must-see attractions for decades now. Head Harbour Light (also called East Quoddy Light) dates from 1829 and is thought to be the most oft photographed lighthouse on the Bay of Fundy coast. Photographs dating back to the beginning of the 20th century show it has hardly changed at all in the past 100 years.

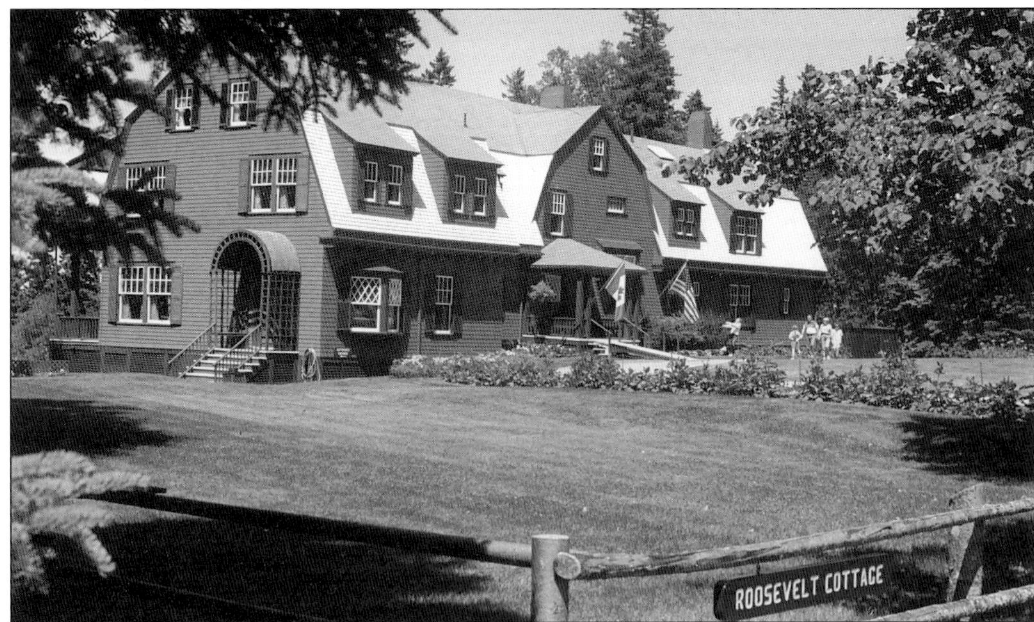

The Roosevelt cottage, where Pres. Franklin D. Roosevelt spent the summers of 1909 until 1921, was built for the Kuhn family in 1897 at a time when Campobello Island was still an all-summer destination for well-to-do American families, including the Roosevelts who bought the cottage for just $5,000. In 1964, the house became the main focus of an international park, and many visitors miss other attractions, such as bog and beach walks, lookouts, and carriage trails, in their quest to see this most popular site. (Courtesy Goss.)

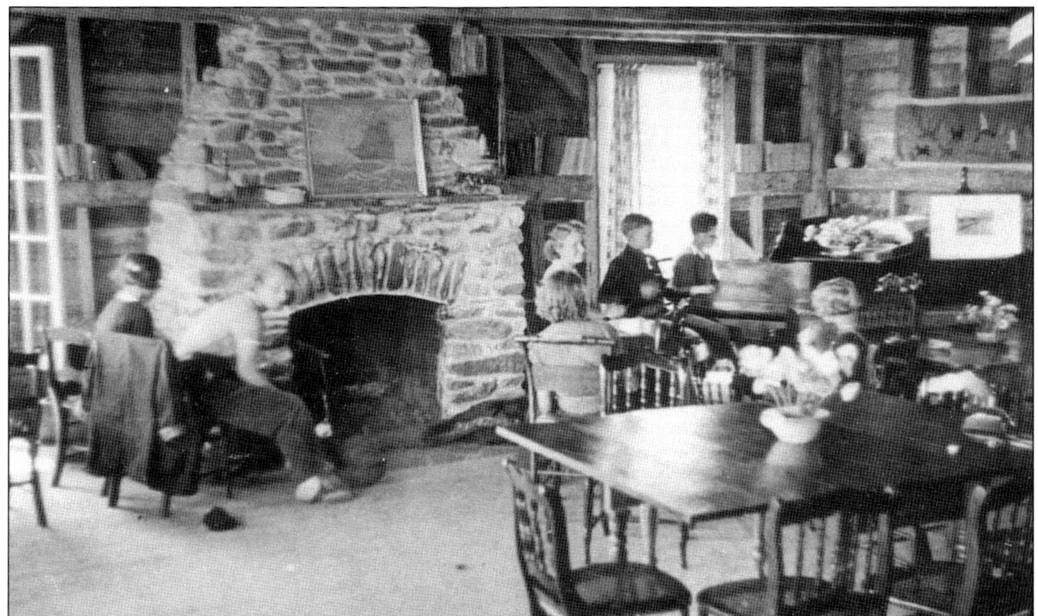

Tourists have been coming to Grand Manan Island since the late 1870s by convenient rail connections from Boston to Eastport, Maine, and then by steamer to the island. The Anchorage property was built by Jerome Daggett in 1909 where his family farmed and fished. In the 1930s, New Yorker Sabra Briggs opened the Anchorage to tourists who stayed in cabins in the woods and came to the lodge to dine in the rustic room shown here.

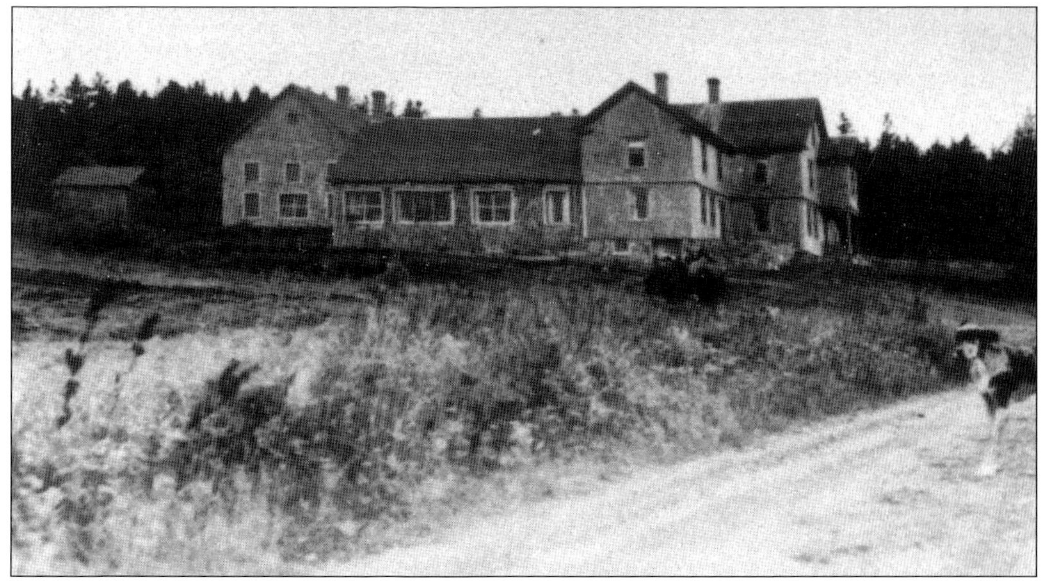

Grand Manan is an accessible island, yet seems remote. Its step-back-in-time look, combined with challenging hiking, world-class birding, and rare flowers makes it attractive to nature lovers looking for quiet getaways. Many chose and still choose the Anchorage, though it is no longer a cottage but a camping opportunity. Among writers who have enjoyed the island's charms is Willa Cather and among actresses is Greta Garbo.

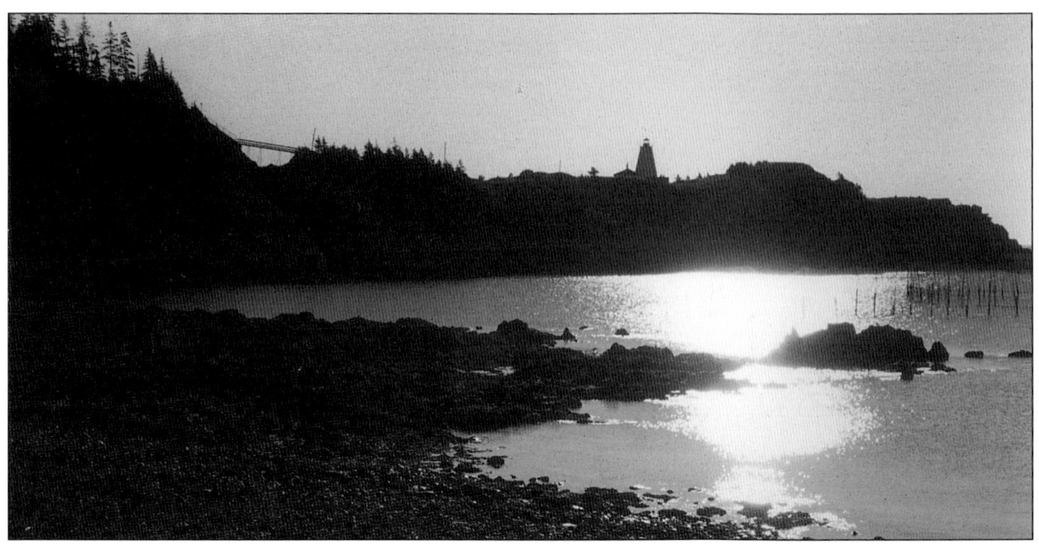

The view is of Swallow Tail Light from Pettes Cove. The bridge shown silhouetted against the morning sun was the only way light keepers could get to this station. Swallow Tail Light is undoubtedly the most oft shot photograph of Grand Manan and has come to be a symbol of the island's rugged charms. (Courtesy Goss.)

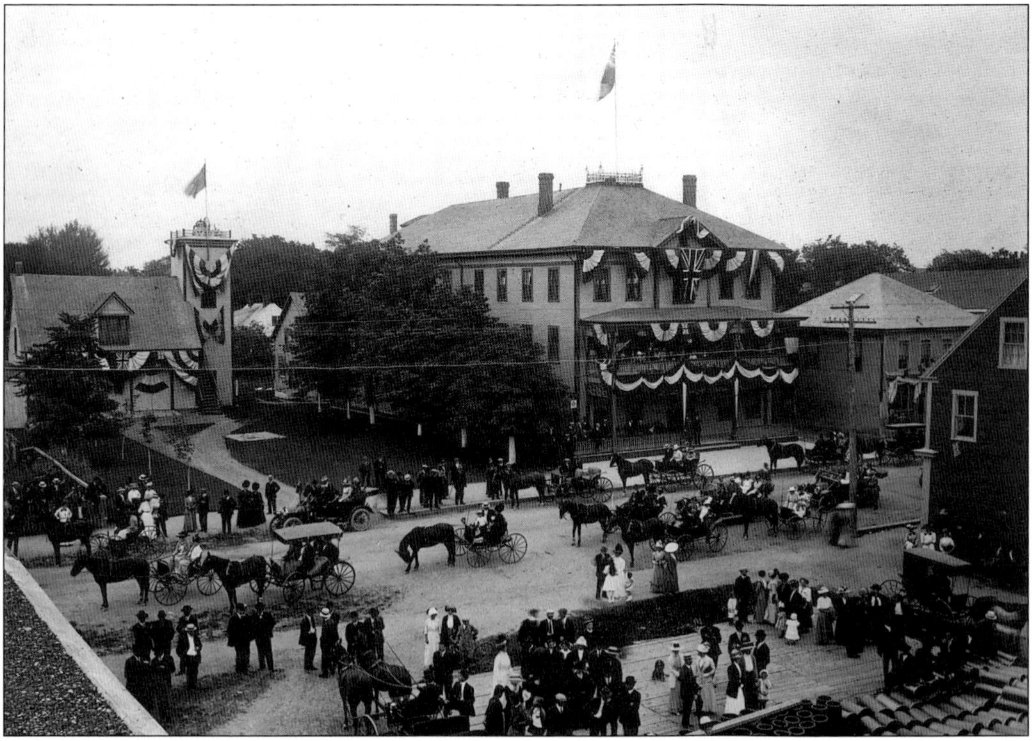

The Anchorage boasted it was "neither a hotel nor an inn not even a camp just an anchorage for those who loved the out of doors." If the rural simplicity became too much, visitors could always take a boat over to St. Andrews. This is how the town looked when the Duke of Connaught, Queen Victoria's third son and the governor general of Canada (1911–1916) came to visit St. Andrews in August 1912. (Courtesy PA, 23-23.)

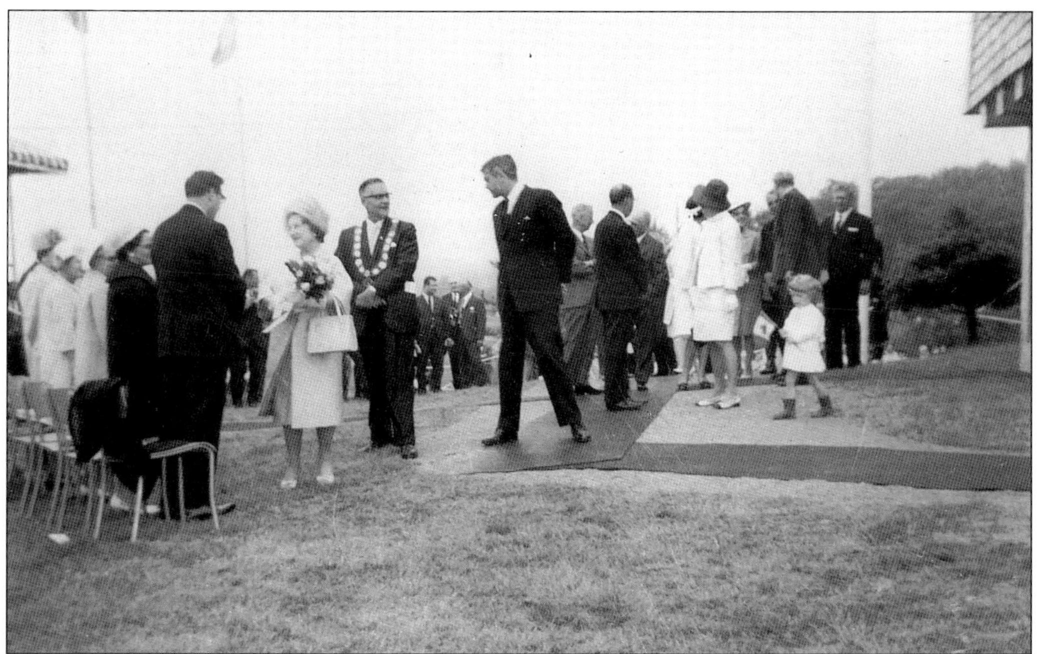
On July 15, 1967, the Queen Mother came to St. Andrews and dedicated Centennial Park, located just across the street from the National Historic Site War of 1812 Block House, just barely visible at the right edge of this photograph. Thousands came to see the beloved mother of the present queen, who Elizabeth Toy had traveled to Saint John to see in 1939. (See page 77.)

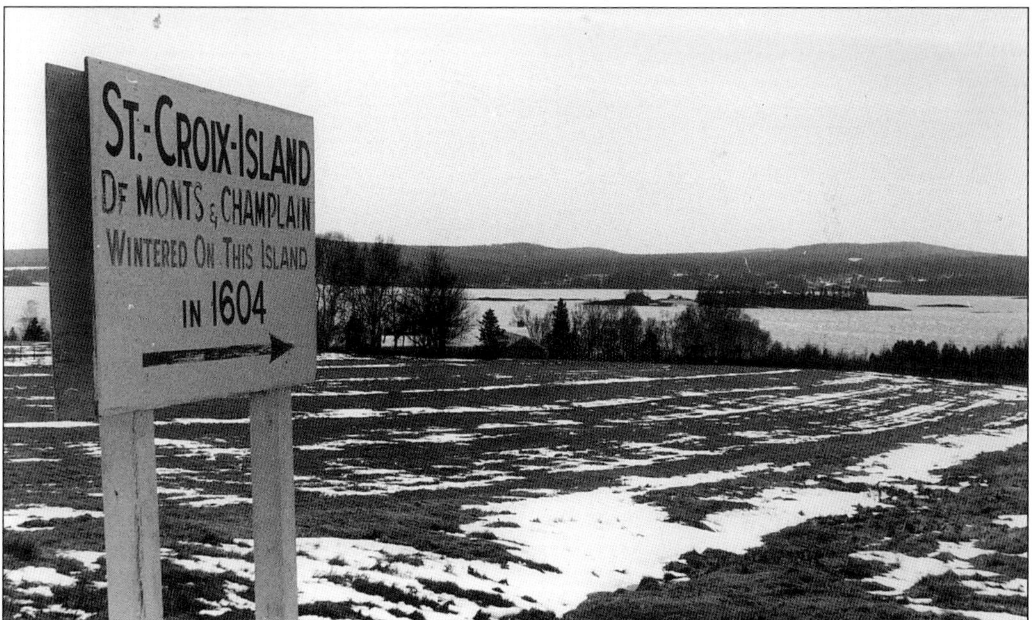

As one travels down the coast of St. Stephen, one passes Dochet's Island. The St. Croix Island is where Champlain and DeMonts spent the winter of 1604–1605. Half of their men perished in the severe weather, and they moved across the Bay of Fundy to Port Royal and set up a second settlement. In 2004, celebrations will be held to mark the initial attempt to colonize the area.

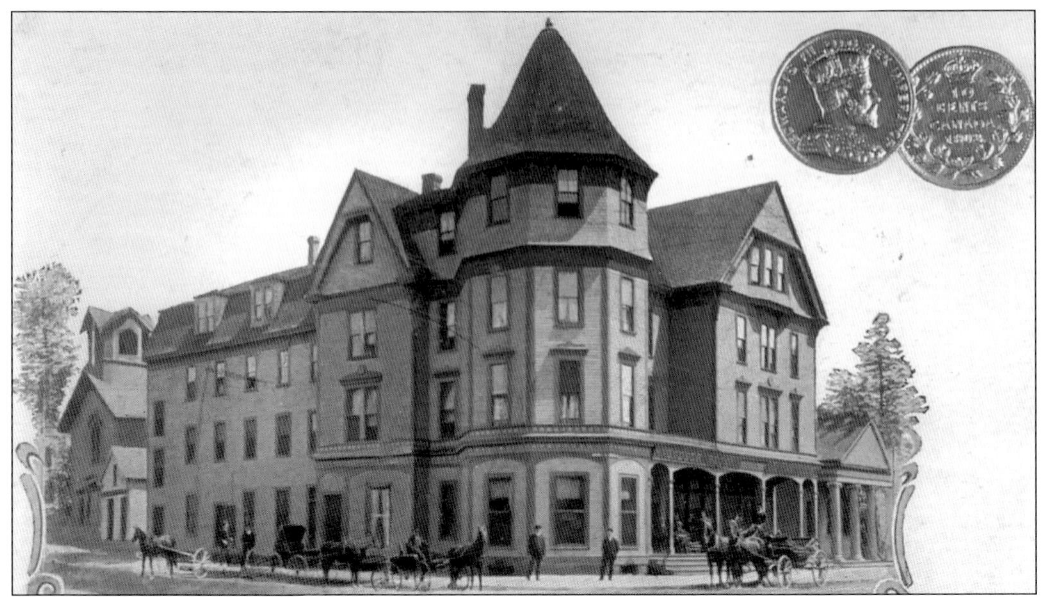

This postcard view of St. Stephen's Windsor Hotel was taken at the turn of the 20th century when the hotel was considered one of the best in the Maritime Provinces. It advertised 50 "guest chambers" at a rate of "two or two-and-a-half dollars per day." Built in 1891, it boasted at that time that it offered "hot water heat, gas lights, hot and cold water baths and electric bells in every room."

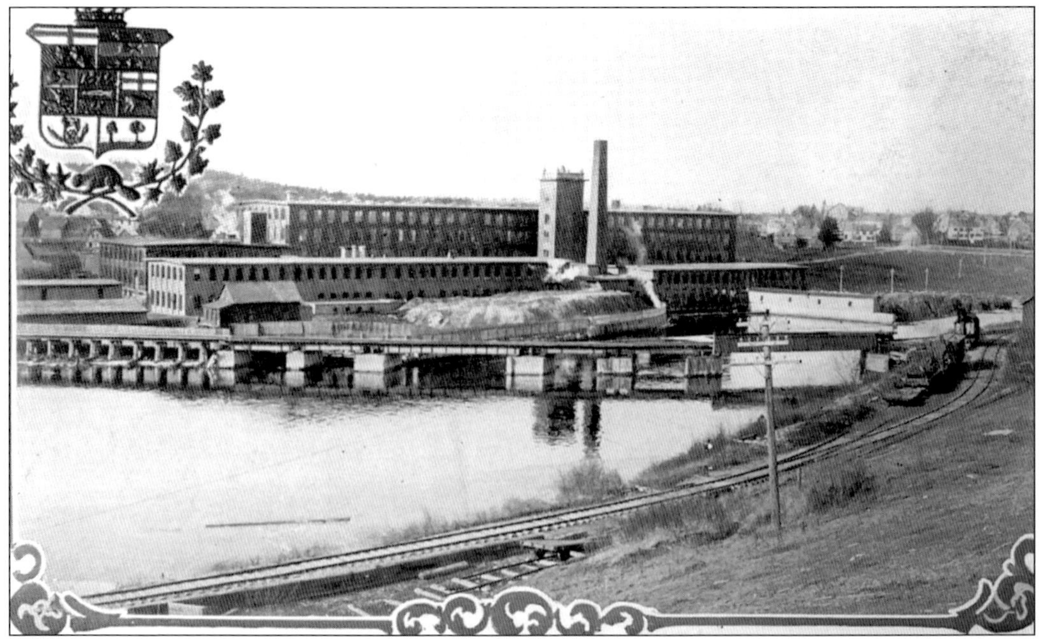

Here is a postcard view of the 1881 Milltown Cotton Mill. Power from this mill lit the streets and homes of St. Stephen. The mill is now gone, but its power plant still serves the town as part of the Milltown Generating Station.

Eight

Utopia: Four-Season Pleasure Spot

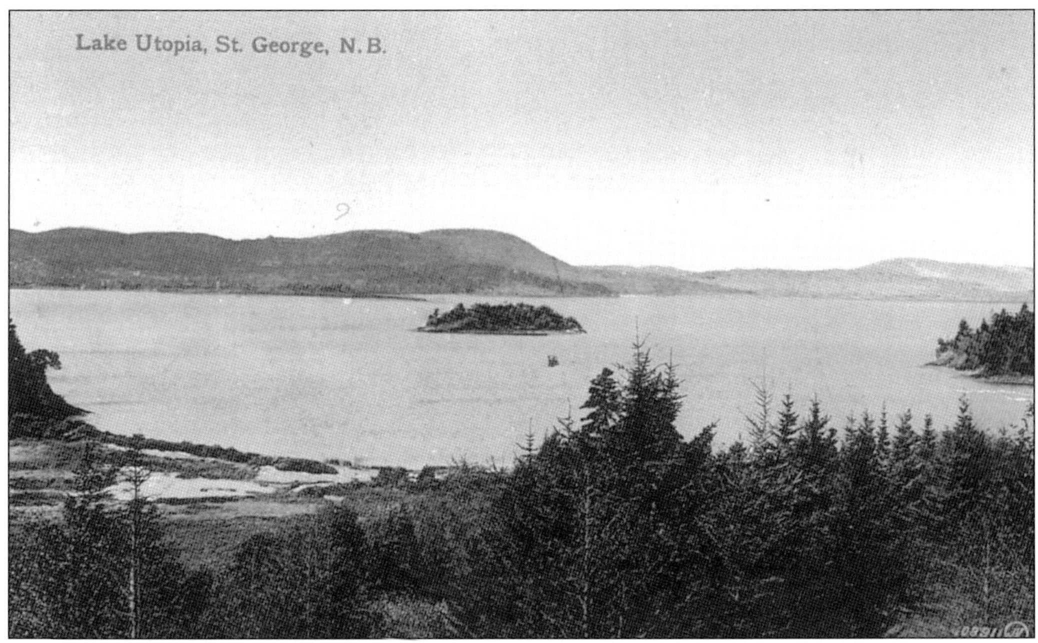

This postcard view of Lake Utopia was published by the Frauley brothers of St. George and printed in far-off Great Britain. Lake Utopia is a popular retreat on the outskirts of the town of St. George. It is an eight-kilometre-long lake, which gets its name from a plan by Buffington when it was discovered that some of the grants to the first Loyalist settlers were under the water of the lake. Capt. Peter Clinch or Lt. Gov. Thomas Carlton was believed to have reported the impossibility of acquiring the grants was comparable to the impossibility of achieving the perfection and abundance described as the ideal of *Utopia*, a 1516 novel written by Sir Thomas More. Many St. Georgers maintain camps on the shore of the lake, the most popular portion being Cabin Cove which is only a few minutes walk in from the road, or in times past, the railway line to Saint John. Others approached the lake by boat via the natural canal that flows into the Magaguadavic River. Still others used lumbering roads to the east of the lake as far as McLeans Beach and took boats to cabins or enjoyed the lake's fishing, canoeing, and sailing opportunities from that point. Studying the map on the next page will make the lake's features clearer. All of the pictures in this section have come from Elizabeth Toy's collection as the Toy's had a cottage on the beach below Gray's Mountain (also spelled Grey's Mountain).

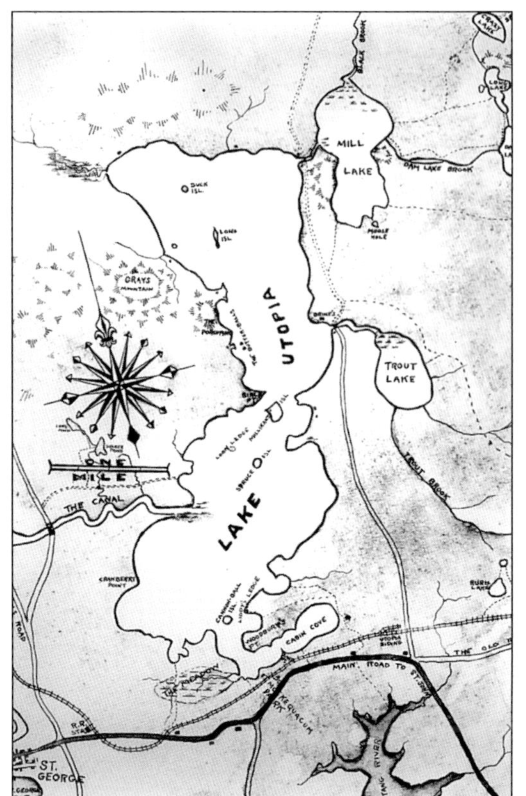

On this map, note Cannon Ball Island, which Pennfield airmen used for firing practice during World War II training. The Two Butterballs though, have nothing to do with butter, though a moose is likely to be seen at Moose Hole, loons on Loon Ledge, and cranberries can be found at Cranberry Point. Why Crazy Lake has that name is unknown, and if Clinch and his men had not come along with the name Utopia, the lake might still be called Meskeequagum, "grassy lake" in Passamaquoddy. Oh, yes, it was a great trout lake as can be seen from the lower photograph.

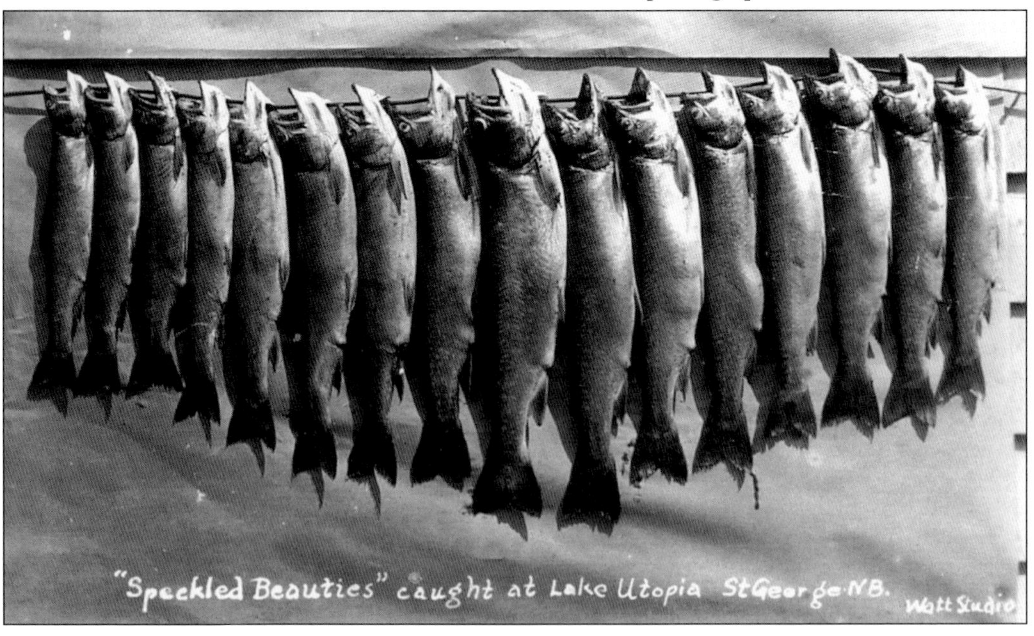

There are two interesting stories connected with the lake. One tells of a red granite medallion that was found on its shores with a carving of a native on the face of the stone. It now resides in the New Brunswick Museum and is thought by some to have been carved in 1604 when Champlain's band were spending the winter on Dochet's Island. He had artisans in his party, so it is a possibility, though not provable. Neither is the legend of the Monster of Lake Utopia, which has been seen with regularity from about 1870 to the early 1980s. There have not been any recent sightings but, still, the legend lives on. It is assumed to be some sort of sea creature that came in the natural canal linking the Magaguadavic River with Lake Utopia. It was usually seen in the springtime of the year in earlier times, and it took great delight in breaking up the log booms that were being towed across the lake. There are no photographs, but an illustration first appeared in 1872 in the *Canadian Illustrated News*, Canada's most popular magazine of the time. On a misty night, someone spotting Eugene Toy standing atop Racer's Reef might wonder if he had discovered the monster itself. In the photograph to the right, Eugene is skimming across the lake in his self-built boat hoping to catch a glimpse of the monster.

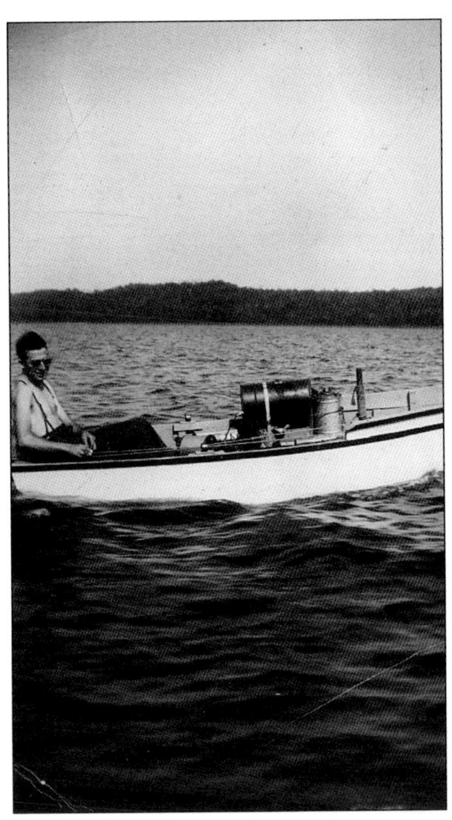

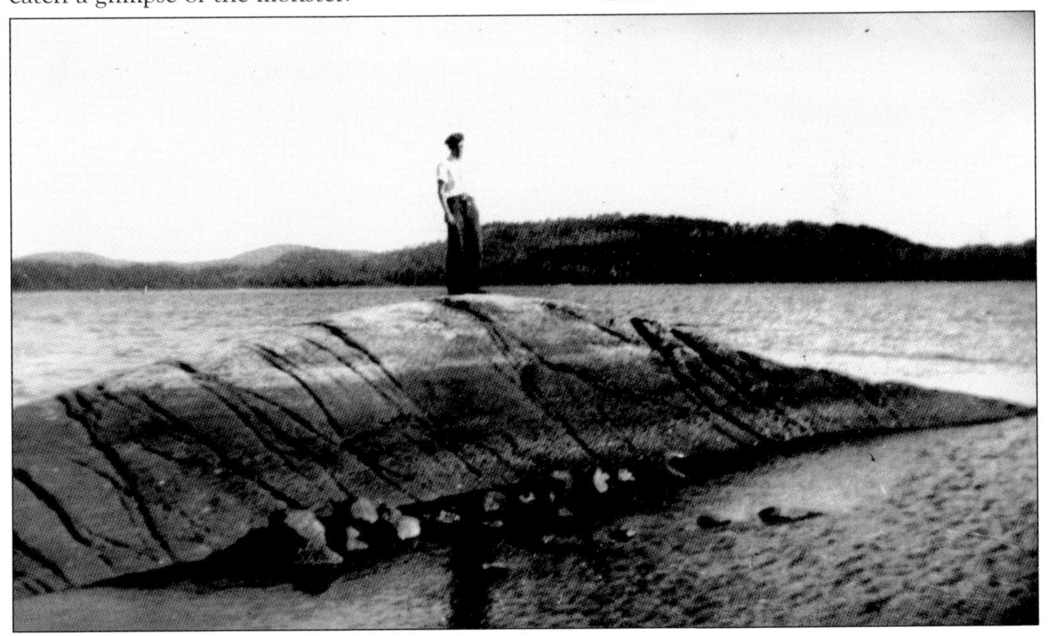

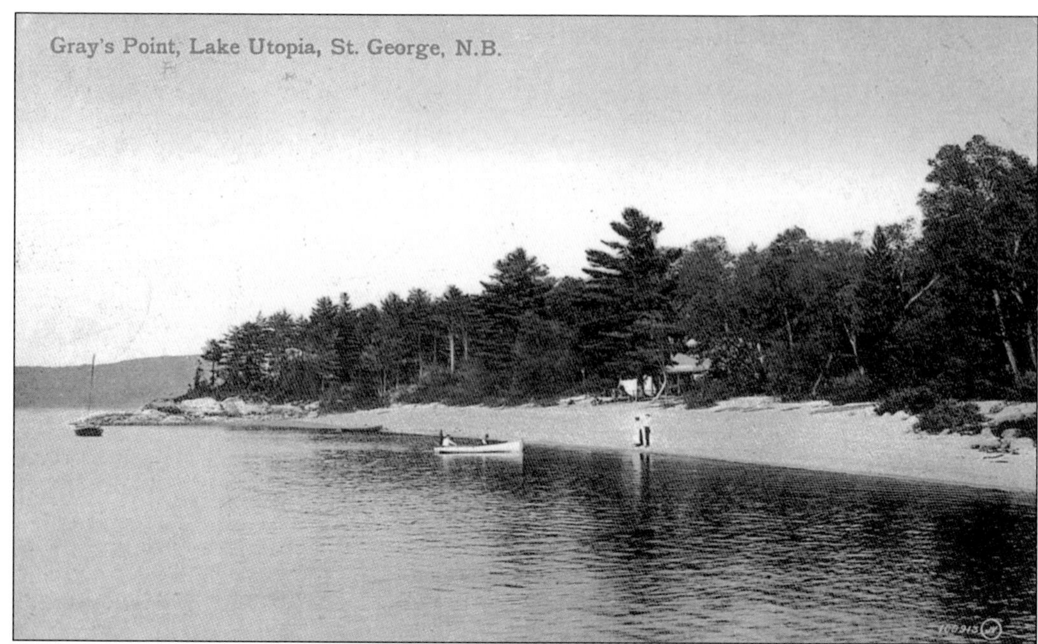

Gray's Point on Lake Utopia is the location of the Toy's camp from where they enjoyed many adventures on and around the lake. The bottom photograph is a postcard view of the area known as the Bluff, where Bryn Derwyn, a summer hotel, stood on the shore of Lake Utopia. It was used as a boys' camp in the early part of the 20th century but burned to the ground on June 5, 1918, when a brush fire got out of control. (Photograph below courtesy PA, 223-397.)

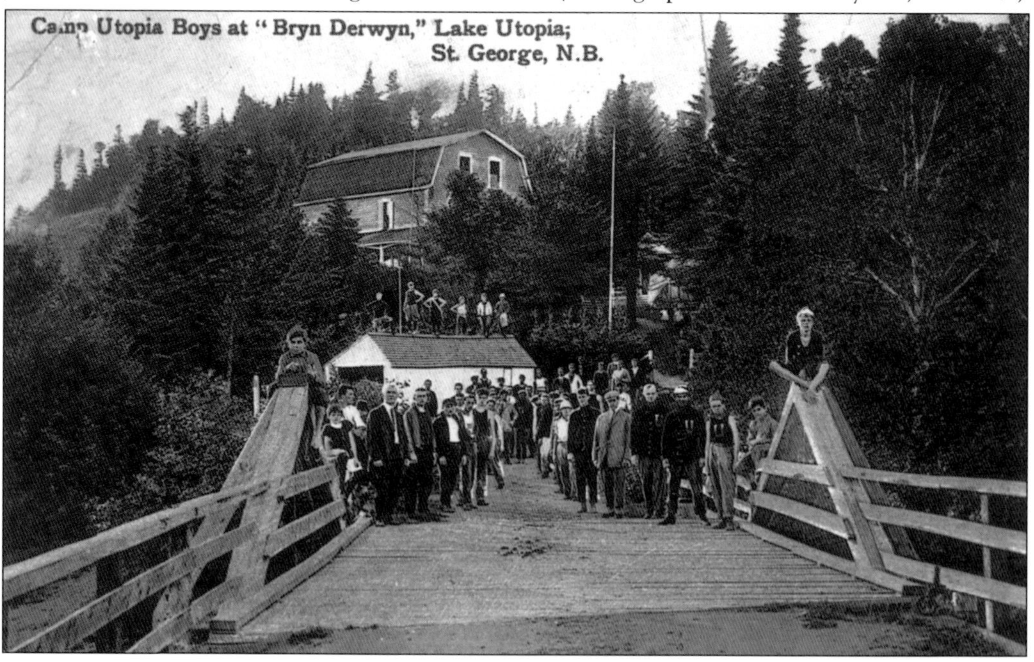

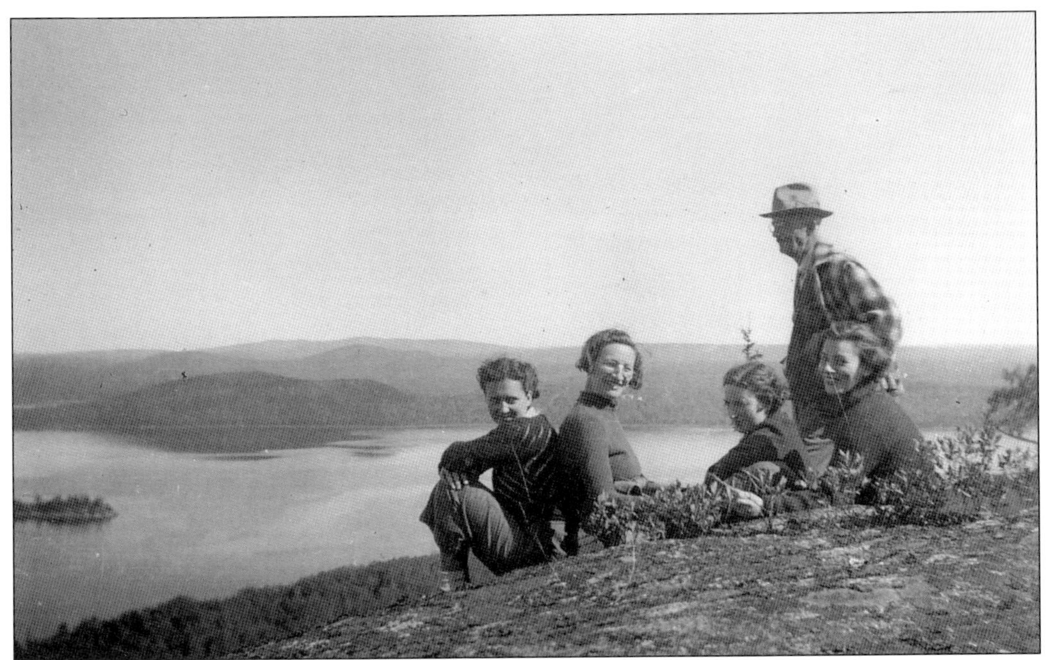

Elizabeth Toy has fond memories of many hikes to the top of Gray's Mountain, and the view of the lake she saw is shown in the bottom photograph. The aptly named Little Island is nearest the shore, just in front of the beach where the Toys' cottage stood. Long Island is in the middle of the lake, and Mill Lake is on the horizon. The picture above depicts a hike that was held on October 4, 1936, and Elizabeth took the photograph showing, from left to right, Frances Toy, Jane Britton, Mable MacDonald, Mary Clinch, and her father, Alvah C. Toy, standing behind the four girls.

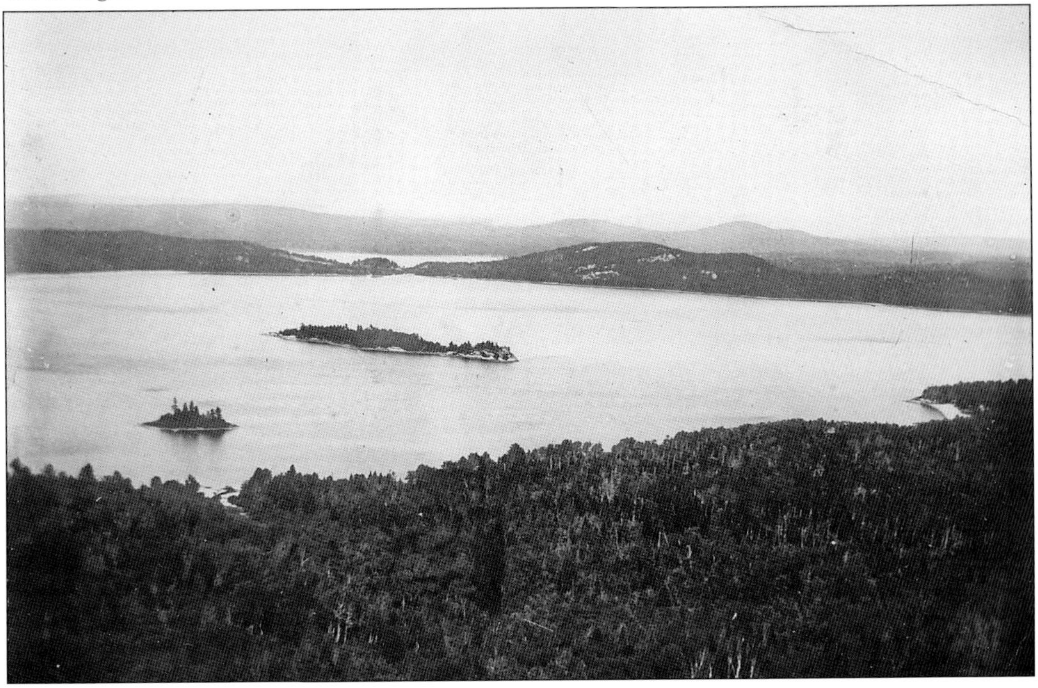

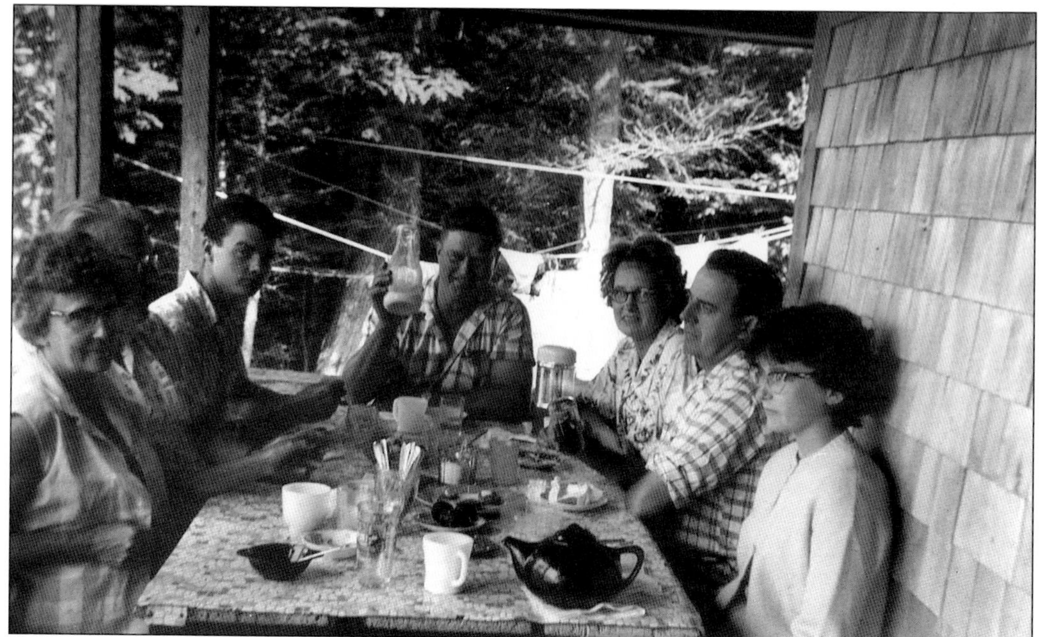

Gathered at what they called "grain time" at Toy's Gray Point Lodge on Sunday, August 15, 1965, from left to right are Frances Waycott, James Waycott, Russel Waycott, Bill Spinney (holding up the milk bottle), Lillian Spinney, Eugene Toy, and Elizabeth Waycott.

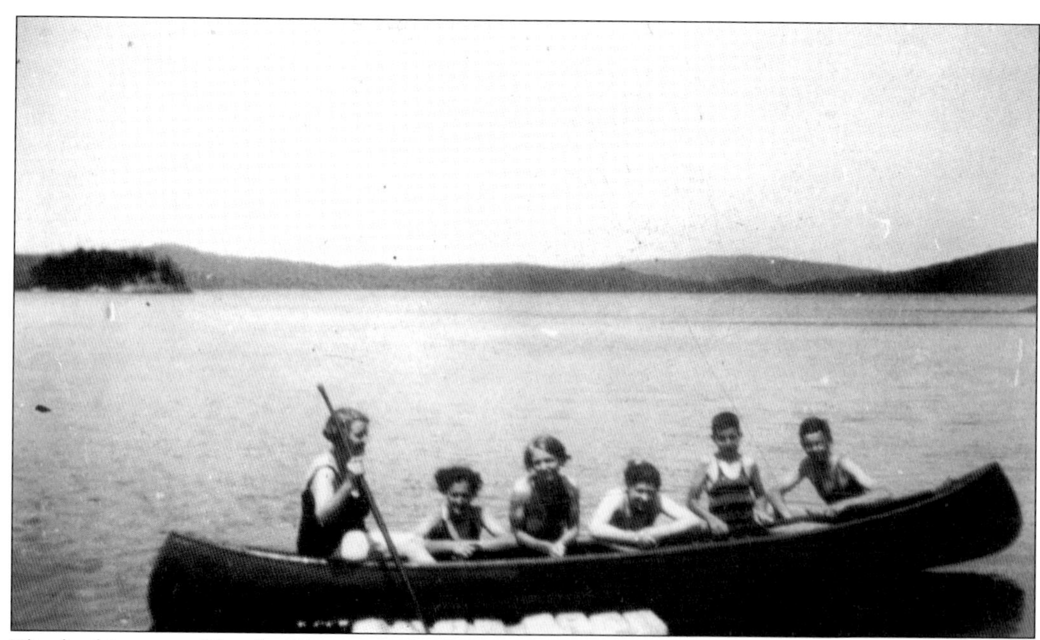

Elizabeth's mom, Phoebe Toy, is at the left in this picture of canoeists enjoying an outing on Lake Utopia, with Eugene Toy, her son, next to her. Beryl Parks and Phoebe Moran are the next two adults. The two boys are unidentified visitors. The salty Bay of Fundy was considered far too cold for comfortable swimming, and its tides made canoeing difficult, thus the popularity of the freshwater of Lake Utopia.

If a better location were found for a cottage, the ingenious cottagers would build a raft, roll the cottage across the shore on fallen trees, and then float it down the lake to a new location.

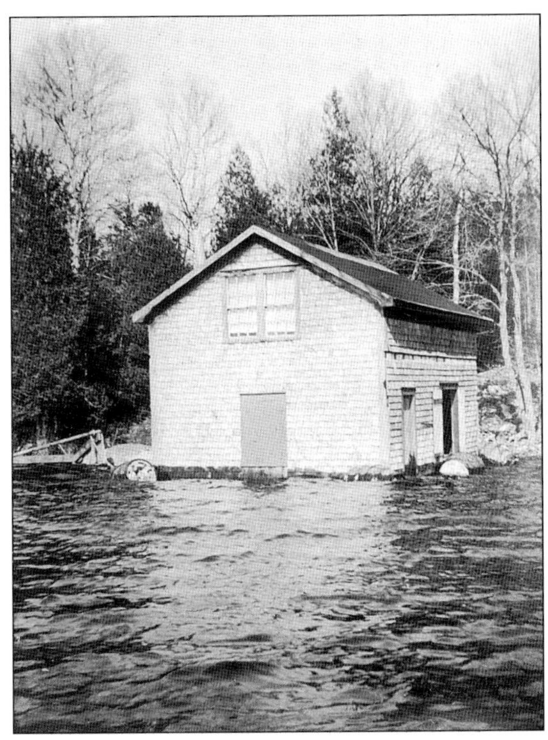

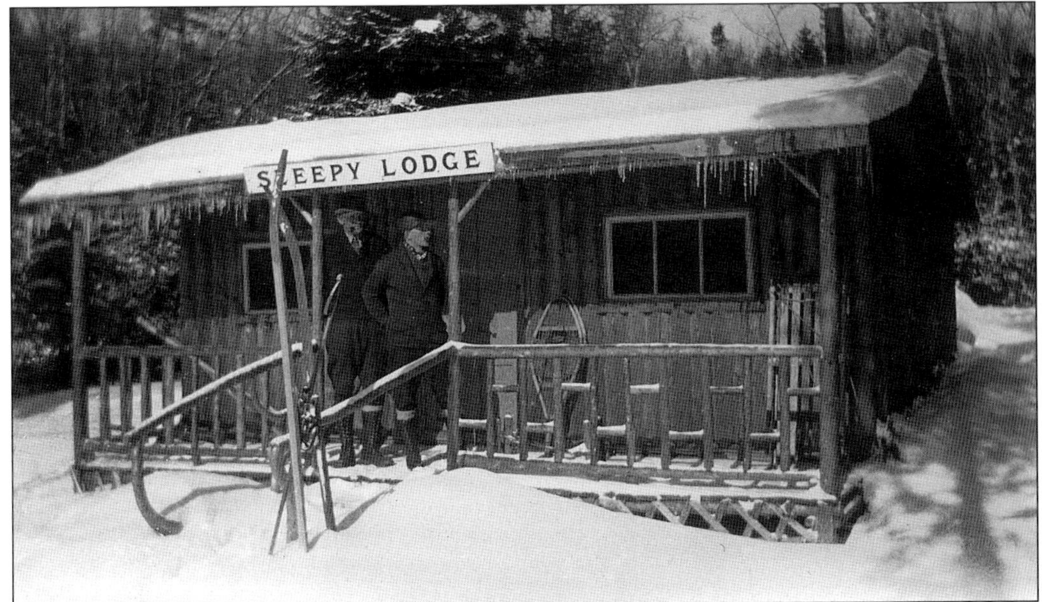

Cottages were enjoyed throughout the four seasons of the year, though high water, sometimes almost to the top of the veranda, made camps un-useable in the spring. Sleepy Lodge is seen here being enjoyed in the winter by Fred Goodeill and Sherman "Nim" Allen who have come to its comfort on a winter day on cross-country skis.

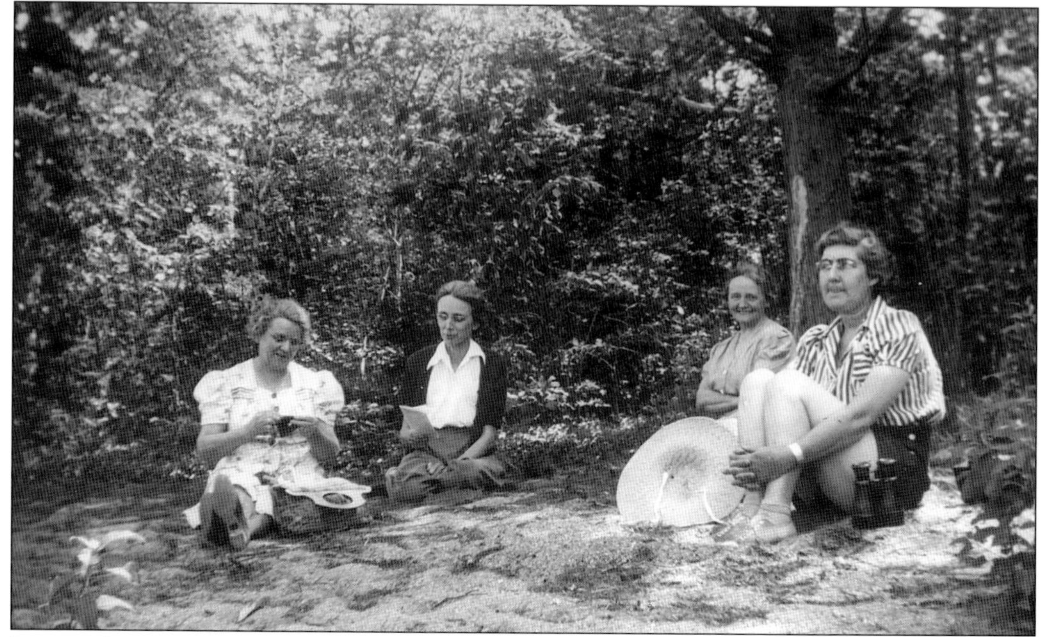

Picnics during the day and campfires during the evening under the trees were always a lake delight. In August of 1942, when this photograph was taken, the war was raging, and training was ongoing at nearby Pennfield. But at the lake, (from left to right) Phoebe Toy, Etta Armstrong, Myrtle Trynor, and Eola Grearson escaped from the problems of the world, as cottagers do to this day.

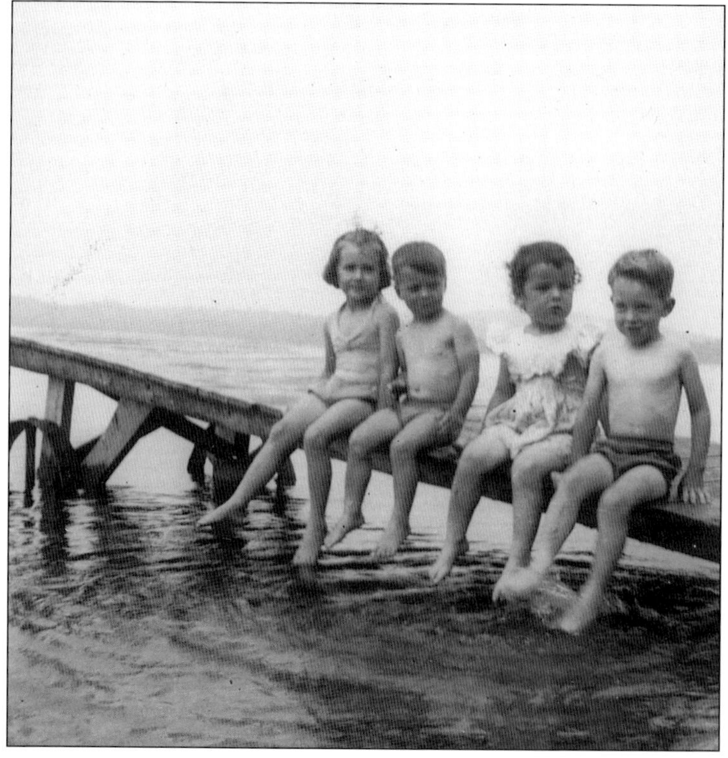

Children and water just go together, and this view is idyllic in its simplicity. From left to right, Beth and Russell Waycott, Valerie Goodeill, and Jamie Corey are shown here on July 11, 1951, at the Toy's boat ramp on wheels, used to easily accommodate the drop in water levels as the summer passed.

Here is Alvah Toy extending a welcome to his wife, Phoebe, on September 20, 1940. Elizabeth Toy calls this "courtesy extending its hand."

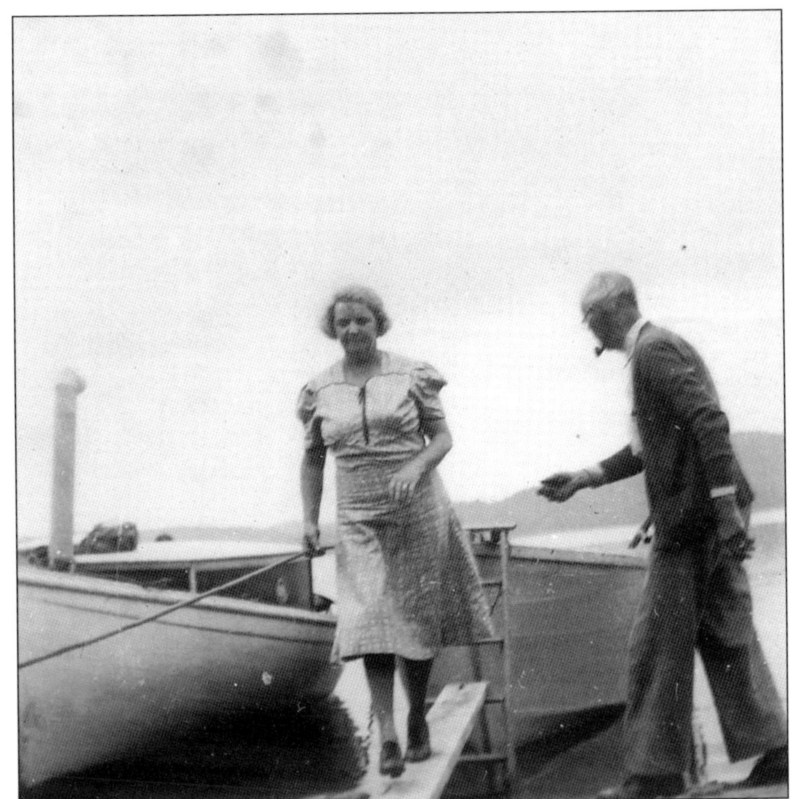

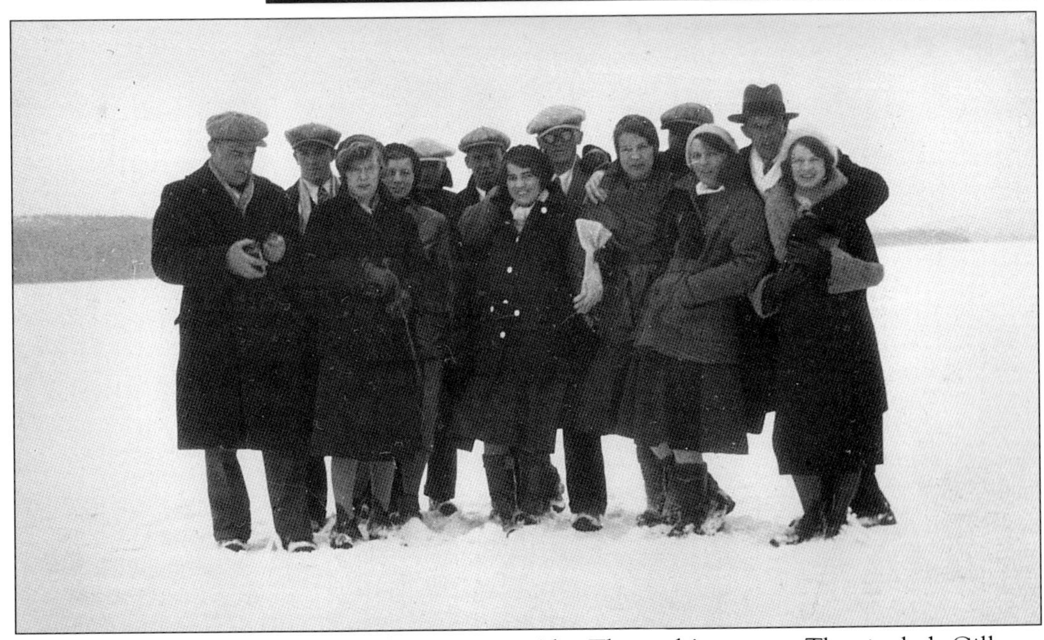

This group was on a walk across Lake Utopia to Algy Theriault's cottage. They include Gillman Brown, Joe Reardon, Edgar Baldwin, Max O'Malley, Stephen Campbell, John Clinch, Frank Dodds, Elizabeth Toy, Mary Clinch, Kay Hyslop, Florence Baldwin, Marjorie Baldwin, and Josephine Campbell. Seventy years later, Stephen Campbell is still leading hikes in the area.

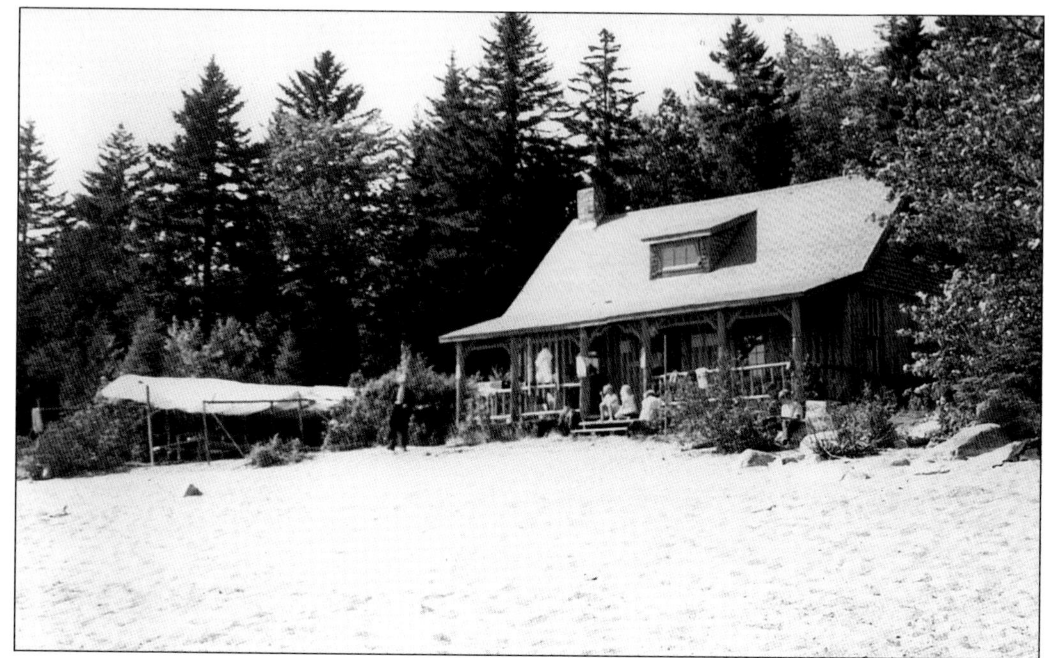

At the very upper end of the lake was the Frauley's camp or cottage that later became the Boy Scout cottage and could be reached only by boat from McLean's Beach—a trip which made it seem even more remote to the many Scouts and other youth who used it over the years.

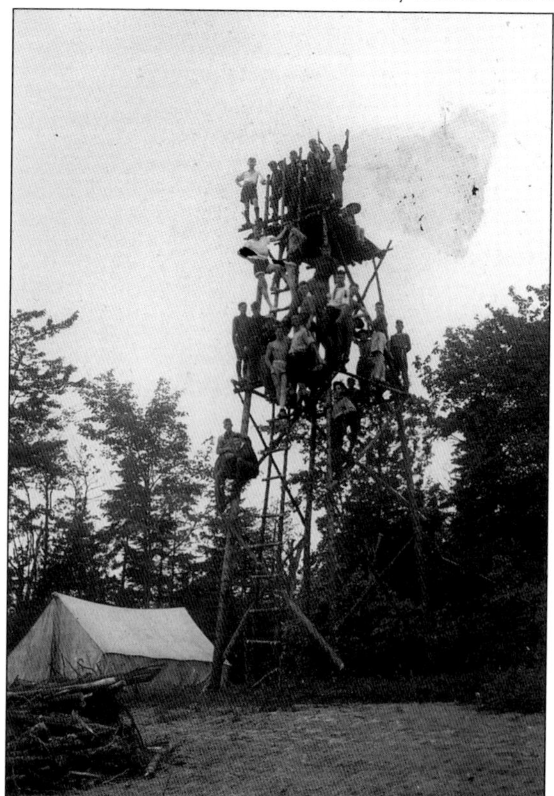

In this picture, we have the scout's pioneering tower built at Rocky Point in 1944. No nails were used in this tower, yet it could still support the entire troop, as the photograph shows. The scoutmaster who had this tower built, Steve Campbell, recalls when his scoutmaster, Henry Austin, somehow had the famed storyteller Thornton W. Burgess visit their camp on the lake when Steve was a boy in the 1920s.

Nine

Last Look and Ephemera

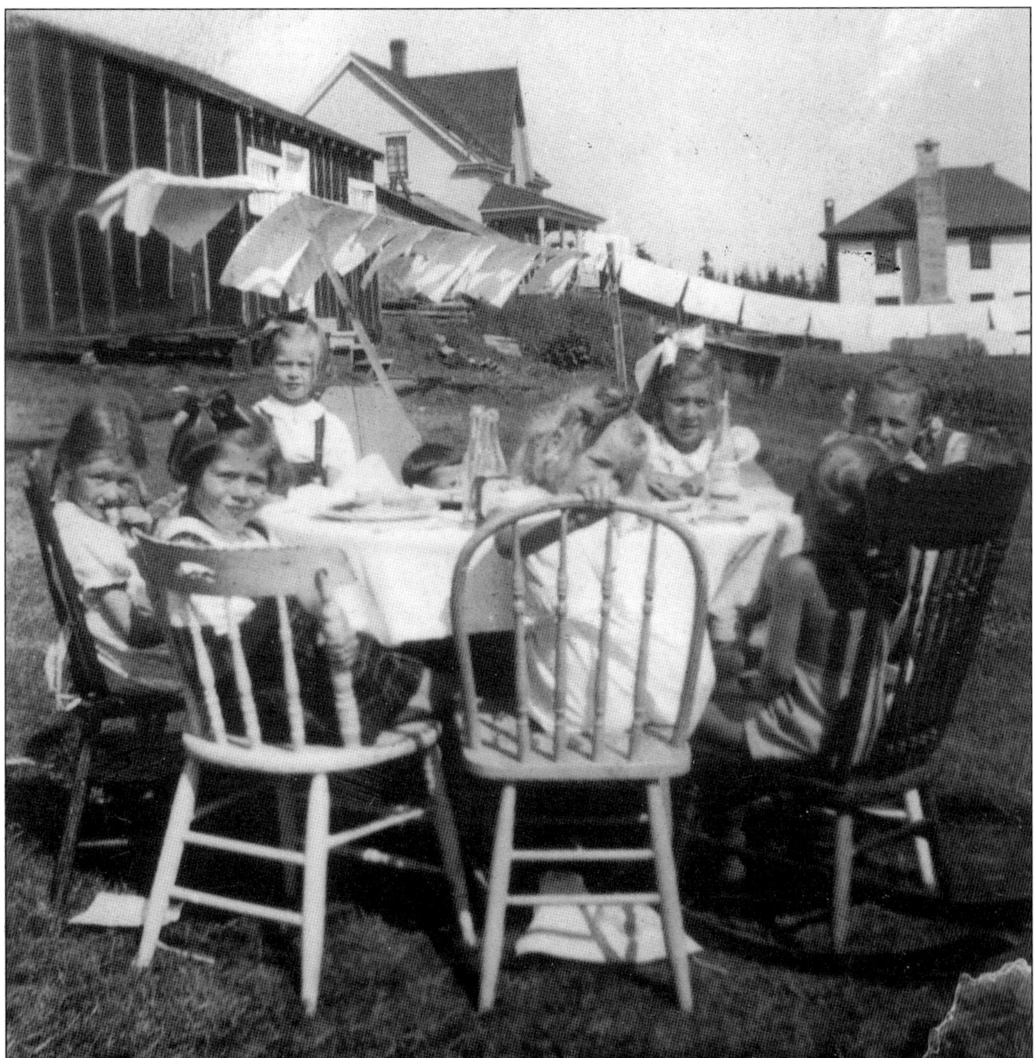

Life is like a night fog on the Bay of Fundy that dissipates at the dawning of a new day. One day, we are children sitting in the summer sun on the shores of Pocologan enjoying a party as shown above. The next day, we are old and gray, trying to remember the things that happened along the way. How lucky Alice (Conde) Garner and her friends were to have their picture taken while celebrating a birthday party at Pocologon in 1944.

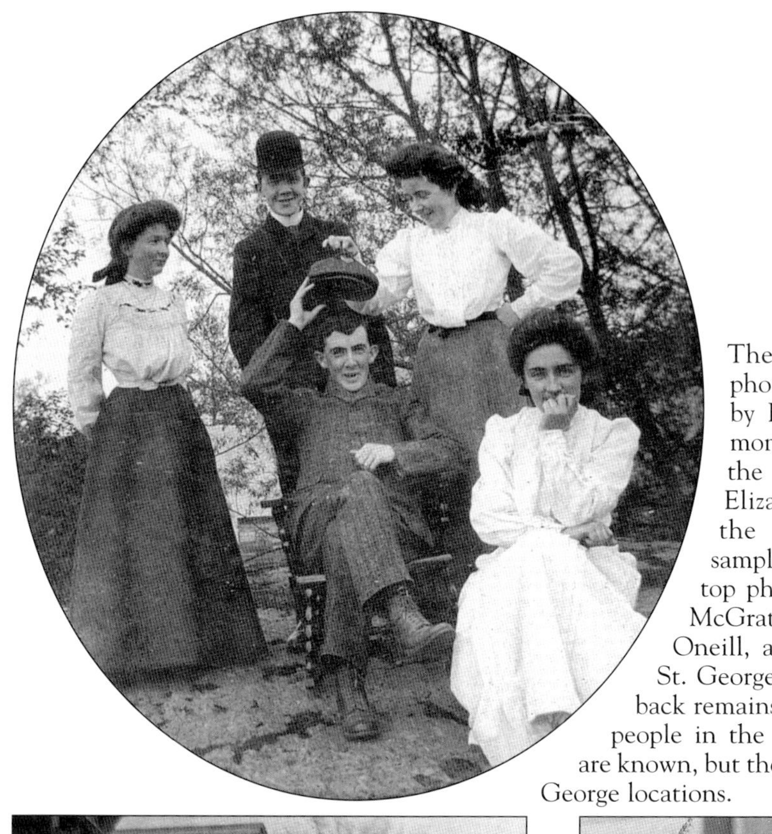

These are three faded photographs that were taken by Phoebe Toy, Elizabeth's mom. Her efforts instilled the joy of photography in Elizabeth, which led to the extensive collection sampled in this book. In the top photograph, we have Bess McGrattan, Annie Oneill, Clair Oneill, and Eddie Oneill, all of St. George. The gentlemen at the back remains unknown. None of the people in the two lower two pictures are known, but they are in recognizable St. George locations.

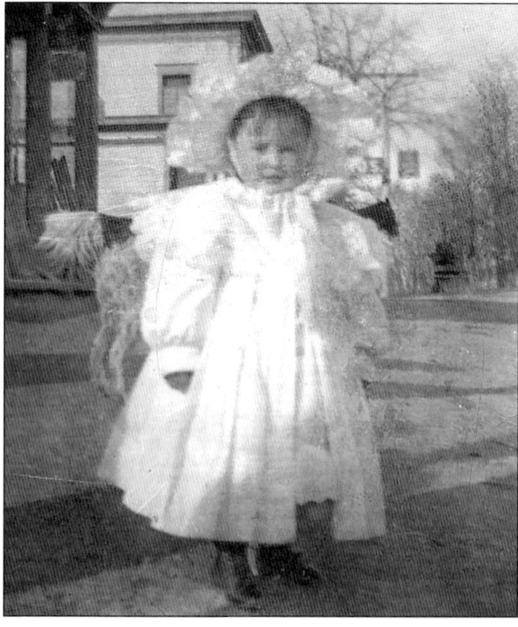

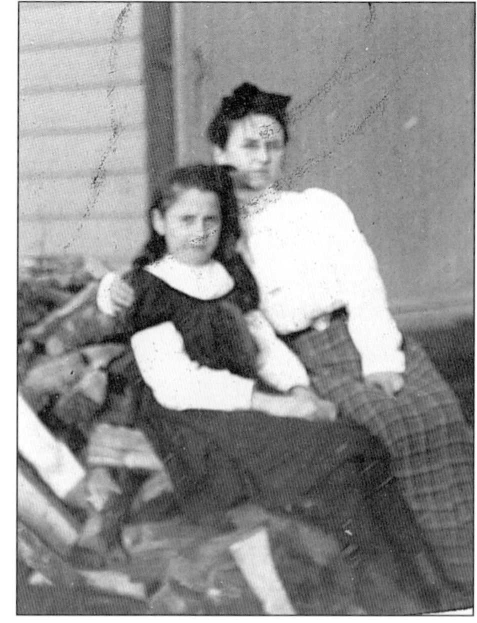

There is no one alive today that remembers the rebuilding of Saint John after the great fire of June 20, 1877, which destroyed almost all the area seen in this picture. What was rebuilt is shown on this postcard commemorating the city's 300th anniversary in 1904. The area today is little changed and considered one of Canada's finest collections of 19th century heritage buildings.

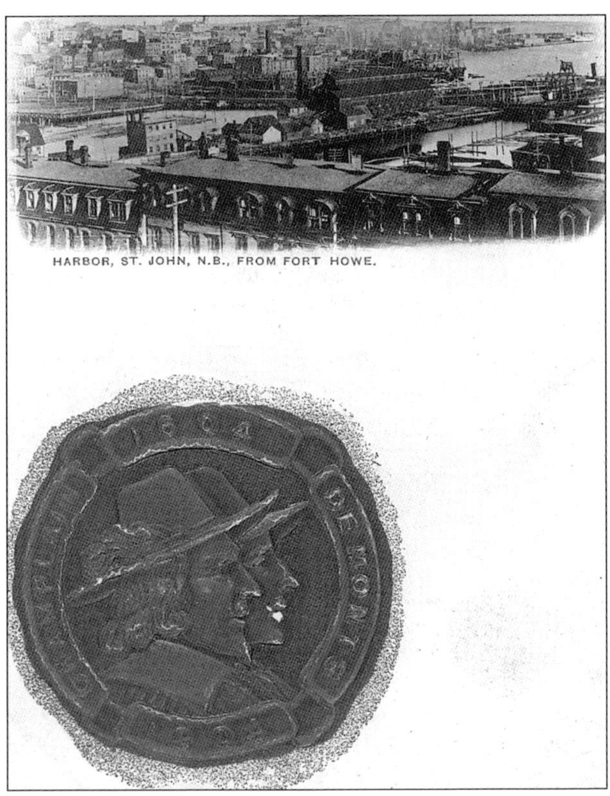

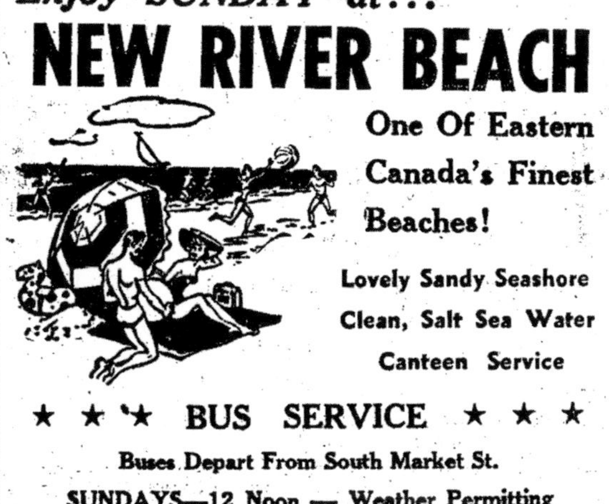

Though New River was not chosen as the territory for the national park in 1948, it remained a popular destination for inland New Brunswickers. The shoreline train service was not regular as the 1950s came in, so the bus companies began offering "tours to no where," and one of the destinations, as seen in this 1952 advertisement, was New River on Sunday afternoon.

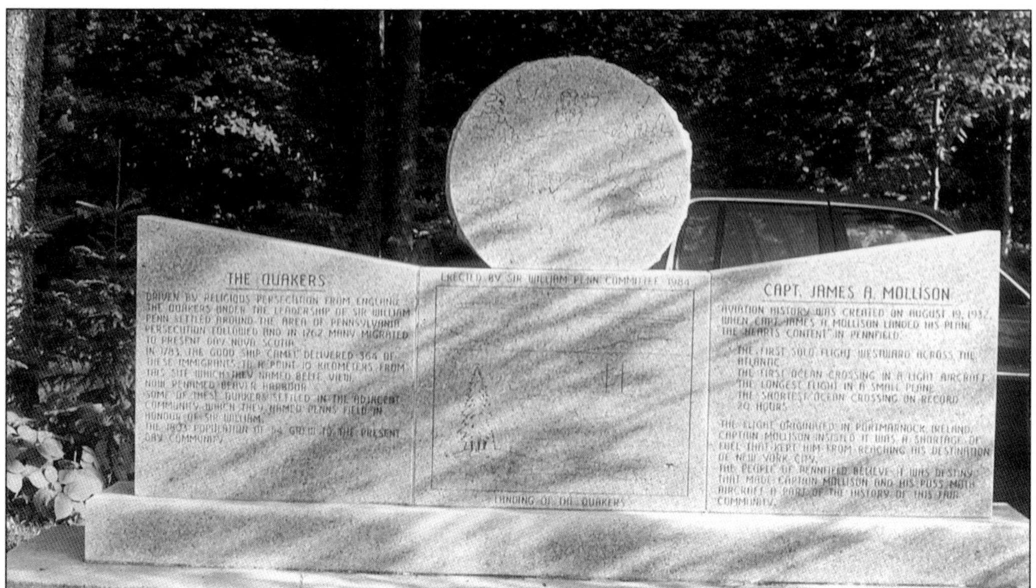

A stone on Route One at Pennfield commemorates the founding of Belle View in 1763 by 364 followers of William Penn. The blueberry barrens behind the community became known as Penn's Field, in honor of the Quaker leader. The right of the stone commemorates the landing of the first nonstop westward air-flight across the Atlantic on August 18, 1932, by James A. Mollison. (Courtesy Goss.)

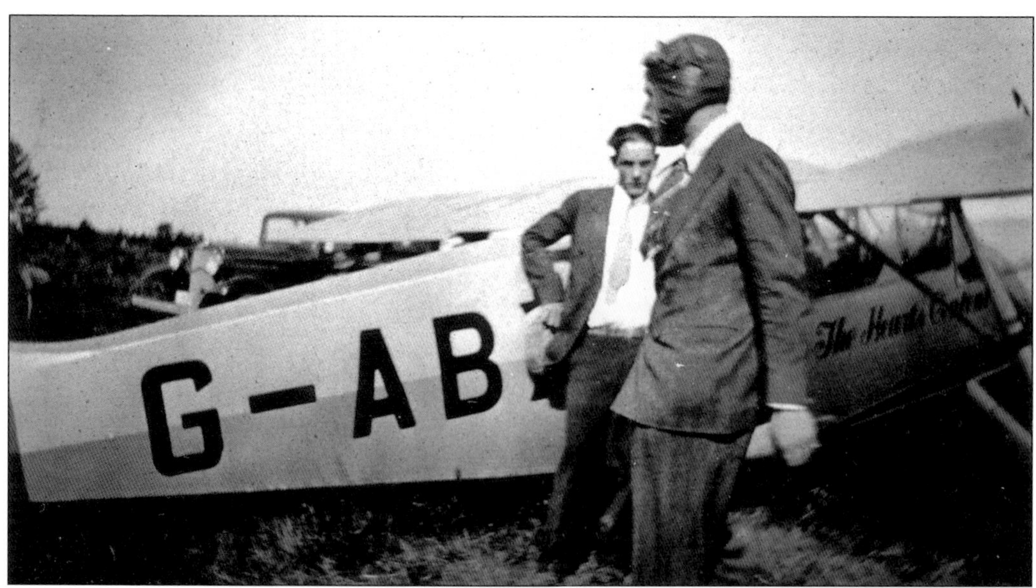

Mollison was a well-known long distance flyer who had taken two days off the flight time to Australia in 1931. A year later, he tackled the Atlantic leaving from Portmarnock, Ireland, for New York. After 30 hours of nonstop flying, he circled over Saint John, Musquash New River, and St. George before setting his Heart's Content Puss Moth airplane down in A.B. Hawkin's field with less than 10 gallons of fuel left. (Courtesy PA, 370-62.)

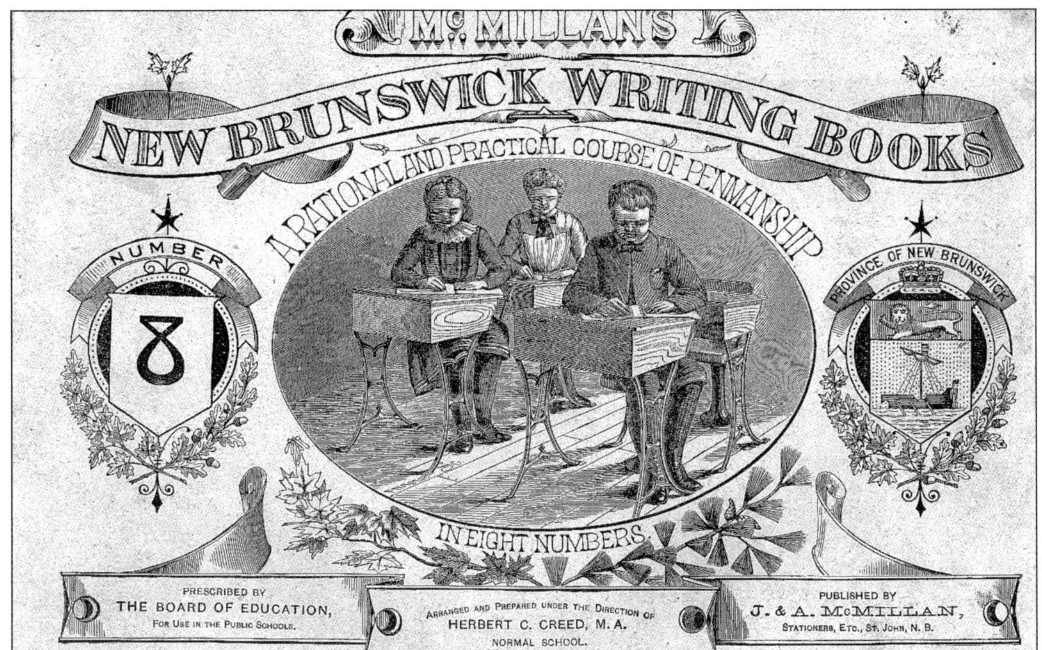

At a roadside antique and craft shop in the former Pocologan School, this century-old New Brunswick writing book showed up. It would have been used by many residents in Charlotte County for practicing their writing skills in times past. It was produced by J.A. McMillian in Saint John as part of a series that children used in the one-room schoolhouses in each seaside community mentioned in this book.

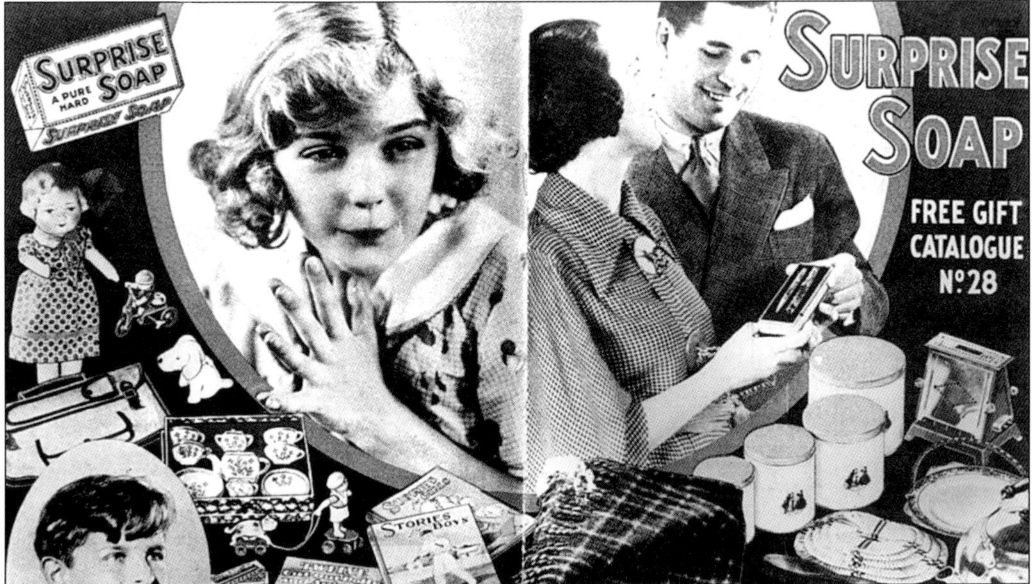

Residents of Charlotte County would save up their soap wrappers in order to get the gifts pictured above from the Surprise Soap Company. Though the packaging notes the premium department was in Montreal, the actual manufacturing of the soap was done in St. Stephen, and such work, combined with making candy at Ganong's and the prints and fabric of the Milltown Cotton Mill, helped St. Stephen grow to be the biggest of the Charlotte County towns.

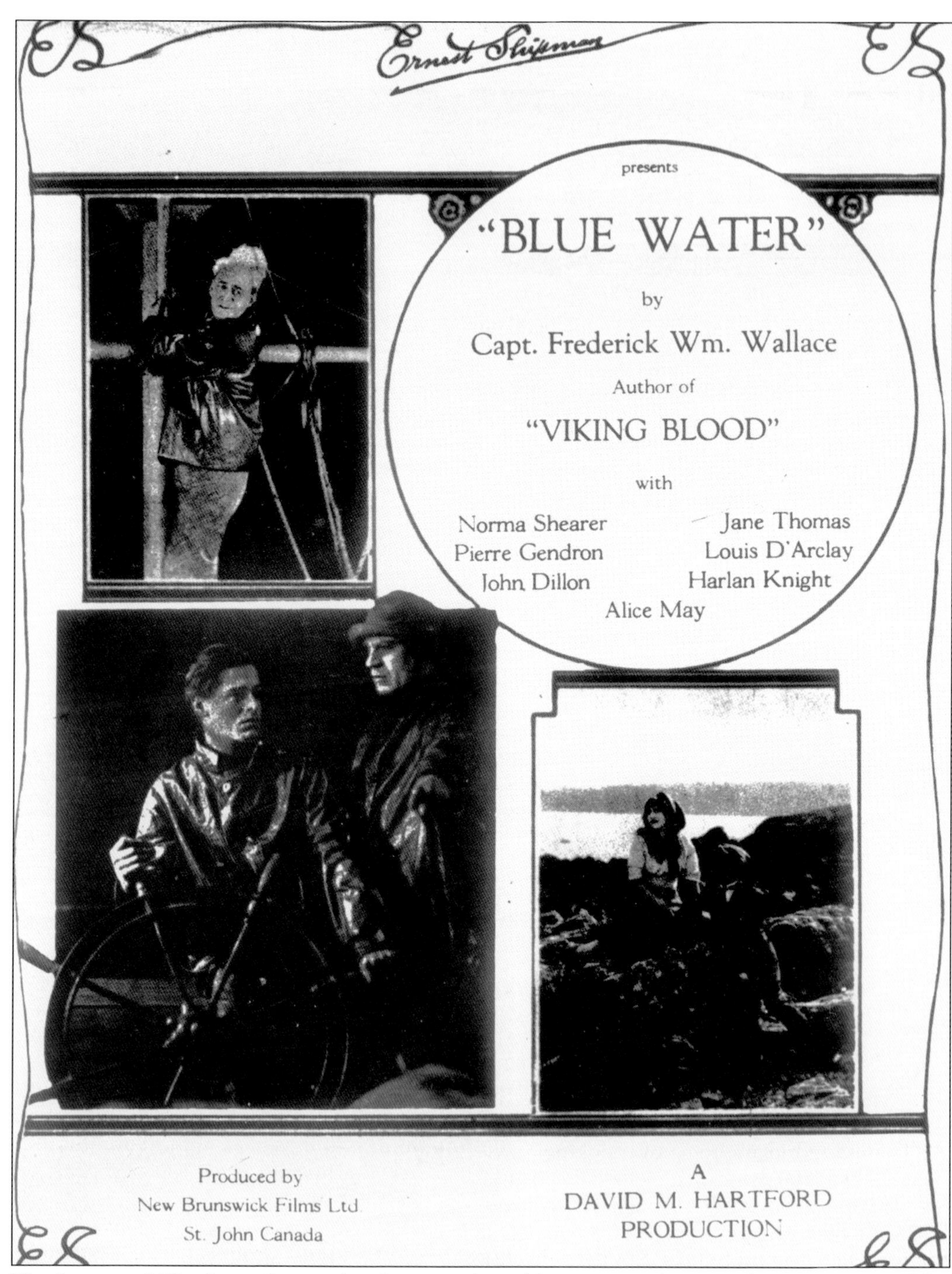

The beauty of Charlotte County has been exploited by moviemakers on three occasions. *Blue Water* (shown here) was the first in 1922, produced by Ernest Shipman with Norma Shearer as its star. Warner Brothers filmed *Sunrise at Campobello*, based on the Roosevelt's love of the island, with stars Ralph Bellamy and Greer Garson in 1960. William Hurt and Marlee Matlin were the stars of *Children of a Lesser God* filmed in 1986. (Courtesy NFA, 2046.)

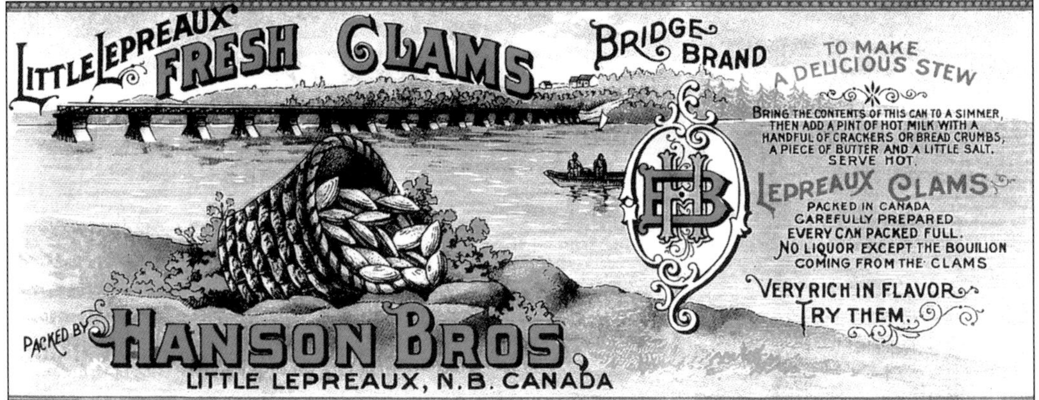

The Hanson Brothers canned clams, blueberries, and rabbits at Little Lepreau, and did so well, they actually issued their own money for use in their many business concerns and built a school to serve the area. The quality was such that some canners won world-fair ribbons. Clams are still dug recreationally and commercially, with deep-frying the preferred way to prepare them these days.

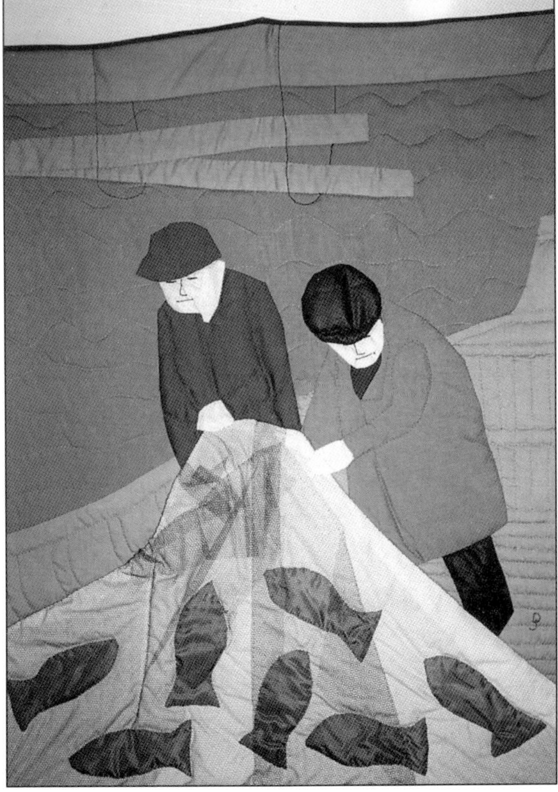

At Theresa Eldridge's home overlooking Beaver Harbour (the former Belle View mentioned before), this fisher folk quilt is on display. It represents the long-standing tradition along the Bay of Fundy shore of craftsmanship celebrating the sea, which gave the resources for living to so many of the area's residents when major industries, like the granite and the pulp mill industries, were idle.

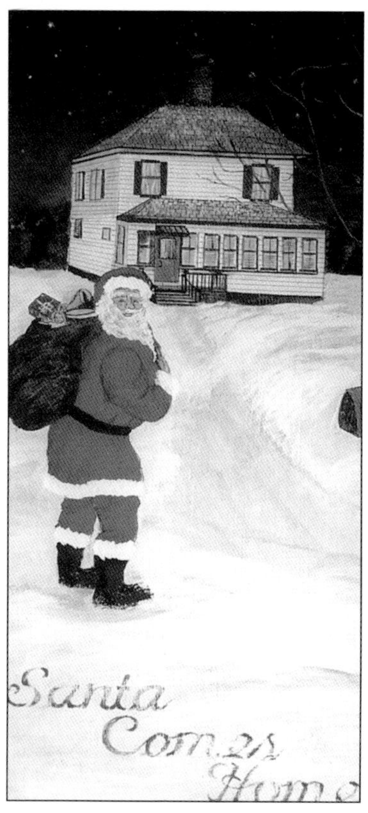

To the right is a painting by my sister Barbara Foss, in which she shows my father playing the role of Santa Claus outside the home where he was born in St. George and first met Santa Claus. Two things he loved in life: to play Santa Claus's role and to share stories about his early life in St. George. Some of his tales led me to Elizabeth Toy, who chose the photograph below, which shows family and friends honoring her on her 90th birthday in December of 2000. From left to right are Elizabeth Toy, James and Russell Waycott, Helena Toy, and St. George Mayor Stan Smith.

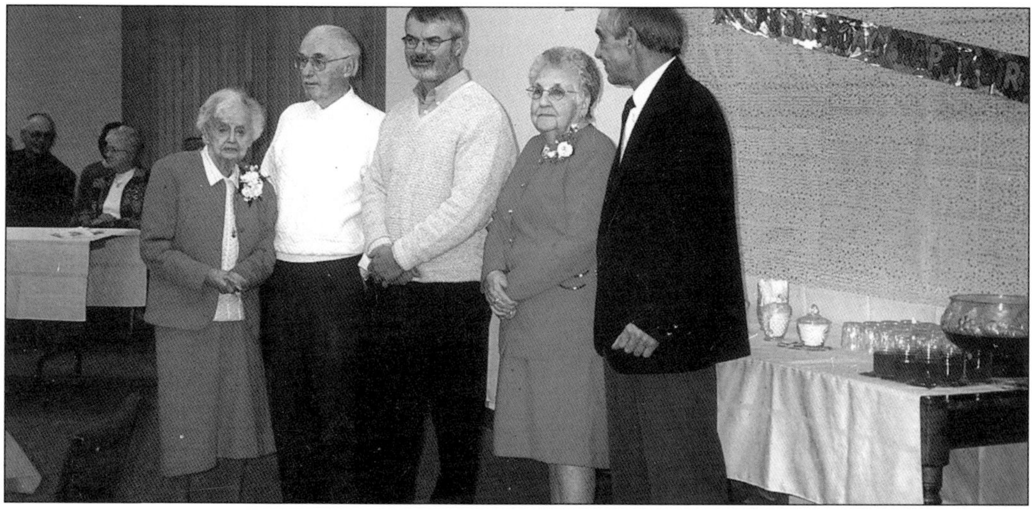